Contents

THE OPEN COLLEGE *of* EQUINE STUDIES

SUCCESS IN STAGES

ESSE... GUID... with ... and ...

...GE 2

...ent

JULIE BREGA

J. A. Allen
LONDON

DEDICATION

This book is dedicated to Holly, Josh and George.

ACKNOWLEDGEMENTS

I'd like to thank Ilona Loftus for reading through and contributing to the content of this book, Erica Dorling for help with Section 9, Frances White for being the rider model, Diane Harvey who provided the basis of the text for Sections 13 and 14, and Carole Vincer and Dianne Breeze for the line drawings.

I'd also like to thank The British Horse Society for the assistance given in relation to the content of this book.

Finally, thanks to my editor Martin Diggle, and to Lesley Gowers of J. A. Allen for being very patient!

© Julie Brega 2011
First published in Great Britain in 2011

ISBN 978 0 85131 980 3

J.A. Allen
Clerkenwell House
Clerkenwell Green
London EC1R 0HT

J.A. Allen is an imprint of Robert Hale Limited

www.allenbooks.co.uk

The right of Julie Brega to be identified as author of this work has been asserted by her in accordance with the Copyright, Designs and Patents Act 1988

British Library Cataloguing in Publication Data
A catalogue record for this book is available from the British Library

Design by Judy Linard

Printed in Singapore by Craft Print International Limited

Introduction

People become involved with horses for many different reasons. Some ride for exercise and the challenge of acquiring new skills, to socialise and enjoy the countryside. Some simply want to look after horses for love of the horse.

There are many riders who attend their local riding school once a week, some of whom hope one day to be a horse owner. Whether you own a horse or not, so much can be gained from knowing more about the horse and his care.

This book has been written for the novice enthusiast, professional or not, with the particular aim of working towards the British Horse Society (BHS) Stage 2 Certificate in Horse Knowledge, Care and Riding.

Once you decide to take the BHS exam it is important that you check the British Horse Society website (www.bhs.org.uk) for exam updates – the syllabus will be updated from time to time. (This book is arranged in the order of the Spring 2011 BHS Syllabus.)

HOW TO USE THIS BOOK

The start of each section describes the required skills and knowledge covered in that section. You will also find a subject box, organised as follows:

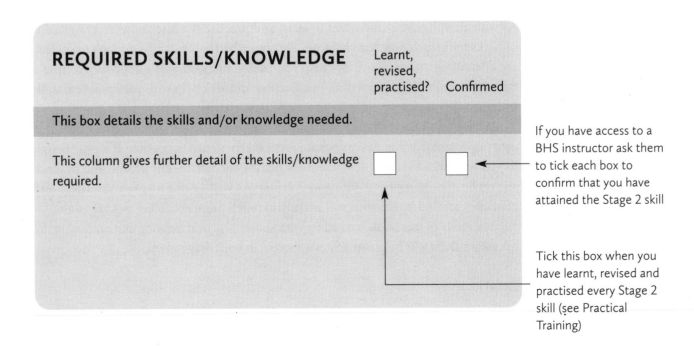

ITQ 0.0

What is an in-text question?

Throughout the book you will see in-text questions (ITQs) in boxes. These are revision aids for you – they are deliberately positioned somewhat further on than the relevant information in the main text. Write your answers in the box – you can check your answers at the end of the book.

EXAM TIP

Throughout the book you will find tips to help you in your exam.

SAFETY TIPS

Specific safety points are flagged up.

PRACTICAL TRAINING

As with all things, it is important to learn and practise the safe and correct methods of performing each practical skill from the outset; bad habits can be difficult to correct, are often dangerous and will not help you pass your exam. It is a good idea to find a BHS approved riding school or training centre and seek help with your practical skills training.

Whilst this book will help you prepare theoretically for your Stage 2 exam, it is very important that you gain as much practical experience as possible. It is not enough to just read about each topic – you must put the theoretical knowledge into practice so you become competent, safe and efficient. As well as improving your safety and efficiency around horses, this will make you much more confident in your exam.

The study of this book, backed up with sound practical training and practising the necessary skills will help you achieve success in your Stage exam.

Good luck!

1 Health, Safety and Efficiency

REQUIRED SKILLS/KNOWLEDGE	Learnt, revised, practised?	Confirmed
Work safely and with efficiency.		
• Safe handling and working practices, with regard to preserving health, safety and welfare of yourself, others and horses at all times.	☐	☐
• Be able to a maintain a clean working environment.	☐	☐
• Efficient time management.	☐	☐
Safe working procedures on a yard.		
• Know what actions should to be taken in the event of an accident on the yard.	☐	☐
• Know how to work safely on the yard.	☐	☐
Be familiar with relevant health and safety legislation.		
• Be able to outline health and safety legislation and codes of practice relating to working with horses.	☐	☐

HEALTH AND SAFETY LEGISLATION

Health and safety legislation and guidance exists to try to prevent deaths, serious injuries, diseases and other accidents from harming people at work, so having an understanding of it is a very important part of your working life.

The **Health and Safety Executive** (HSE) and the **Health and Safety Commission** (which merged in April 2008) are a division of the government **Department for Work and Pensions** and are responsible for proposing new legislation surrounding health and safety at work, updating current legislation and enforcing the law. Local authorities, like your local council, also have some involvement in the enforcement of health and safety law in the UK and work alongside the HSE to assist in monitoring the vast numbers of workplaces to make sure that they are safe for employees, employers and members of the general public – the local authority employees responsible for this are known as **Environmental Health Officers**.

A representative of the HSE or an Environmental Health Officer from a local authority can serve two types of notices on businesses under the Health and Safety at Work Act 1974 if they do not comply with the law:

- **Improvement Notice** – this alerts the employer to a specific issue that needs to be rectified in order that the business operates within the law, and gives them a specific timeframe in which to complete the necessary action(s).

- **Prohibition Notice** – this notice is the more serious of the two and is used to immediately stop businesses carrying out a certain activity when people are at risk of serious injury, and might stop a business from trading altogether until the situation has been fully rectified to the satisfaction of the HSE.

The HSE website carries a list of all of the Improvement and Prohibition notices served on businesses in the UK which can be accessed by anyone, so it is possible to check whether a company you are working for, you are considering working for, or one which your company might be working with, has ever had a notice served on them and for what reason the notice has been served.

The Health and Safety at Work Act 1974

All employers have a legal responsibility to ensure the health and safety of their employees so far as is reasonably practicable. The term 'reasonably practicable' means that your employer should put safety measures in place that make the risk of activities as low as possible, provided that the measures are not disproportionate to the risk itself. For example, for an employer to spend £1 million to prevent four staff getting bruised knees would be disproportionate to the risk, but spending £1 million to prevent an explosion that could kill 150 people would be proportionate to the risk.

The **Health and Safety at Work Act 1974** compels employers to maintain safe equipment, premises and procedures. The conditions of the Act encompass employers, employees and all visitors to the establishment; so it is not only your employer who has a legal obligation to operate in a way that reduces the likelihood of accidents or injuries – it is partly your responsibility too! However, the Health and Safety at Work Act indicates that, although employees have some responsibilities, ultimately the overall responsibility for health and safety is that of the senior partner/s of the practice or the director of the business.

The HSE issues three types of information under the Health and Safety at Work Act: **Guidance**, **Approved Codes of Practice** and **Regulations** and, when you are looking at health and safety documents it is important for you to know the status of each type of information. Guidance documents are just that – they provide guidance about ways in which you might consider doing something – they are not law and so it is not compulsory to follow them. However, if you and your employer are using guidance documents then you will normally be doing enough to comply with the law so it can be a good idea to use HSE guidance to your advantage in this way.

Approved Codes of Practice set out practical examples of good practice surrounding certain specific activities, for example the use of veterinary medicines. Approved Code of Practice documents contain information regarding how to comply with the law and take consideration of what is 'reasonably practicable' in terms of controlling risks.

Regulations are laws made by parliament under the Health and Safety at Work Act 1974 in order to address specific risks that *must* be dealt with by your employer. They include regulations such as the **Reporting of Diseases and Dangerous Occurrences Regulations (RIDDOR) 1995** and the **Manual Handling Regulations 1992**.

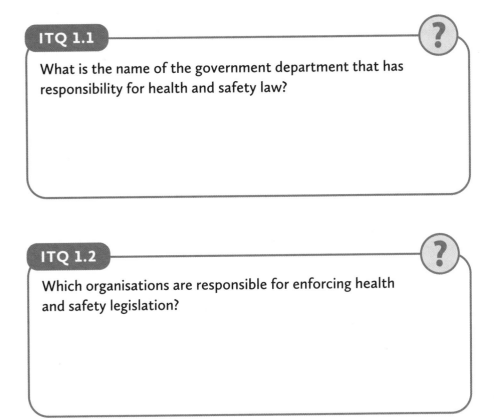

ITQ 1.1

What is the name of the government department that has responsibility for health and safety law?

ITQ 1.2

Which organisations are responsible for enforcing health and safety legislation?

Whilst it is beyond the scope of this book to discuss the Health and Safety at Work Act fully, everyone involved in a professional capacity with horses should be familiar with their responsibilities under the Health and Safety at Work Act. Up to date information should be obtained from The Health and Safety Executive – their website is very comprehensive and can be found at www.hse.gov.uk

General responsibilities under the Health and Safety at Work Act 1974

Under the Health and Safety at Work Act 1974, employers and employees have the following general obligations:

- Employers with more than five employees must prepare, and when necessary revise, a written health and safety policy statement and this be made known to all employees.

- Employers must ensure the safety of their employees by maintaining safe systems of work, safe premises and equipment, and by regularly assessing risks.

- Employees and self-employed persons must take reasonable care to avoid accidents or injuries to themselves and others.

- Employers, employees and the self-employed must not endanger the health and safety of third parties.

- Employers must ensure that all employees and others (for example volunteers) are instructed and trained in the jobs they have to do and in the use of all equipment.

- A named person must be specified to whom any potential hazards, faults in equipment or accidents can be reported.

- All employers must have Employers' Liability Insurance and the certificate must be displayed.

- A trained first-aider and well-equipped first aid kit must be accessible to all.

ITQ 1.3   **?**

Name the two types of enforcement notices that can be served on businesses:

1.

2.

ITQ 1.4   **?**

Explain the difference between the two types of enforcement notices.

As well as abiding by the responsibilities set out in the Health and Safety at Work Act 1974, your employer should also clearly display a Health and Safety Law poster entitled 'Health and Safety Law: What you should know' (see Figure 1.1) somewhere on the premises. The boxes on the poster should be filled out to include details of the health and safety arrangements for your place of work – an organisation can be fined if it fails to display an appropriately completed poster. The poster summarises the Health and Safety at Work Act 1974 and provides specific information about which people and organisations are responsible for certain aspects of health and safety management and advice within your workplace – if the poster is displayed but the boxes are not completed then your employer might be subject to a fine from the HSE.

Health and Safety Law
What you need to know

All workers have a right to work in places where risks to their health and safety are properly controlled. Health and safety is about stopping you getting hurt at work or ill through work. Your employer is responsible for health and safety, but you must help.

What employers must do for you

1 Decide what could harm you in your job and the precautions to stop it. This is part of risk assessment.

2 In a way you can understand, explain how risks will be controlled and tell you who is responsible for this.

3 Consult and work with you and your health and safety representatives in protecting everyone from harm in the workplace.

4 Free of charge, give you the health and safety training you need to do your job.

5 Free of charge, provide you with any equipment and protective clothing you need, and ensure it is properly looked after.

6 Provide toilets, washing facilities and drinking water.

7 Provide adequate first-aid facilities.

8 Report injuries, diseases and dangerous incidents at work to our Incident Contact Centre: **0845 300 9923**

9 Have insurance that covers you in case you get hurt at work or ill through work. Display a hard copy or electronic copy of the current insurance certificate where you can easily read it.

10 Work with any other employers or contractors sharing the workplace or providing employees (such as agency workers), so that everyone's health and safety is protected.

What you must do

1 Follow the training you have received when using any work items your employer has given you.

2 Take reasonable care of your own and other people's health and safety.

3 Co-operate with your employer on health and safety.

4 Tell someone (your employer, supervisor, or health and safety representative) if you think the work or inadequate precautions are putting anyone's health and safety at serious risk.

If there's a problem

1 If you are worried about health and safety in your workplace, talk to your employer, supervisor, or health and safety representative.

2 You can also look at our website for general information about health and safety at work.

3 If, after talking with your employer, you are still worried, phone our Infoline. We can put you in touch with the local enforcing authority for health and safety and the Employment Medical Advisory Service. You don't have to give your name.

HSE Infoline: **0845 345 0055**

HSE website: **www.hse.gov.uk**

Fire safety
You can get advice on fire safety from the Fire and Rescue Services or your workplace fire officer.

Employment rights
Find out more about your employment rights at:
www.direct.gov.uk

Your health and safety representatives:

Other health and safety contacts:

 Health and Safety Executive

1.1 Health and safety law poster

Employee training

The Health and Safety at Work Act 1974 implies that employees must receive instruction, training and supervision in order to carry out their job safely. Some accidents at work are caused through lack of skill and experience on the part of the employee or through lack of appropriate supervision by the employer. Anyone working with horses should receive thorough training in all aspects of their management. The training should include a summary of employee responsibilities and should also involve safety and accident prevention measures.

When young (under the age of 18 years) or inexperienced employees start work they should work under the close supervision and guidance of an experienced person. Inexperienced employees must not work with difficult horses alone or be asked to carry out any task for which they have not been thoroughly trained beforehand.

New members of staff should receive a health and safety briefing at the start of their employment. This is often referred to as an **induction.** Employers should keep a record of the induction procedure, who was involved and the date(s) on which induction took place and the employee should sign a statement specifying that they have received health and safety induction training.

If, at the end of an induction, a routine health and safety training session or a training session regarding a new procedure or piece of equipment you will be using, you are still unsure about what you need to do then you should not be afraid of making your employer aware of this – this way they can go back through things with you to clarify anything that you don't understand. It is very important that you receive enough training to ensure that you can work safely, not just for your benefit but for that of the other people and animals you work with too!

ITQ 1.5   **?**

List four responsibilities of employers under the Health and Safety at Work Act (1974):

1.

2.

3.

4.

Consequences of poor workplace health and safety practices

Employers and employees who do not observe health and safety laws and guidance put themselves and others at risk of injury, disease or even death. Another consequence of not observing the law is that an employer or person deemed to be responsible for health and safety in the workplace (for example a senior partner) could be subject to prosecution in the courts and may be liable to pay fines and/or face a prison sentence depending on the severity of the breach and the resulting effects.

In terms of other consequences, the effects of poor workplace health and safety practices, whether they be injury, illness or a fine, have (aside from other issues) an economic cost. For example, if a practice does not observe good hygiene measures and as a result of this an employee contracts a zoonotic disease and has to have a period of time off work, the practice is likely to have to pay the employee sick pay (depending on the length of time they have been employed at the practice) and would need to arrange cover whilst the employee is recuperating. In cases where poor health and safety practices have resulted in an employee or member of the public getting injured or contracting a disease, the business might be sued and forced to pay damages to the injured party as part of the court ruling; this can be a very costly process in terms of both money and the time taken for the case to go to court and be heard.

Any events that have resulted from a failure in health and safety practices that are made public, for example court cases, accidents or the serving of improvement or prohibition notices by the HSE or local authority, can damage the reputation of a business, in some cases beyond repair, which might ultimately lead to a business ceasing to trade and to individuals losing their income and livelihood.

SAFE WORKING PRACTICE

Handler training

Handling horses involves an element of risk and many accidents are caused through a lack of skill and experience on the part of the handler. Anyone working with horses, or even simply handling them, should receive thorough training in all aspects of their management. This should involve appropriate safety and accident prevention measures.

Horses are flight animals: if they feel threatened or frightened their first natural instinct is to take flight, normally at high speed. This means that when a problem happens, e.g. a horse gets his headcollar caught on a catch or similar, he will make matters far worse by panicking and trying to pull away violently. If a horse's initial flight reaction is prevented (perhaps by confinement within a stable or constraint under a rider) he may resort to the secondary 'fight' reaction of his species. It is therefore very important that handlers learn to calm and reassure a horse in 'flight mode' whilst being firm and assertive enough to take on a role as 'herd leader' and thus ensure the safety of the horse and themselves.

Inexperienced handlers should work under close supervision and under the guidance of an experienced person. The inexperienced handler must not work with difficult or very young horses. Therefore, if you are a novice handler in the early stages of training and learning about horses, you should ideally work under experienced supervision and deal mainly with quiet, well-behaved horses. With experience you will recognise potentially hazardous situations and how to reduce the chance of an accident occurring.

Just as horses respond positively to a calm, confident and authoritative handler, they can also sense when the handler is inexperienced or nervous and some will take advantage. With experience you will learn when you need to be more assertive with horses, and when you need to be quieter. The temperament of each horse and the individual situation will determine how you need to react. For example, an unruly, 'bolshy' horse who is not nervous or frightened but simply misbehaving will need firm and authoritative handling, whereas a nervous individual is more likely to respond to a quiet approach.

Dress guidelines

When working with horses you should appear workmanlike and practical, looking as neat and tidy as possible. Each yard will have its own dress code.

Working with horses involves being outside in all weathers including everything from freezing wind, rain and snow to heatwaves, therefore it is important to have the right clothing to be able to work effectively. In addition to being appropriate for different levels of cold and heat, clothing worn when working with horses must take account of other practicalities, such as protection from tread injuries and rope burns. Outdoor pursuit shops sell a huge range of technical outdoor clothing including base layers, gloves, hats, fleeces and jackets, which are all ideal for working outdoors.

Base layers. Depending on the weather you should aim to use layers of breathable clothing so you can adjust the amount you wear according to your body temperature. In hot weather it looks more professional to wear short-sleeved polo shirts rather than skimpy sleeveless vest tops (and helps stop you getting sunburnt shoulders).

Jacket. You will need a decent waterproof jacket, preferably one with breathable qualities so as you warm up it wicks perspiration away, keeping you dry. A decent hood is essential.

Overalls. If you are mucking out several stables, overalls can protect your clothes, keeping them clean and stopping them from smelling. Overalls are also very useful to wear when clipping as they prevent most of the fine hairs from getting under your clothes.

Waterproof overtrousers. In torrential rain, waterproof overtrousers are needed. Again, these should ideally be of a breathable material, with the lower section zipped so they can be pulled on and off over wellington boots. It is possible to buy waterproof overtrousers suitable for riding.

Footwear. Boots or shoes must always be sturdy, secure and non-slip, even in very hot weather. Clogs, flip-flops and soft shoes are unsuitable. It is not essential to wear steel toecap boots, as these can cause further injury if a horse treads on the steel rim. Wellington boots are needed for walking in muddy wet fields and for mucking out. Don't wear leather boots for mucking out as the urine rots the stitching and damages the leather.

Socks. When riding or standing around (e.g. if teaching or lungeing) in very cold weather your feet can get extremely cold, to the point of being painful. It is worth investing in decent hiking socks, including thermal inner socks, to keep your feet warm. These are much better than wearing several pairs of ordinary socks, which can restrict your feet to an uncomfortable degree.

Gloves. Non-slip gloves are needed all year round for leading and lungeing horses. When working in cold weather you will need warm, preferably waterproof gloves. If trying to preserve your fingernails and prevent calluses, gloves should be worn for stable duties, especially mucking out.

Hat. In very cold weather you will need a warm winter hat. In hot, sunny weather a baseball cap can help keep the sun off your face.

Crash cap. A correctly fitted crash cap should be worn when riding or lungeing. It should also be worn when leading and handling youngsters and unruly horses.

Hair ties. Long hair should be tied back when working with horses, or riding.

Body protector. When jumping, especially for cross-country jumping, a current BSI standard body protector should be worn. At most competitions, and many schooling courses, these are now obligatory.

Dust masks. When working in dusty conditions, e.g. when unloading hay or grooming, you may need to wear a dust mask, especially if you are prone to a dust allergy or asthma.

Jewellery. Ideally no jewellery should be worn but if it is, it must be kept to a minimum. Loop earrings, necklaces and studded rings, etc. can be dangerous as they can get caught. Rings can scratch saddles.

Perfume. Strong perfumes should not be worn as horses are very sensitive to smell.

Accident prevention

As the saying goes, 'Prevention is better than cure' – it is essential to be aware of what can cause an accident and how to prevent them happening in the first place. When working with horses there are many risks to consider.

In the yard and stable

- Keeping the working environment clean and tidy will improve efficiency and reduce the risks of accidents. The yard must always be kept tidy, free of debris, tools, haynets etc., which could injure a horse or trip someone over.

- Keep the yard gates closed at all times – then if a horse breaks loose, he is contained.

EXAM TIP

It is often wise to make sure that you have a change of clothing with you in an exam situation as the examiner will usually push on regardless of the weather. This also applies to the work environment; changing into a new set of dry clothes is preferable to spending the entire day wet and muddy!

- To prevent horses from escaping from their boxes, make sure top and bottom bolts on doors are securely bolted, especially last thing at night.

- Don't leave a horse loose in a stable wearing a nylon headcollar. The headcollar can become caught on the top bolt of the stable door, causing the horse to pull back and panic. The nylon headcollar wouldn't break and the horse could be injured.

- Stables should be solidly constructed. Flimsy materials will splinter or break if the horse kicks out whilst rolling, etc. Make sure that stables are free of sharp projections such as nails. Try to keep additional stable furniture to a minimum as this reduces the risk of an accident occurring.

- Stables should be well bedded down to prevent the horse from slipping. Well banked-up sides can help to prevent the horse from becoming cast. Horses can damage themselves thrashing about when they become cast.

- Do not allow empty haynets to hang low in the stable as the horse may get a foot entangled.

- When mucking out with the horse in the stable, keep all of the equipment outside of the stable when not in use. Make sure the horse cannot get entangled in wheelbarrow handles. Always position yourself safely, ensuring that you do not get trapped between the horse and a wall.

- In icy conditions do not empty water buckets onto the concrete. Spread grit or rock salt on all areas where horses are to be led and where people walk.

Manual handling

When working on the yard, many heavy items have to be moved around. Training should be given in correct handling procedures.

Points to remember when moving heavy loads are:

- Estimate the weight of the load and if necessary seek help.

- If lifting by yourself:
  - Stand close to the bale or sack.
  - Square up the sack in front of you.
  - Keep your spine straight and bend the knees – don't lean over the sack to lift.
  - Lift by straightening your knees rather than using arm strength alone.

- When putting heavy items down, remember to bend your knees, not your back.

- Heavy items should be transported on a sack barrow rather than being carried and assistance should be sought where possible.

- When moving hay bales, wear gloves to protect your hands from the twine.

- If moving hay from a stack always take bales from the top – never pull out the lower bales as the stack may collapse.

- When carrying water buckets make sure the buckets are evenly filled and not too heavy. Carry one in each hand to balance the load. If using large tubs for water it is advisable to part-fill them and use a bucket to top them up, or ask someone to help you carry them.

Tying up

- Only tie horses to tying rings securely fitted to a solid object, e.g. the wall. The tying ring should never be fixed onto something which may pull away, e.g. a loose rail or similar.

  Attach a weak link to the tying ring. This can be a loop of baler twine or string. Always tie the horse to the weak link so that in the event that he pulls backwards, the weak link will break, rather than the headcollar. Use a quick-release knot so you can undo the rope in an emergency.

- Never leave horses tied up close to each other as they may fight, and never tie a horse up in an area where there are loose horses.

- Tie up so that the rope is not so long that the horse can put a foot over it, nor so short that the horse becomes upset.

- Never tie up by the reins. The horse will injure his mouth if he pulls back.

- Never leave a horse unattended when tied up.

- When a young horse is tied up, e.g. for the farrier, have an assistant who can hold the horse if necessary. If the horse continually pulls back and breaks free, the farrier may be tempted to tie the horse directly to the ring with potentially disastrous results. You have a responsibility to assist the farrier – it is for the farrier's benefit as well as the horse's.

ITQ 1.6

Why should a horse never be left wearing a nylon headcollar when he is loose in the stable?

In the field
Fencing, fittings and the environment

- Never use barbed wire as fencing for horses at grass. Very serious injuries are regularly caused when horses become entangled in barbed wire.

- Check fencing materials for safety – broken rails need to be repaired promptly and protruding nails removed.

- Check that no rails protrude into the field, e.g. slip rails must be fully opened before leading horses through. Slip rails must never be left partially closed when horses are loose in adjoining fields. Serious injuries can result if the horses canter past protruding rails.

- The fencing should be high enough to deter the horses from jumping out. The top rail should be at least 1.2m (4ft) high. The bottom rail should be high enough to stop a horse putting a foot over it but not so high that a pony or foal could roll underneath it. In addition, rails must be nailed to the inside of posts to prevent horses pushing through them.

- If plain wire fencing is used, a wooden top rail must be added to help the horses see the fence when galloping around. It also prevents them from leaning on the fence and causing the wire to sag.

- Serious injuries can be caused by horses getting a foot caught in the gate. Ideally gates should have vertical bars or a wire mesh base. Metal five-bar gates are particularly dangerous as the horse can get a foot trapped in the 'V'-shaped sections between the bars.

- Horses are particularly prone to injuries when they are in adjoining fields as they may fight at the fence. This is when they are more likely to put a foot through the fence or gate, or try to kick each other. Use a strip of electric fencing along the top of the rails to keep the horses away from the fence.

- Make sure the water trough doesn't have any sharp protrusions. If you use an old bath as a water trough, make sure that you remove the taps.

- Trim back any sharp branches on hedges and trees.

- As far as is practical, fill in rabbit holes as a horse can be injured if he puts a foot down one whilst cantering in the field.

ITQ 1.7   **?**

Give four safety points to observe when tying horses up:

1.

2.

3.

4.

The horses

- Never leave a horse out in the field wearing a nylon headcollar. If the headcollar became caught up, it wouldn't break and could cause serious injury. If the horse is very difficult to catch it is best to turn him out in a leather headcollar which will break under pressure; another option is a headcollar designed specifically for use in the field, i.e. one that has a weak link that will break under pressure.

- Turn horses out in small groups known to get on with each other. The smaller the group, the less likely they are to fight. It is often safer to turn out in same-sex groups to reduce squabbling.

- Introduce new members to the group carefully. Let the horses meet in the yard before turning them out together. Keep a close watch on them and remove one or other if they don't get on. In particular you should check for bullying.

- When turning out a horse for the first time, e.g. after box rest or similar, use the smallest paddock available to prevent him from galloping around too energetically. Put brushing and overreach boots on if the horse is likely to charge around at first.

- When turning horses out, lead them into the field, close the gate and, keeping the horses apart, turn them to face the gate. Everyone should undo headcollars and release the horses at the same time, stepping back as they do so to avoid being kicked.

Tack and equipment

Tack should ideally be cleaned after each use, or at least on a weekly basis. The tack should be thoroughly checked for state of repair. Faulty, brittle or damaged tack is more likely to break when put under strain. A quick wipe-over after each use saves time in the long run as it reduces build-up of grease and dirt, making the full tack clean much easier. It will also increase the lifespan of your tack.

Before starting any lesson for novice riders, the instructor should check the tack. Check that all buckles are done up on the bridle, all straps are through their keepers, that the girth is secure and the stirrup bars are down. If the stirrup bars are up the stirrup leather will not pull free in the event of the rider's foot becoming wedged in the stirrup after falling, and if the rider's foot is caught up in the stirrup, the rider will be in danger of being dragged.

It is also important that the stirrup irons are the correct size for the rider's feet – neither too large nor too small. The former may result in the foot going right through the stirrup and getting caught; the latter in it becoming wedged. It is also important to check that riders' safety equipment is undamaged and up to current standards and to ensure that all equipment used in the lesson (jump wings, poles, fillers, etc.) is in good order.

ITQ 1.8

Give two examples of accidents that can happen whilst a horse is turned out in the field:

1.

2.

ITQ 1.9

List three safety measures that can be taken to prevent accidents in the field:

1.

2.

3.

ITQ 1.10

How would you introduce a new grazing member to a group of horses?

ITQ 1.11

What do you need to check at the beginning of a lesson for a novice rider?

BASIC ACCIDENT PROCEDURE

This section is intended to introduce basic accident procedure. Everyone working with horses should train with a recognised organisation and gain the First Aid at Work Certificate. Refresher courses need to be undertaken at regular intervals to maintain skills and keep up to date with new developments. The British Horse Society organises Equine Specific First Aid Courses which, as the name suggests, cover the type of accidents which affect those handling and riding horses.

Action to be taken after a fall or accident

1. The ride should halt somewhere safe.

2. Depending on the circumstances, the most experienced rider or the instructor should assume control unless one of the other riders is medically qualified.

3. Assess whether there is danger to you – it is important that you do not become another casualty.

4. Assess the situation so that suitable control procedures can be delegated. For example, if the accident occurred on the road, someone should be positioned on either side of the accident to slow down and control the traffic in front and behind. If the horse is loose, someone competent should be sent to catch him.

   At this point, your assessment of the situation will indicate whether the casualty needs to be moved or not. For example, an injured person lying in an icy, water-filled ditch on a freezing day is in danger of drowning or becoming hypothermic so needs to be moved.

   Because of the risk of spinal injury, never move the casualty unless it is absolutely necessary. Incorrectly moving a casualty with a spinal injury can result in permanent paralysis.

5. When the safety measures above have been taken to prevent the situation becoming worse, you can turn your attention to the injured rider. You must establish whether the casualty is conscious or not and provide emergency care as necessary.

Do not remove the casualty's crash cap unless it is essential.

Remember the letters **DR ABC**:
D – Danger – check that you and the casualty are not in danger.
R – Response – try to get a response by asking questions and gently shaking their shoulders.
A – Airway – the airway should be clear and kept open. Place one hand on the forehead, two fingers under the chin and gently tilt the head back.
B – Breathing – normal breathing should be established. Once the airway is open check breathing for up to 10 seconds by looking for the rise and fall of the

chest, feeling for their breath on your cheek and listening.

C – Compressions – if the casualty is not breathing you should call for an ambulance and start cardio-pulmonary resuscitation (CPR) (also known as mouth-to-mouth resuscitation) straight away. CPR is a combination of rescue breaths and chest compressions to keep blood and oxygen circulating in the body.

a

b
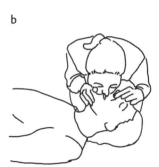
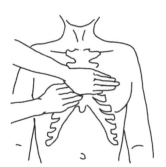
c
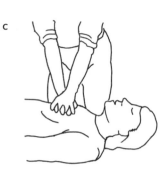

1.2 The ABC of first aid

CPR method for adults

- Place your hands on the centre of the casualty's chest and, with the heel of your hand, press down (4–5cm) at a steady rate, slightly faster than one compression a second.

- After every thirty chest compressions, give two breaths.

- Pinch the casualty's nose. Seal your mouth over their mouth and blow steadily and firmly into their mouth. Check that their chest rises. Give two rescue breaths, each over one second.

- Continue with cycles of thirty chest compressions and two rescue breaths until they begin to recover or emergency help arrives.

CPR method for children

- Open the airway by placing one hand on the forehead and gently tilting their head back and lifting the chin. Remove any visible obstructions from the mouth and nose.

- Pinch their nose. Seal your mouth over their mouth and blow steadily and firmly into their mouth, checking that their chest rises. Give five initial rescue breaths.

- Place your hands on the centre of their chest and, with the heel of your hand, press down one-third of the depth of the chest using one or two hands.

- After every thirty chest compressions (at a steady rate, slightly faster than one compression a second) give two breaths.

- Continue with cycles of thirty chest compressions and two rescue breaths until they begin to recover or emergency help arrives.

The recovery position

A casualty who is breathing but unconscious should be placed into the recovery position to ensure the airway remains clear and open and prevent vomit or fluid from causing choking.

- Place the casualty on their side so they are supported by one leg and one arm.

- Open their airway by tilting the head back and lifting the chin.

- Monitor breathing and pulse continuously

- If injuries allow, turn the casualty onto their other side after 30 minutes.

If you think a spinal injury may have been sustained, do not move the casualty; place your hands on either side of their face and gently lift their jaw with your fingertips to open the airway. Take care not to move the neck. If breathing is or becomes noisy then place the casualty in the recovery position.

If the casualty is conscious:

- Offer reassurance and tell them not to move until their injuries have been assessed.

- Ask them if there is any pain and, if so, where.

- Ask them whether they can move their fingers and toes. If they are unable to do so, there is a strong possibility of damage to the spine, so the casualty *must not be moved* until skilled help arrives. Loosen clothing around the neck and waist and cover the casualty with a jacket to keep them warm.

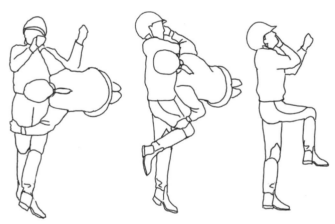

1.3 The recovery position

Further procedure

If necessary, send someone to call an ambulance. Make sure the person calling the ambulance knows the exact address/location of the accident. Searching for a telephone in a rural area can waste time – this is where the mobile phone is so useful. Always keep the phone battery charged for this reason and take it with you on hacks.

Meanwhile, continue to reassure the casualty and check bleeding, which should be stemmed (see next heading) unless pressure to the wound would make matters worse e.g. pushing foreign matter further into the wound. Immobilise fractures as best you

SAFETY TIP

▶ If there is any possibility that a casualty has spinal damage they must not be moved until skilled help arrives.

can with the equipment you have with you. Jumpers can be made into slings and clean handkerchiefs make useful pressure pads to stem bleeding. The casualty should not be offered anything to drink in case surgery is necessary, for which the stomach needs to be empty.

Controlling bleeding

Heavy blood loss leads to a reduction in blood pressure, which causes life-threatening shock. To control bleeding:

1. Apply direct pressure with the fingers to the bleeding points. If the wound area is large, press the sides of the wound together firmly but gently.

1. If the wound is on a limb, raise the injured part and support it in position. *Don't* do this if you suspect an underlying fracture.

3. Do not try to remove foreign bodies from a wound as this could cause further damage to veins or arteries.

4. When you have a clean dressing available apply it to the wound and press down gently but firmly. Cover with a pad of soft material and bandage in position.

Take the casualty to the nearest Accident and Emergency Department.

How to continue

If the fallen rider gets up straight away and doesn't suffer dizziness, double vision or complain of a headache, and has no obvious injury (other than to their pride!), they may be permitted to remount and continue the ride.

However, if there is any doubt as to their well-being, someone from the stables should be contacted to come and collect them by car and the horse should be led home. A rider who has been unconscious, even for a short time, must not be allowed to remount and should be taken to hospital for a check-up. There is a risk of delayed concussion in these cases, so such a person should not drive themselves to hospital.

The injured horse

If the horse is injured it may be possible to lead him home, or transport may need to be arranged. A vet may need to be called to meet the horse back at the stables or, in more severe situations, the vet may need to attend the scene of the accident. Try to keep the horse calm and, in cold weather, keep him warm with jackets or blankets. It may be necessary to keep one of the other horses beside the injured horse while waiting for help to stop him fretting about being separated.

The accident report book

All riding schools and livery yards should keep an *Accident Report Book* to ensure all details of incidents are recorded in case claims are made against the insurance. All falls and any accident, whether it occurred whilst riding out or in the yard, should be recorded in the *Accident Report Book*, no matter how minor the incident may seem at the time.

ITQ 1.12

In the event of a rider falling off whilst out riding, what would be your immediate course of action?

SAFETY TIP

▶ If there is an object embedded in the wound try to pack and apply pressure around it to prevent pushing it further in whilst attempting to stem the bleeding.

ITQ 1.13

What is the main danger of moving a casualty who is unable to get up unaided?

ITQ 1.14

What should you do with a breathing but unconscious casualty?

ITQ 1.15

What should you do if the casualty is conscious but injured?

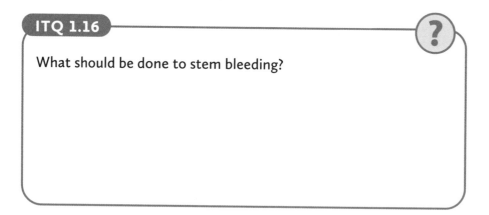

ITQ 1.16

What should be done to stem bleeding?

This is best done whilst everything is still fresh in your mind and while witnesses are available to sign the book to confirm your description of events.

The information to be recorded in the *Accident Report Book* includes:

- Date, location and time of the accident.

- A diagram depicting the location of those involved and how the situation progressed.

- Names and addresses of those involved, including witnesses.

- Description of events, i.e. what happened and why.

- Record of injuries sustained and to whom.

- Record of any treatment given and by whom.

- Details of admission to hospital if that was necessary.

- Signatures, preferably of all parties involved, including the escort or instructor in charge at the time.

Advising insurers

The relevant insurance company should be advised if there is injury to a horse or rider, or damage to property, a motor vehicle or similar which could result in a claim. If in doubt it is always better to err on the side of caution and advise the insurance company.

Learn the sequence of priorities in the event of an accident so that if you are ever involved in one you will know what to do, and will not waste time panicking.

The golden rules if you are in an accident involving other people are:

- Never admit liability.

- Never apologise.

- Never accept the blame.

- Exchange names and addresses with the people involved in the accident.

- Ask for the name and address of their insurance company.

- Take the names and addresses of all witnesses and note registration numbers of vehicles involved.

If the police are involved they will also take everyone's details, but you will need to know them for your insurance company, as well as to fill in the *Accident Report Book*.

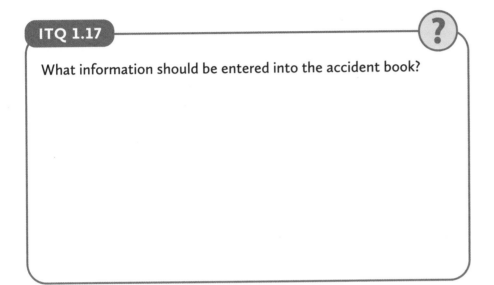

ITQ 1.17

?

What information should be entered into the accident book?

EFFICIENCY AND TIME MANAGEMENT

Without exception, professional involvement with horses is hard work. Depending on the type of yard, certain times of year may be quieter but, on the whole, horses are very labour-intensive animals to care for and most yards tend to be busy places.

The majority of the tasks need to be repeated every day, with many needing to be carried out more than once a day, e.g mucking/skipping out, feeding, watering, exercising, etc. and a great deal of time can be saved by planning the layout of the yard and organising the way in which you work to maximise efficiency.

Taking into account individual horses' temperaments you should aim to work to a high standard, quickly and safely. If you are hurried and sloppy you are more likely to make a mess, upset the horses and cause an accident.

Being set a good example at the start of your training and actually working with horses is the best way to learn good practice. Most employers very much value a yard assistant who works hard and maintains high standards.

Planning the layout of the yard and amenities, e.g. tack room, feed room, muck heap, etc. to improve ergonomics and keeping everything tidy and in its place saves time spent looking for and gathering tools and equipment, moving feed, hay, tack, wheelbarrows, etc.

② Grooming and Plaiting

REQUIRED SKILLS/KNOWLEDGE	Learnt, revised, practised?	Confirmed
Strapping a horse.		
• Select and use equipment for grooming fit horses.	☐	☐
Know the procedure for grooming a rugged-up horse.		
• Know how to groom a stabled horse before and after exercise.	☐	☐
Mane and tail plaiting.		
• Prepare the mane and tail for plaiting.	☐	☐
• Plait a mane using bands/thread.	☐	☐
• Plait a tail using bands/thread.	☐	☐

GROOMING

Clothing/equipment notes:

Remove gloves.

Gather and check grooming kit, keeping it in a container.

Have to hand a small bucket partially filled with water.

Have to hand a headcollar and lead-rope.

2.1 The grooming kit

a. Dandy brush – used to remove dried mud and dirt.

b. Plastic curry comb – used to remove dried mud and dirt.

c. Rubber curry comb – used to remove loose hair.

d. Water brush – used to wash off stable stains and to 'lay' the mane.

e. Body brush – used to remove grease and dust; it can also be used to brush out the mane and tail.

f. Metal curry comb – used to clean the body brush.

g. Hoofpick – used twice daily (more frequently if necessary) to clean out the hooves. You must also have a rubber skip to pick the foot into.

h. Leather 'banger' or massage pad – used to strap the fit horse to tone the muscles.

i. Stable rubber – used to wipe off dust following strapping.

j. Sponge – each horse should have his own separate sponges for eyes, nostrils and dock region, and a water bucket.

Quartering

Quartering (brushing off) is a short groom used to tidy up the horse or prepare him for a ride. After you have ridden it is correct to give your horse a more thorough groom, known as **strapping**.

1 Put on a headcollar and tie up the horse to stop him from wandering around. If grooming in the stable, remove the water buckets to prevent them becoming soiled by the dust which is generated when grooming.

If the horse's coat is particularly dusty and/or you have a dust allergy or suffer from asthma you should wear a protective dust mask.

2 Start by picking out the hooves. Position the skip behind the horse's foreleg. Stand facing the horse's tail and run your hand down the back of the foreleg and ask him to give his foot. You may need to take hold of some hair from the back of his heel – this hair is called **'feather'**. If he is reluctant to pick up his foot you may need to lean on him to make him shift his weight. This often makes it easier for you to pick up the foot. Hold the foot securely around the coronet/pastern.

Use the **hoofpick** from heel to toe to prevent digging it into the frog or your own hand. Clean the foot out very thoroughly, making sure that you get all the dirt out from the clefts of the frog. If dirt is allowed to collect in the clefts it can cause a bacterial infection which results in a foul-smelling black discharge called **thrush**.

Most horses will allow you to pick out all four feet from the nearside, which saves time. When holding the outside forefoot, bring it across behind the closer foreleg. When holding the outside hind foot bring it across in front of the closer hind leg. However, if the horse appears unfamiliar with this, pick out the nearside hooves from the horse's nearside; the offside hooves from the horse's offside.

Always clean the feet out into a **skip** to keep the yard or bedding clean.

The hooves need to be picked out before and after a ride.

Always clean out the feet at least once a day, preferably twice, even if you are not riding, and check on the condition of the shoes while you do so.

The hooves should always be picked out when you bring the horse out of his stable and again upon return from exercise or the field.

3 If the horse is rugged up on a cold day, undo the front buckle and belly straps of the rug. Loosely knot the belly straps together to stop them hanging down. Fold the front half of the rug back. Brush the exposed areas then replace the rug and re-fasten the front buckle. Fold back the rear half of the rug and brush off the hindquarters. Once this is done, fold the rug back down again, unknot and fasten the belly straps to prevent the horse from getting cold.

4 Your choice of brushes will depend on the thickness of the horse's coat, how sensitive the horse is likely to be and how dirty his coat is. If the horse has a reasonably thick coat and is not a 'ticklish', sensitive sort use the **dandy brush** or **plastic curry comb** to remove the worst of the dried mud or dirt. Start at the top of the neck and brush briskly. When using the dandy brush you should use a flicking action at the end of each stroke to flick the dirt and dust off the coat. Fine-coated horses, e.g. Thoroughbreds, are likely to object to the use of a dandy brush or plastic curry comb – a **body brush** or soft dandy brush will have to be used instead.

Make sure you brush all over the horse; it is easy to miss areas such as the inside of the legs and underneath the belly. Take care when brushing around the flanks and belly as horses are quite sensitive here. Careless brushing can make a horse bad-tempered and more likely to nip.

If trying to remove a stable stain you can use the dandy brush backwards and forwards across the lie of the coat to help shift the stain. Once the stain has gone, brush the coat flat again.

5 Whilst working on the horse's neck, brush out his mane using the **body brush**. Starting just behind the poll, separate out a segment of hair and brush down to the roots to remove scurf. Continue down the length of his mane. Once you have brushed out the mane, dampen the water brush and lay the mane down flat on the offside (right) of the neck. Dirt from the mane will have been flicked onto his neck so you should brush his neck after brushing out the mane.

6 To groom the horse's head, untie the quick-release knot and slip the headcollar around his neck. Steady the horse's head with your hand. Using the body brush, brush the head and forelock carefully, taking care not to bang the facial bones. Replace the headcollar and retie the quick-release knot.

7 To brush out the tail, stand to one side and hold the tail. Release a small amount of hair and brush out all knots using a body brush. Carry on doing this until the tail is free of tangles. You may find that using your fingers to untangle the hairs helps to prevent the hairs from breaking. A small amount of baby oil brushed through the tail prevents tangling but this is not feasible in the Stage 2 exam. If the horse has a very thick tail you should use a fairly stiff body brush.

8 The last thing to do when quartering is to wipe the eyes, nose and dock region with separate clean, damp **sponges**. Always wash the sponges well after use. Have a different coloured sponge for each or use a permanent marker pen to label the sponges. To prevent the spread of disease, each horse should have his own sponges.

SAFETY TIPS

▶ Never brush the horse's head without untying the quick-release knot as the horse may be head-shy and prone to pulling backwards.

▶ Never slip the headcollar around the horse's neck with the quick-release knot still tied. If the horse pulls back it will have a noose effect, causing the horse to panic.

Strapping

Strapping is normally done after exercise because the coat is then warmed and the pores of the skin are open. This means that the oil in the skin, which gives the coat its shine, will come out more easily – the dirt in the coat will also loosen off more easily. Any sweat on the coat will be brushed off when strapping, which promotes good hygiene.

1 Start off as with the quartering by tying up the horse and then picking out the hooves. Undo and fold back any rugs, as described previously. Unless the horse is thin-skinned and sensitive, remove the worst of the dirt with the dandy brush.

1 Next, take the body brush in the hand nearer the horse's body and have the **metal curry comb** in the other hand. Starting at the top of the neck, use the brush vigorously in circular motions. Every three or four strokes, clean the brush on the metal curry comb. Occasionally tap the dirt out of the metal curry comb and you will see how much dirt you are getting out of the coat.

　　The body brush has soft bristles and removes grease from the coat. This brush is not used on grass-kept horses as the grease in the coat acts as a waterproofer and helps to keep the horse warm.

Groom the horse's entire body. Make sure you brush inside the horse's legs, around the girth area and under his belly.

When grooming the neck on the side upon which the horse's mane lies, put the metal curry comb down and brush the mane out as previously described.

Groom the head as previously described.

③ If the horse is stable-kept and has a pulled tail, you can dampen the tail and put on a tail bandage to improve the appearance. Never leave a tail bandage on for more than a few hours as it could interfere with circulation within the dock bone.

④ To tone up the horse's muscles you can 'bang' them with a wisp. This is referred to as **banging** or **wisping**. Traditionally this was carried out using a wad of plaited hay but is now more likely to be carried out using a folded **stable rubber** (a clean tea towel makes a good stable rubber), or a special leather **massage pad** may be used in a banging action on the main muscles on the body. This helps to tone the muscles and produce a shine. Most horses enjoy it once they get used to it. Wisping is done on the shoulders, neck and hindquarters – never wisp any bony areas, or over the loins. The kidneys lie beneath the loins, so wisping here would cause pain and damage.

⑤ Remove the last traces of dust by wiping the horse over with a stable rubber.

⑥ Sponge the eyes, nostrils and dock. Lay the mane and top of the tail with a damp water brush. Put hoof oil on the walls of the hooves for the final shine up.

Some people advocate cleaning geldings' sheaths. Unless they are extremely dirty, sheaths should not be cleaned, particularly not with a soapy product. Male horses are supposed to have smegma, which contains a balance of healthy bacteria, in the sheath and excessive cleaning can cause irritation and disturb the natural balance of bacteria.

Grooming machines

Grooming machines are used in some busy yards. There are two main types – the vacuum type, suitable for removing dust and loose hair, and the revolving brush type, useful for strapping the horse. Grooming machines must only be used every three days or so to prevent the skin becoming sore. A circuit-breaker plug should be used.

Grooming and cleaning after exercise

The horse should be warmed down after exercise – walked either in hand or under saddle until his breathing is back to normal, i.e. he has stopped blowing.

If the horse is dry and cool he can be strapped as described above. If he has sweated or is wet from the rain he can be washed off using a sponge or hose. Hosing is more appropriate in hot weather and should be done cautiously, making sure the horse is allowed to become accustomed to the process. In warm weather cold water can be used; in cold weather it is more pleasant for both horse and handler to use warm water. The water should be scraped off immediately using a sweat scraper.

Make sure that sweat marks are removed from the bridle, saddle and girth areas using the sponge.

In warm weather the horse will dry quickly without a rug. In cold weather a thermal cooler rug should be applied to wick the moisture from the horse's coat and prevent him catching a chill. Some yards have the luxury of infra-red solarium dryers (heat lamps) which the horse can be held or tied beneath to warm and dry. In cold weather avoid leaving the horse standing without a rug once you have washed him off.

The hooves must be picked out after exercise, not only for reasons of hygiene, but because the horse may have picked up a stone or other foreign body which could cause injury if not removed.

If the horse is to be stabled his legs and feet can be washed if they are muddy. Dry the heels thoroughly after washing. Stable bandages can be applied to increase drying rate. Some people advocate packing the heels with petroleum jelly prior to washing to act as a barrier and prevent cracked heels. If the heels are very muddy and the horse has a lot of feather this is impractical. It is better to wash the heels, dry thoroughly and then apply a protective moisturising product such as udder cream or petroleum jelly.

Once dry the horse can be strapped and rugged as appropriate.

EXAM TIP

Practise grooming efficiently. The examiner will want to see you groom and handle the horse efficiently, in a workmanlike manner with due regard for safety at all times.

ITQ 2.1

What is the main difference between quartering and strapping?

ITQ 2.2

Why is strapping carried out after exercise?

EXAM TIPS

Strapping is hard work so, unless it is very cold, it is preferable not to wear a jacket. This is an important point to remember when grooming in an exam. Show a workmanlike approach in exams by removing your jacket, gloves and crash cap.

Check the contents of the grooming kit and make sure you have everything. If anything is missing, ask the examiner.

Move around the horse in a quiet yet confident manner.

Work efficiently – just as you would if you worked in a busy yard.

Keep all equipment tidy in the grooming box – never put brushes down in the bedding as they will get trodden on, soiled or lost.

ITQ 2.3

Whilst picking out the hooves, what can you check at the same time?

SAFETY TIP

▶ Long hair must be tied back – this is very important when using a grooming machine. In your exam you will be wearing a crash cap and, unless you have very short hair, or are male, a hairnet.

ITQ 2.4

What should you do with the rug when quartering a clipped horse on a cold day?

ITQ 2.5

a. Which brushes are suitable for use on a thick-coated horse with a dirty coat?

b. Which brush is most suitable for a thin-skinned horse?

c. How can a stable stain be removed?

ITQ 2.6 ?

a. What is the first thing you must do when brushing the horse's head?

b. Why must this be done?

c. Which brush will you use for brushing the horse's head?

PLAITING

Horses are most frequently plaited when taking part in a turnout class at a show, or going hunting, or to a dressage competition. Plaiting greatly improves the horse's appearance, helping to show off the neck.

Ideally you will have a well-lit stable with a rubber floor in which to plait your horse. It is not safe to use needles in a bedded stable as, in the event that you accidently drop a needle, it will be difficult to find and could be ingested by the horse with potentially serious health consequences.

Plaiting the mane

Preparation

- The mane must be reasonably well pulled (thinned and shortened), otherwise the plaits will be too large. Traditionally the mane is 'trained' to lie on the right-hand side of the horse's neck.

● The equipment needed includes:
  – Body brush, water brush and water.
  – Blunt plaiting needle(s) with large eye(s).
  – Waxed plaiting thread or small elastic plaiting bands the same colour as the mane.
  – Scissors.
  – Sturdy box to stand on.
  – Mane comb.
  – Plastic comb cut to correct size.
  – Butterfly hair clip.

● There is an old tradition regarding the number of plaits, which states that there should be an uneven number down the neck, plus the forelock. It is, however, unlikely that when at a show, the judge will count your plaits! It is more practical to plait in a way that enhances the horse's appearance. A horse with a long, fine neck will look better with fewer, larger plaits whereas smaller plaits can improve the appearance of a short, thick neck. In your exam you may only be asked to make a small number of plaits.

● The horse must be tied up, preferably without a haynet – it is virtually impossible to plait a horse who is tugging to pull hay out of a net.

SAFETY TIP

▶ Never hold the needle in your teeth! In addition to the risk of swallowing it, you are more likely to drop it.

Method 1 – using thread

1. Cut about 20cm (8in) of thread and thread through the needle. Put the scissors in your back pocket. Secure the needle and thread by tying a knot at the eye – this helps to prevent needles dropping off the thread and being lost in the bedding or on the yard. Secure the needle firmly in your sleeve while you plait the hair.

2. Starting just behind the ears, brush out the mane thoroughly and measure one plait width. To be sure that your plaits are even, decide how many plaits you wish to put in and cut a cheap plastic comb to the appropriate width. Use this comb to measure each plait. Keep the rest of the mane out of your way by clipping to the side with a butterfly clip.

3. Dampen the section of hair and divide it into three even sections. Plait it as tightly as possible and go as far down to the ends as you can – this is a fiddly job which takes practice!

4. Pass the needle through the end of the plait and wind the thread around the hair twice before passing the needle through the end of the plait again. This should secure the thread well.

4. Fold the end of the plait underneath to the base and pass the needle through the base of the plait.

6. Fold or roll the plait underneath, forming a neat ball, and sew securely in place by passing the needle and thread through the base. Draw it around one side of the

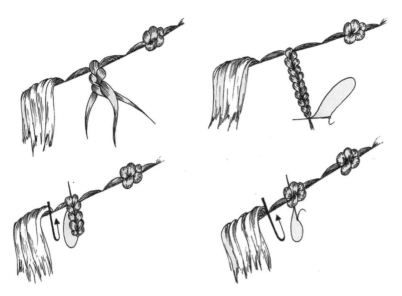

2.2 Plaiting the mane

plait, back through the base and then around the other side of the plait and back through the base. The thread is then kept neatly out of sight.

7 To finish, pass the needle down through the centre of the base of the plait to the underside, back up through the base of the plait to the top and once more down through the centre of the base to the underside. The plait will now be very secure, with the thread unobtrusive. You will have the scissors in your pocket so you can reach them without letting go of the needle – snip the cotton carefully.

8 Carry on with this procedure until the whole mane is plaited.

It is not ideal to leave plaits in overnight as they pull on the hair, causing discomfort. The hair may also be pulled out by the roots as the horse flexes his neck, the horse may rub the plaits out and bedding will become stuck in the plaits.

To remove a plait, take hold of it, turn it upwards to reveal the thread underneath the plait and snip carefully at the thread. Unplait the hair using your fingers or the mane comb. Brush out the mane and dampen down with a water brush to straighten the hair.

Method 2 – using rubber bands

1 This method is similar in all respects to the above, except that rubber bands are used instead of needle and thread. Plaiting with bands is normally quicker than using thread.

2 Wrap two plaiting bands around your index finger so they are easily to hand. Prepare the mane in exactly the same way as above and, once you have plaited a section of hair, wrap a rubber band securely around the end.

3 Turn or roll the plait up until you get it into the required position and size. Wrap a second band around the base of the plait to hold it securely in place. You cannot wrap the band too close to the base or it will slip off and the plait will unroll.

Rolling the plait gives a round shaped plait; folding it tends to give a more upright, rectangular shape. Round plaits look better on most horses.

Plaiting the tail

This greatly improves the appearance of an unpulled tail. You will need:

- Body brush, water brush and water.

- Rubber bands or needle and thread.

1. Brush out the tail thoroughly, removing all tangles. Dampen the hair to make it easier to handle. Starting at the top of the tail, take a small section of hair from either side and a small section from the centre. Start off a plait and, if you find that the hair is not quite long enough, wrap a rubber band around these three sections of hair to hold them together.

2. Next, take a small section from either side and begin to plait down the tail, introducing hairs from each side of the tail as you plait down the length of the dock bone.

3. Having completed this, plait all of the remaining hair into a long pigtail. Secure the ends using either a needle and thread or a rubber band. Now fold the pigtail upwards to the end of the tail plait and secure, then stitch the folded pigtail together to form a double thickness plait.

4. If travelling to a show, protect the tail with a bandage, remembering when you remove it to unwind the bandage rather than pull it off.

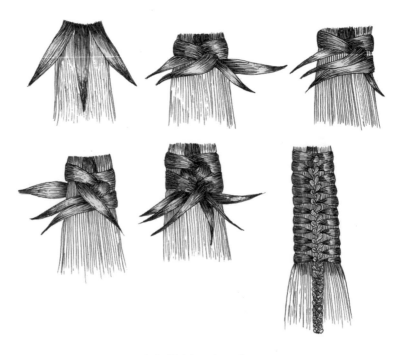

2.2 Plaiting the tail

3 Horse Clothing and Travelling Horses

REQUIRED SKILLS/KNOWLEDGE	Learnt, revised, practised?	Confirmed
Be able to prepare a horse for travelling.		
• Select and fit equipment suitable for travelling a horse relevant for the distance travelled and weather conditions.	☐	☐
• Fit a travel bandage and travel boot.	☐	☐
Know procedures for fitting and storing clothing and equipment.		
• Understand the importance of clothing and travelling equipment.	☐	☐
• Describe methods for washing clothing and equipment.	☐	☐
• Know how to store clothing and equipment when not in use.	☐	☐
• Describe how to maintain clothing and equipment in good condition.	☐	☐

RUGS

The following rugs are in common use.

Stable (night) rugs

The old-fashioned stable rugs were made from jute, a heavy woollen-lined hessian-type material. There is now a wide range of quilted synthetic rugs available in a variety of styles, weights and thicknesses. There are specially designed under-rugs for additional warmth.

The majority of stable rugs are held in position by cross-over belly straps which pass beneath the horse's abdomen, with the front strap passing under the belly and fastening to the rear clip and the rear strap passing under the belly to fasten at the front clip. Some have adjustable interlocking leg straps. The advantage of these straps over rollers is that there is never any pressure on the horse's spine – the majority of rugs now have belly straps, and rollers are becoming much less common.

All rugs without leg straps must have a fillet string or strap to prevent the rug from slipping forwards.

Rollers and surcingles

The old-fashioned types of stable rugs are often held in position by a **roller** – a padded strap which buckles on the nearside. A roller can be used to hold extra blankets in position beneath the night rug. If a roller is used, extra padding such as a square of thick sponge should always be used beneath it to stop the roller pressing on the spine.

A **surcingle** is similar to a roller, but has no padding. Surcingles are sometimes used to hold anti-sweat rugs or day rugs in position and, like rollers, should have a pad placed underneath them to relieve pressure on the spine.

Rollers and surcingles are not in common use nowadays as belly straps are so much more effective at holding rugs in place without the risk of pressure on the spine.

Turnout (New Zealand) rugs

Turnout rugs (often called New Zealand rugs) are waterproof, designed for outdoor use, to be worn when the horse is in the field.

There are many types of turnout rug on the market. They vary in weight and thickness and most have cross-over belly straps instead of interlocking hind leg straps, which were once popular. Some old-fashioned rugs have surcingles attached, the main danger of which is that too much pressure will be exerted on the spine by the surcingle. Most of the new types of rug are made from synthetic non-rip material making them lighter than the old-fashioned canvas ones.

If a rug does have interlocking hind leg straps these should be fastened fairly loosely around the hind legs. If it does not have interlocking leg straps it must have a fillet strap which passes under the tail to stop the rug from slipping forwards or blowing up over the horse's back in windy weather.

3.1 Interlocking leg straps

You must always check that the rug does not slip too far back and chafe the horse's shoulders and that the leg straps do not rub the insides of the hind legs. It is a good idea to have two turnout rugs so that one can be drying off, cleaned or repaired whilst the horse wears the other – in fact, in the British climate, this can be considered pretty much essential.

Rugs for other purposes

Anti-midge sheets

Lightweight anti-midge rugs are available for horses who suffer from sweet itch (an allergy to the saliva of the biting *Culicoides* midge) to wear in the field; these can be very effective provided that they fit snugly enough to prevent the midges getting under the rug and biting the horse.

Anti-sweat sheets

These are lightweight cotton mesh rugs used to prevent a horse who has sweated up from catching a chill whilst he dries off in the stable. They should be used beneath another rug to allow pockets of warm air to be trapped, helping to dry the horse. Once an anti-sweat rug is wet it must be replaced with a dry one. The modern cooler rug has virtually superseded anti-sweat sheets.

Cooler/thermal rugs

These are specially designed to draw moisture away from the horse's coat and to promote cooling and drying without chilling. Most cooler rugs are fitted with crossover belly straps and a fillet string.

Day rugs

These are normally used when travelling to a show and are smart woollen rugs with coloured binding. They are not normally used in the stable, as they would be easily spoilt. Woollen day rugs can make a horse sweat and the sweat is not easily absorbed by the wool. These rugs often have a matching surcingle.

EXAM TIP

Try to look at as many rugs and types of fastening as possible so that in an examination you are more likely to have seen and/or used all the rugs and fastenings given to you. Tack shops are a great place to wander around and glean information.

Size and fit

In the UK, rugs increase in size in 3-inch (7.5cm) stages. (They remain commonly marketed in imperial sizes, as well – but the metric equivalents are given here for comparison and the sake of consistency.) As approximate guides – a chunky 14hh pony will need a 5ft 9in (175cm) rug, a lightweight 15hh horse, a 6ft (183cm) rug and a chunky 16.1hh horse will need a 6ft 6in (198cm) rug. Rugs are measured from the centre of the front of the horse's chest to the point of buttock. You need to take into account how chunky or light the horse is, as well as the fit and type of rug.

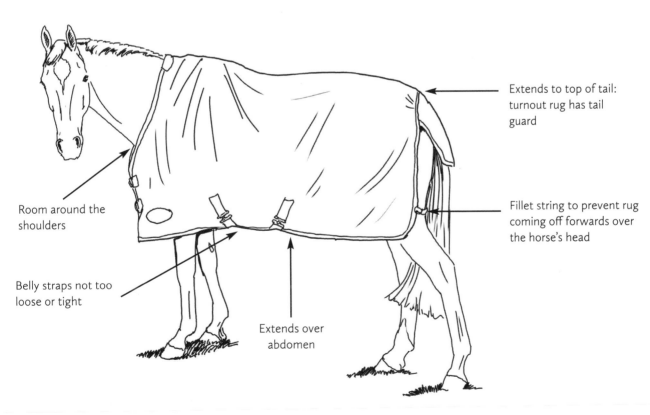

Extends to top of tail: turnout rug has tail guard

Fillet string to prevent rug coming off forwards over the horse's head

Room around the shoulders

Belly straps not too loose or tight

Extends over abdomen

3.2 Correct rug fitting points

Rugging-up

1 The horse should be tied up to prevent him from wandering around.

2 Fold the rug in half so that the back half lies on top of the front half.

3 From the nearside (left), place the rug over the horse's withers and straighten. Unfold the back half. Do not pull the rug too far back – the end of the rug should just reach the top of the tail. Rugs tend to slip back so put it on well forward so it is loose around the shoulders. A rug that is tight on the shoulders may cause chafing and soreness.

4 If the rug has belly straps – fasten the front buckles first, then the cross-over belly straps. These should not be too tight against the horse's belly. Likewise, they must not be so loose that they hang down in loops. The horse may put a foot through a loop whilst lying down in the stable. (There is however, a disadvantage to having only the front buckles fastened. This is explained in point 5 below.)

If the rug has a surcingle, the order of buckle fastening is different. Put on the roller or surcingle with thick sponge for padding, just behind the withers, buckles on the nearside. Check the offside in case the roller is twisted. Fasten the buckles on the nearside quite tightly and smooth out creases in the rug, beneath the roller.

5 Next, fasten the front buckle. A rug that is fastened by the front buckles only is in danger of slipping around the horse's chest. If the rug has hind leg straps, for example on a New Zealand rug, you should always fasten these last.

Always finish rugging up properly before leaving the horse. Don't leave him standing with only the front buckles or belly straps fastened for any length of time.

6 In cold weather it may be necessary to use more than one rug. Some rugs are fitted with neck hoods for additional warmth. If using a blanket beneath a jute rug, fold the blanket in half and place it well up onto the horse's neck. Unfold the lower half to cover the back, just reaching the top of the tail.

Put on the top rug in the way described earlier. Fold the two front corners of the blanket to the withers, forming a 'V' shape. Fold the 'V' back down. It should cover the withers and part of the horse's backbone.

Put the roller and padding on top of this 'V' shape and fasten to hold the blanket in position and prevent it from slipping back. Then fasten the front buckle.

To keep the horse warm and to prevent pressure on the spine, it is more satisfactory to use additional stable rugs which have belly straps, rather than having to use a roller.

EXAM TIP

Make sure that you have the rug ready before you put on the headcollar and tie up the horse; don't tie up the horse then go looking for the rug as it is potentially dangerous to leave the tied-up horse unaccompanied.

SAFETY TIP

▸ The reason for fastening the front buckles first is to prevent the horse from standing with the rug held in place by only the belly straps as the rug may, potentially, slip backwards, causing the horse to panic as the belly straps would become entangled around the horse's hind legs.

3.3 A correctly fitted underblanket

Unrugging

① Check to see if the rug has hind leg straps. If it has, undo them first. Once undone, refasten the clips to prevent the straps from hanging down. Next, undo the belly straps and then the front buckle. If the rug has a roller, undo the front straps first. Finally, undo and remove the roller.

② The rug can then be simply pulled off backwards over the horse's tail and folded up, or it can be folded, front half over back, and then removed.

③ The rug must then be hung up safely, not placed on the ground where it can get soiled and become a trip hazard.

SAFETY TIP

▸ Make sure that you don't stand directly behind the horse to remove the rug in case he is irritated or startled by the movement and kicks out. Stand approximately level with his flanks on the nearside.

ITQ 3.1 ?

How can you tell if a rug fits the horse correctly?

ITQ 3.2

Why should a horse not be left standing with only the belly straps holding a rug in place?

ITQ 3.3

Why should a horse not be left standing with only the front buckle of the rug fastened?

ITQ 3.4 ?

Which rug has now largely superseded the anti-sweat sheet?

BANDAGES

Reasons for use

Bandages are worn for the following reasons:

- To provide warmth in the stable.

- To provide protection when travelling.

- To provide protection and support during exercise.

- To hold a dressing or poultice in position.

- To help dry wet legs.

- To provide support to the sound leg when the opposite one is being treated for injury.

- To prevent filling of the lower leg during enforced rest.

- Tail bandages improve the appearance of a pulled tail and protect the dock bone whilst travelling.

Types of bandage

Stable/travelling bandages. These are wide bandages made from synthetic materials, wool or towelling. They fasten with tie strings or Velcro.

Support/exercise bandages. These are narrow, elasticated bandages which normally have tie strings. This type of bandage is often used for tail bandaging.

Crêpe bandages. Used for veterinary purposes.

Vetrap. These are self-adhesive stretch bandages which are ideal for holding dressings in place.

Tail bandages. Narrow, elasticated bandages which can also be used as exercise and support bandages.

Bandage padding

Padding is always used beneath leg bandages to even out the pressure, help guard against over-tightening and provide extra protection. **Gamgee** or synthetic bandage pads are used to provide padding.

Gamgee is similar to cotton wool, but much tougher. It comes on a roll which is cut to size. It is not washable and tends to tear so although a very good form of padding, it can work out expensive. Gamgee is ideal for veterinary purposes.

Fybatack/Fybagee is a spongy, specially designed leg pad, which is available in different sizes and is machine washable. It has a much longer life than Gamgee but is not so useful for veterinary purposes. Many Fybagee/Fybatack pads are now shaped to match the contours of the leg and provide a good level of protection for the knee and hock.

Applying stable or travelling bandages

1. Always have the horse tied up to prevent him wandering off while you are in the middle of bandaging. If you try to bandage a loose horse you are likely to get trodden on or kicked. (Even if he just fidgets, the bandaging process will probably be destroyed).

2 Wrap the padding around the lower leg. It should reach the knee/hock and the coronet. Pull the padding fairly tightly and neatly around the leg.

3 Hold the bandage on the outside of the leg, midway down the cannon bone and start to unwind the bandage around the leg, overlapping half the bandage in each turn. Bandage downwards in the same direction as the padding overlaps, i.e. if the padding is wrapped around the leg left to right, wrap the bandage around the leg left to right. Keep a firm and even pressure on it to prevent it slipping down. You are not likely to pull it too tight as the padding prevents this.

4 When you reach the coronet, wind back up the leg to just below the knee or hock. If you still have spare bandage, start to bandage back down the leg until you run out of bandage. If the bandage has Velcro, simply fasten the Velcro straps. If the bandage has ties you must tie them on the outside of the leg. Do not tie them:
– On the back as this puts pressure on the tendons.
– On the inside as the horse may rub and the knot may come undone.
– On the front, as this puts pressure on the cannon bone.

Never tie too tightly as it could interfere with the circulation. The ties should be no tighter than the bandage.

3.4 Applying a stable bandage

EXAM TIP

When you have fastened the ties you can fold a section of bandage down over them to tuck the loose ends in and keep them secure to give a neat look whilst ensuring that you do not create any pressure points. Alternatively you can apply bandage tape to secure the fastening; remember that this should be applied at the same tightness as the bandage and fastening.

SAFETY TIPS

▸ When bandaging be aware of your positioning. Never position your face in front of the horse's knee – if he were to bring his knee up and forwards it could cause injury.

▸ Position yourself to the side of the leg you are bandaging facing the leg and assume a squatting position (do not kneel on the ground), to ensure you can move with the horse safely should he try to fidget whilst you are bandaging.

▸ Never touch the ground with your hands when bandaging – if the horse were to move he could step on your fingers.

ITQ 3.5

List four reasons for using bandages:

1.

2.

3.

4.

ITQ 3.6

Why is padding needed beneath leg bandages?

EQUIPMENT USED FOR TRAVELLING

Clothing and protective equipment are usually necessary when transporting horses. Rugs are provided for comfort, normally to keep the horse at a comfortable temperature and to prevent chilling through sweating. Protective clothing should always be used, especially for valuable competition horses. Hunters tend to travel to the meet tacked up, without protective clothing, as the meet is often not too far from home. Youngstock and mares with foals are also travelled without protection as the risk of entanglement and panic in the event of a boot or bandage coming undone poses a greater risk.

Protective clothing generally consists of:

● Travelling boots and/or bandages: Table 3.1 compares the merits of boots and bandages.

● Tail bandages and/or guard.

● Poll guard.

● Rugs – make the horse comfortable and protect against adverse temperatures.

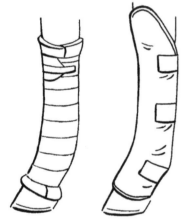

3.5 Travelling bandage and boot

EXAM TIP

When applying travelling boots fasten the middle strap(s) first, followed by the top and bottom straps; in this way you are securing the boot in the correct position in the first instance, allowing you to fasten and adjust the following straps more easily.

Protective equipment

Travelling bandages/pads

The horse's legs should be protected with woollen stable bandages over Gamgee or bandage pads (Fybatack). Travelling pads/boots are easy to put on. They normally have Velcro fastenings and must be fastened tightly enough to prevent them from slipping down.

Knee and hock boots

Although bandages are sufficient on most horses, some need additional protection in the form of knee and hock boots. Knee boots protect the horse from injury if he should trip whilst going up or down the ramp. Hock boots protect the hocks from rubbing against the back of the lorry or trailer. Leg bandages are applied first, then the knee and hock boots are fitted.

There are two main types of knee boot. The skeleton knee boot is used for exercise purposes: the travelling type of knee boot has an additional material edging.

Knee boots have two straps. The top strap is secured first, firmly enough to prevent it slipping down. The lower strap is fastened quite loosely to allow joint flexion. The buckles are always fastened on the outside with the ends of the straps pointing forwards. When removing knee boots, always undo the lower strap first. If the top strap is unfastened first the boot may slip down and become entangled around the foot.

Hock boot straps are fastened in the same manner as knee boots.

Tail bandage and guard

The tail bandage is applied first, over which a tail guard is then fitted. This normally fastens with Velcro. If the journey is to last longer than 4 hours, a tail guard only should be used, as a bandage could interfere with circulation in the dock bone if left on for longer than this.

Apply the tail bandage without padding underneath; bandage firmly but not overly tight.

Begin as high up at the top of the tail as possible and leave the beginning of the bandage protruding above the top of the tail during the first turn, then fold it down over the first bandage turn and complete the second turn. This will add to its security.

Continue to bandage down the tail to the end of the dock bone and wind back up, fastening the ties at the side of the tail (to prevent them being rubbed undone), around halfway up and fold a section of bandage down over it for protection.

Bandages	Travelling boots and pads
If applied correctly they are secure and don't tend to slip down.	Some types tend to slip down unless fitted very securely. If they slip down, the hind boots can become very soiled. They may cause the horse to slip or trip on unloading if they slip down covering the heel or sole of the foot.
Provide a degree of support.	Unless the boots have elasticated fastenings they do not offer any additional support.
Offer a very good level of protection.	Provided they don't slip they offer a good level of protection.
Can be time-consuming to put on.	Very quick to put on although some horses can object to the feel of them initially.
Once removed they can be time-consuming to roll up.	Once removed there is no additional work.
Fybagee/Fybatack bandages pads can be shaped to protect the knees and hocks.	Most travelling boots are shaped to protect the knees and hocks.
After competing, cold dressings can be held in place.	Boots are not usually secure enough to hold cold dressings in place.

Table 3.1 Comparisons between travelling bandages and boots

EXAM TIP

When bandaging, try to keep the bandage as close to the horse's leg as possible to avoid unrolling large lengths of bandage before you are ready to use it. In addition, being close to the leg will enable you to bandage more efficiently and go with the horse should he move his leg.

SAFETY TIP

▶ When applying travelling boots, especially hind ones, stand clear of the horse immediately after fitting them as some horses can react quite violently to the new sensation. The horse may lift his legs up and out to the side or kick out in an effort to remove the strange sensation. Some horse may hop or jump about a little when first walked on in the boots. In such cases try to encourage the horse to settle and walk properly by reassuring him and giving a firm 'Walk on' command; he will usually settle with three or four strides.

EXAM TIPS

In an exam always check that your bandages have been rolled up correctly before attempting to apply them. Sometimes Velcro-fastening bandages may be rolled the wrong way, making it impossible to fasten them when you have bandaged the leg; this is not only frustrating but time-consuming in an exam. If in doubt, unroll and reroll the bandage ready for use.

Always make sure that you roll bandages with the ties or Velcro to the inside of the roll to ensure that they will fasten correctly when unrolled and applied.

Poll guard

If the horse has a tendency to throw his head up, a poll guard should be attached to the headpiece of the headcollar to protect the sensitive poll area from injury. A leather headcollar should be used as this is safer than nylon; if the horse became hooked up leather would break, whereas nylon would not.

When preparing a horse to travel in an exam you must fit all of the above items (travelling bandages *or* boots).

Travelling rugs

Factors affecting the choice of rug

● The weather – in hot weather the horse may not need a rug. Always take rugs with you however, as the weather may change later in the day.

● Clip – in winter a clipped horse must not be allowed to get cold. An unclipped horse may be prone to sweating and must not get chilled.

● Number of horses in the lorry – the more horses there are, the hotter it gets in the back of the lorry.

● The horse's temperament – some horses are prone to sweating when travelling.

Always have spare rugs with you in case the weather conditions change and/or rugs become damp. It is not a good idea to travel horses in their stable rugs as this can lead to sweating and the rug becoming damp. Try to avoid travelling a horse in damp rugs as he could catch a chill.

If travelling to a hunt meet that is fairly close it is acceptable to travel tacked up with a suitable rug on top. However, if the meet is quite a long way away, it is more comfortable for the horse to travel untacked and to tack up on arrival.

Types of travelling rug

Woollen day rug. These are smart and warm but do not wick sweat away effectively.

Summer sheet. Lightweight and suitable in warm weather.

Anti-sweat sheet. If the horse is prone to sweating he could wear an anti-sweat sheet underneath another rug. This allows air to circulate, helping to keep the horse cool and dry.

Thermatex rug. These provide the ideal clothing for travelling in cold conditions as they are warm but draw sweat away from the horse's coat, keeping him drier and less likely to get chilled.

Cooler sheet. Specially designed sheets that draw sweat away from the coat and encourage drying. Suitable for use in warm conditions.

3.6 A horse prepared for travelling

EXAM TIP

In an exam, try to use equipment that you estimate will fit the horse you are given; if this is not possible because appropriate equipment has already been used by another candidate then you should use the equipment available to you but explain to the examiner why this is not your first choice and what you would change in an ideal situation.

ITQ 3.7 ?

Give two advantages of using bandages as leg protection when travelling:

1.

2.

ITQ 3.8   **?**

Give two advantages of using travelling boots as leg protection:

1.

2.

ITQ 3.9   **?**

List two factors that affect the choice of rug worn when travelling:

1.

2.

ITQ 3.9   **?**

What is the longest length of time that a tail bandage should be left on for and why?

ITQ 3.9   **?**

What is a poll guard and why would you use one?

WASHING AND STORING CLOTHING

- Muddy brushing boots should be wiped straight away after use. Leather boots should be cleaned and saddle-soaped.

- Do not roll up soiled bandages – they should be laundered and dried thoroughly before being rolled and stored. Store in pairs or sets of four in a dry vermin-proof labelled box.

- Send rugs away to be laundered and repaired after each winter. Most tack shops offer a rug cleaning and repair service.

- Turnout rugs should be re-proofed at the same time.

- Smaller rugs, bandages, bandage pads and numnahs can be laundered at home.

- A drying rail or hooks in the rug room are useful for hanging up wet rugs.

- All leather straps must be oiled and saddle-soaped. Most modern rugs, however, have nylon straps.

- Rugs must be stored in a dry vermin-proof area.

- If there is a large number of turnout rugs on the yard they could be folded and stored on shelves labelled with the respective horses' names. If the rugs are shared amongst a yard of horses it is a good idea, having folded and placed each rug on its shelf, to write the size of the rug in marker pen on the rug where it can be seen. This saves a great deal of time when trying to find rugs to fit, avoiding having to pull rugs off of the shelf to see what size they are.

- Never put a rug folded back on a shelf if it is damaged and in need of repair. It is very frustrating to take a rug out to the field, walk miles up a hill to the horse, only to find it has a buckle missing or similar. Have rugs repaired as soon as the damage is noticed.

SAFETY TIP

▶ If using travelling boots, the hind boots must be applied last. Horses will often react to the feel of the hind boots by over-flexing their hocks, even kicking out. It is not safe to apply a tail bandage after putting on hind leg boots.

④ Tack Fitting and Maintenance

REQUIRED SKILLS/KNOWLEDGE	Learnt, revised, practised?	Confirmed
Fit and remove tack for exercise.		
• Prepare and control the horse in readiness for tacking up.	☐	☐
• Fit suitable tack for exercise, including:	☐	☐
i) bridles	☐	☐
ii) martingales	☐	☐
iii) saddles	☐	☐
iv) nosebands and bits	☐	☐
v) breastplate	☐	☐
• Fit suitable boots for exercise.	☐	☐
• Remove tack/equipment after exercise and store it safely and correctly.	☐	☐
Safe working practices.		
• Work in a way which maintains health and safety and security of horses, yourself and others during work which is consistent with relevant legislation, codes of practice and any additional requirements.	☐	☐
Select, use and maintain tack.		
• Check tack for safety and suitability for the specified work.	☐	☐
• Know how to clean, maintain and store tack.	☐	☐
Fit and remove tack for exercise.		
• Reasons for checking tack for comfort and safety.	☐	☐
• Tack in common use and how to fit it.	☐	☐
• Understand the problems which may occur when tacking up or untacking.	☐	☐

	Learnt, revised, practised?	Confirmed
• Be able to recognise ill-fitting tack and the appropriate action to take.	☐	☐
• Describe the process of untacking a horse safely and securely and the reasons for checking condition of a horse after untacking.	☐	☐
• Understand the reasons for checking, cleaning, maintaining and storing tack and know what to do if tack is found to be unsafe.	☐	☐

FITTING A SNAFFLE BRIDLE

Bridles may be purchased in pony, cob or full sizes, with various sizes and weights of leather used. The bit is normally purchased separately.

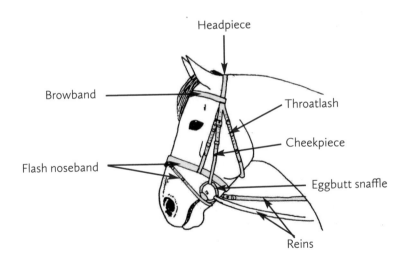

4.1 The snaffle bridle

The **headpiece** passes behind the horse's ears. The **throatlash** extends down from the offside of the headpiece and buckles up on the nearside. It prevents the bridle from being pulled forwards over the horse's head, in the event of the rider taking a fall. It must be buckled up to allow the width of a clenched fist between it and the horse's cheek to prevent interference with the horse's windpipe as he flexes his jaw when working.

SAFETY TIP

▶ Once the bridle is on, and keepers replaced, do up the throatlash first, followed by the noseband; in this way you are securing the bridle on the horse and then adjusting the other fastenings.

The two **cheekpieces** attach one on either side of the headpiece and hold the bit in place. They should be evenly adjusted on the same hole either side. Ideally, if the bridle is a good fit for the horse, this is halfway down the cheekpieces, which allows for adjustment up or down.

The **browband** attaches to the headpiece, preventing it from slipping back. It should not be too tight or it will pull the headpiece forward and pinch the ears. If it is too loose it will flap when the horse is moving and will be ineffective. Ideally you should be able to fit a finger easily between the browband and the forehead.

The **bit** must not protrude more than 1cm (approx. ½in) either side of the mouth and must be just high enough to create approximately two wrinkles (but no more) in the corners of the lips.

Nosebands

EXAM TIPS

When putting the bridle on make sure that you have control of the horse. If the horse is tied up remember to untie him before slipping the headcollar around his neck to allow you to fit the bridle.

Make sure that all the keepers are undone if you are fitting a new bridle or fitting the bridle to a new horse; this will make adjustments easier and less fiddly. Hold the bridle against the side of the horse's head, poll to mouth, to get a rough idea of whether it will fit before putting it on.

While it is part of the bridle, there are many different types of **noseband** available, each having different functions. The most commonly seen are as follows.

Cavesson

This is often worn to make the bridle look complete. It has no effect on the horse's jaw but can be used for attaching a standing martingale. It should be fitted so that it sits two fingers' width down from the projecting cheekbones and is loose enough to permit two fingers' width between the front of the horse's nose and the noseband.

Drop

This is fitted one hand's width from the upper edge of the horse's nostril, on the bony part of the face, and should be buckled around and under the bit. It should be just tight enough to keep the horse's jaws closed but not *so* tight that it pinches the skin. The drop is designed to prevent the horse from opening his mouth and evading the bit. If fitted incorrectly the drop can be uncomfortable for the horse – if too low it will rest on the soft skin of the nasal passages and can interfere with the horse's breathing.

Flash

This has an upper strap that fits in the same way as a cavesson but is tightened rather than left loose. It has a second strap attached to the cavesson part, which fastens around and under the bit. This noseband is more effective at preventing the horse from crossing his jaw and opening his mouth than the drop and is in common use. If adjusted correctly, the way in which it fits makes it more comfortable for the horse than the drop noseband (it does not end up over the soft skin of the nasal passages).

Grakle

Named after the 1931 Grand National winner and often misspelt Grackle, this is also called a **figure-of-eight** or **cross-over noseband.** The Grakle consists of two straps that cross over on the front of the horse's nasal bone and fasten quite tightly in the same position as the Flash.

This noseband can be adjusted fairly precisely as required and is useful on strong horses, particularly when going cross-country. As it acts over a wide area of the head it helps to prevent the horse from crossing his jaws and evading the bit.

Kineton

Named after its place of origin this acts by transferring some of the rein pressure from the mouth to the bridge of the nose, and is useful on strong horses. It consists of a centre strap that passes over the bridge of the nose, to which two metal loops are attached. The loops are held in position by a headpiece. It is used with a snaffle – each loop fits round the mouthpiece of the bit between the bit ring and the horse's face. The snaffle should be fitted as previously explained with the Kineton loops sitting just below, but in contact with, the bit rings, not affecting the positioning of the bit. If fitted or used incorrectly it can, like a drop noseband, restrict breathing.

4.2 The drop noseband

4.3 The Flash noseband

4.4 The Grakle noseband

4.5 The Kineton noseband

BITS

The action of the bit exerts pressure on certain points of the horse's mouth or face. These are referred to as **pressure points** and can include:

- The corners of the lips and mouth.

- The bars of the mouth.

- The tongue.

- The chin groove.

- The roof of the mouth (but only if the bit has a 'port' – an upwardly curved arch in the mouthpiece). Ports are seen mainly on curb bits or some pelhams; high ports are becoming much less common nowadays because they can be very severe in action.

- The nose.

- The poll.

- The side of the face.

Look in any equine products catalogue and you will see new types of bits and new materials. There is a huge range of bits to choose from and this can be confusing.

Broadly speaking, bitting arrangements are based around the following: snaffles, curb bits, double bridles (which combine a curb bit with a slightly 'downsized' form of snaffle, called a bridoon), gags (most commonly specialised adaptations of snaffles, with a potentially severe action) and pelhams. Hackamores are bitless bridles which do not utilise a mouthpiece.

In the Stage 2 exam, you will be fitting and riding in snaffle bridles, so this section will concentrate on them

Snaffles

The mouthpiece is a key component of any bit: the thickness and weight of the mouthpiece varies across most types of snaffle. In principle, a thicker mouthpiece is milder than a thinner one because the pressure of the reins is spread over a wider surface area. However, consideration must also be given to the conformation of the horse's mouth. A horse with a particularly small mouth may find it difficult to close his mouth over a bit that is too 'fat'.

Single-jointed snaffles

Single-jointed snaffles have one joint in the mouthpiece which gives the bit a **'nutcracker'** action when the joint closes, i.e. as pressure is applied to the reins. It also acts on the bars and lips. If fitted correctly, there is less tongue pressure than with a straight-bar snaffle.

One distinguishing feature of these snaffles is how the mouthpiece is joined to the bit rings.

Loose-ring snaffles. With these snaffles, the mouthpiece has free movement on the bit rings, which pass through it. This mobility encourages the horse to relax his jaw and salivate (known as **mouthing**) and such bits are widely used. Care must be taken that the skin on the sides of the mouth does not get pinched in the loose rings. If the holes in the mouthpiece, through which the bit rings pass, become worn and enlarged, the bit must not be used as this increases the risk of nipping. The **German loose-ring hollow mouth** is a very light version of this bit.

Eggbutt snaffles. These very popular designs are acceptable to most horses. The bit rings do not allow the mouthpiece to move, so they are useful for horses with a tendency to be too 'fidgety' in the mouth. However, they are not so useful for horses who tend to be 'set' in their jaw when working, or who have a very dry mouth – these horses would be better in a loose-ring snaffle.

Eggbutt snaffles are also less prone to pinching the horse, as they do not pull through the mouth so easily as a loose-ring (see also Fulmer, below).

As with the loose-ring version, **German eggbutts** are hollow, so therefore very light.

Another variation of the eggbutt is the **D-ring** which, as the name suggests, has D-shaped bit rings.

Fulmer or Australian. These have elongated cheeks on either side which help prevent the bit from being pulled through the horse's mouth. The upper cheeks should be attached to the cheekpieces of the bridle with a small leather keeper to prevent the bit from rotating forwards. The Fulmer may be loose-ring or eggbutt.

Eggbutt snaffle

Loose-ring snaffle

4.6 Single-jointed snaffles

Double-jointed snaffles

These have much reduced nutcracker action compared to a single-jointed snaffle. The main action is on the bars of the mouth and the lips. Double-jointed snaffles can be either loose-ring or eggbutt design.

French link

French link. This has a rounded plate in the centre of the mouthpiece, which lies on the tongue. It encourages the horse to relax his jaw. It must be the correct fit for the horse and not pull through his mouth when pressure is applied to one rein. If it pulls through, the joint with the centre link will nip the corner of the lips.

Dr Bristol

4.7 Double-jointed snaffles

Dr Bristol. This bit has an oblong centre plate which rests on the tongue. The plate has squared edges and should always rest flat on the tongue. If the horse raises his head the plate will sit at an angle of 45 degrees which 'encourages' the horse to lower his head. It is a severe bit, used on strong horses.

Straight-bar snaffles

Straight-bar bits have an unbroken mouthpiece and act mainly on the tongue and, to a lesser extent, the bars of the mouth. Many are of a **half-moon** or **mullen-mouth** shape. As these are shaped to fit the contours of the mouth they are mild in their action.

4.8 Straight-bar (mullen mouth) snaffle

Vulcanite loose-ring. Vulcanite is a very hard, unyielding material which does not encourage the horse to mouth the bit. Vulcanite mouthpieces can be rather bulky, especially those that are completely straight.

Nylon. These are often shaped and provide a hard-wearing, flexible mouthpiece which encourages the horse to mouth and accept the bit. They are ideal for young horses and those who are particularly sensitive. (This material is also now used by some manufacturers to produce jointed mouthpieces.)

Rubber. Rubber mouthpieces have the similar influence on the mouth as the nylon ones, although they are not normally shaped. They can encourage horses to chew on them, so should be checked regularly for wear.

Metal loose-ring. Straight-bar metal mouthpieces are not usually used for riding purposes but may be used on stallion bridles (for leading the stallion).

Correct fitting

- A horse with a narrow mouth, low palate and/or large tongue will need a thinner mouthpiece than a horse of more normal conformation. You must, however, bear in mind that as the rein pressure is concentrated over less surface area, the action of a thinner mouthpiece is sharper than the action of a thicker one.

- The mouthpiece should protrude approximately 1cm (approx. ½in) either side of the mouth without pinching the lips.

- The bit should lie on top of the tongue, resting on the bars of the mouth. The bit must not be too low or it will bang on the incisors, or in geldings, on the tushes. The horse may also put his tongue over the bit if it is too low.

ITQ 4.1   **?**

List six of the pressure points upon which the bit acts:

1.

2.

3.

4.

5.

6.

ITQ 4.2   **?**

What is meant by a 'nutcracker' action?

ITQ 4.3   **?**

What is the difference between a French link and a Dr Bristol?

ITQ 4.4   **?**

Give three qualities of a nylon mouthpiece on a bit:

1.

2.

3.

- If fitted too high it will cause discomfort. The corners of the lips should be slightly wrinkled (one or two wrinkles).

- Whatever the horse's age or standard of training, he should be 'happy' in his mouth. Ideally he should accept the bit with a relaxed jaw, whilst going calmly and freely forward.

Bit evasions

Signs that the horse is unhappy, possibly in discomfort include:

- Working in a hollow outline with the head raised.

- Mouth open.

- Fidgeting constantly with the bit.

- Tilting the head.

- Tossing and shaking the head.

- Drawing the tongue back and putting it over the bit.

- Overbending and moving behind the contact.

- Sticking the tongue out of the mouth (a few horses to do this as a habit, without obvious signs of discomfort).

- Forcing the head down suddenly and 'snatching' at the bit.

- Bolting.

- Rearing.

- General control problems.

The course of action to be taken with a horse showing any of these signs must always start with a check on the teeth and condition of the mouth. Sharp edges, sores, wolf teeth or abscesses must be dealt with immediately.
  Reasons for discomfort include:

- Sharp teeth – molars need rasping.

- Sore mouth – strong-pulling horses often become sore, especially around the corners of the mouth.

- Wolf teeth and any other tooth problems – the vet may need to remove wolf teeth.

- Incorrect size or type of bit – mouthpiece too thick/thin.

- Bit too severe in action.

- Bit incorrectly fitted.

- Noseband incorrectly fitted – too low/high/tight.

- Bad riding – rider's hands too harsh and rough.

- Inexperienced riding – the rider may inadvertently rely on the reins for balance.

THE SADDLE

Types of saddle

Dressage. The dressage saddle is a specialist saddle used only for flatwork. It is designed to allow a longer length of leg as the panels are very straight cut. A short **Lonsdale girth** is used as the dressage saddle has extra long girth straps.

Jumping. Again a specialist saddle with very forward-cut panels and large knee rolls for the shorter leg position used when jumping. The knee and thigh rolls are designed to help the rider maintain leg position.

General-purpose. This is the most commonly used type of saddle. It is a combination of the above two and is suitable for use in general flatwork, jumping and hacking.

In addition there are now a number of specialised saddles available for different purposes, including extra wide-cut cob saddles, endurance and close-contact saddles.

Structure of the saddle

The **tree** is the framework upon which the saddle is made. The majority of trees used to be made from beech wood, but more recently laminated wood has been used, which can be moulded into shape to give a strong, lightweight tree. Also, some trees are now made of high-tech artificial materials. Trees are generally made in three widths – narrow, medium and wide (although some are now adjustable) and in different lengths.

The tree can be **rigid** or '**sprung**'. The **spring tree** consists of two flat panels of steel running from underneath the pommel to the cantle. The panels are thin enough to give a 'springy' feel to the tree. The rigid tree has a more solid framework than the spring tree.

The **stirrup bars**, made of hand-forged steel, are riveted to the **points** of the tree. The stirrup bars are often recessed and have a safety catch *which should always be in the open position when in use.* This ensures that, in the event of the rider falling and a foot becoming stuck in the stirrup, the whole stirrup leather will come off the bar. The catch is only closed when the saddle is being transported or used on a horse who is being lunged without a rider. However, because of the recessing, it is not normally necessary to put the safety catch up in these circumstances, as the leathers are often extremely difficult to put on and take off, especially in new saddles.

Saddles usually have full panels, extending down the same length as the flaps, although some pony saddles only have half panels. Full panels give a greater bearing surface, which is more comfortable for the horse. The panels are best lined with leather as this is easy to maintain and very long-lasting. The panels are normally stuffed with wool fibre (although some innovative designs incorporate air-filling).

Saddles need regular attention (at least once a year), as the stuffing or flocking packs down, often unevenly – the saddler will put this right. If not corrected, uneven stuffing can cause pressure points, which will give the horse a sore back.

There are normally three **girth straps** on each side. It is correct to use the front two straps, keeping the third strap as a spare in case of breakages. The front strap is attached to a separate piece of webbing whilst the second and third straps are connected to the same piece of webbing. To use the second and third girth straps together would increase the risk, should the webbing break. Therefore the second and third straps should never be used together.

Girth straps should be checked frequently for wear and tear, especially the stitching. Leather **buckle guards** should always be used to prevent the metal girth buckles rubbing and wearing through the saddle flap. New saddles tend to have built-in buckle guards.

ITQ 4.5

Why is a bit with a narrow mouthpiece sharper in action than one with a thicker mouthpiece?

ITQ 4.6

List four points regarding the fitting of a bit:

1.

2.

3.

4.

ITQ 4.7

List four points that indicate a horse is uncomfortable in his mouth:

1.

2.

3.

4.

ITQ 4.8

What will you check first if your horse shows signs of discomfort in his mouth?

ITQ 4.9

List four causes of discomfort:

1.

2.

3.

4.

ITQ 4.10

Why should a saddle be re-flocked at least once a year?

ITQ 4.11   **?**

What is the main difference between a spring tree and a rigid tree saddle?

Saddle fitting

It is important that the saddle is a good fit for both the horse and rider. Serious damage can be caused to the horse's spine through using an ill-fitting saddle. The horse may show his discomfort by behaving badly, refusing to jump, and a generally poor performance. Very often though, the poor horse continues to work 'normally', even though he is in pain. It is up to us to make sure that only safe, well-fitting saddles are used.

- When trying a new saddle to see if it fits, make sure that the horse is clean and place a clean stable rubber on his back to stop the saddle from being marked. Do not use a numnah as this disguises the true fit of the saddle. Use buckle guards to prevent the flaps from being marked by the girth. Fasten the girth.

- The saddle should sit level on the horse's back – it should not tilt forwards or backwards as this would make it difficult for a rider to maintain position and would exert uneven pressure on the horse's back.

- The saddle lies on the lumbar muscles, which cover the top of the ribs. It should rest evenly on these muscles and must not touch the loins. The full surface of the panels must be in contact with the horse's back to distribute the weight over the largest area possible.

- The saddle must not pinch the horse's shoulders. The knee roll, panel and saddle flap should not extend out over the shoulder as this would restrict the horse's freedom of movement.

- With the rider mounted there should be sufficient, consistent clearance beneath the pommel when in an upright, flatwork position and a forward, jumping position.

- You should be able to see daylight through the gullet. At no time should the saddle touch the horse's spine. When viewed from behind, the saddle should not appear crooked or twisted.

- If buying a saddle, you must walk, trot and canter in it (with stirrups attached) to see how it feels. It is not sufficient to just sit in it on the yard. If the saddle is to be

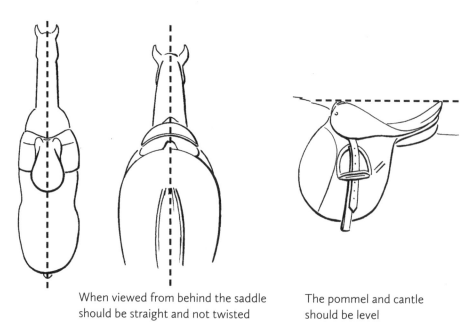

When viewed from behind the saddle should be straight and not twisted

The pommel and cantle should be level

4.9 Saddle fitting points; the saddle must sit straight on the horse and be level on his back

purchased as a jumping or dressage saddle it is important that you test it out over jumps or riding some dressage movements, as appropriate, to ensure it is suitable for both horse and rider in all gaits.

Second-hand saddles

If buying a second-hand saddle it is important that you check the tree. If the tree is damaged it will cause serious problems to the horse's back. *Under no circumstances should a saddle with a broken tree be used as it would damage the horse's back.*

To test for a broken tree, put the front arch on your knee and try to move the cantle towards the pommel. There will be a certain amount of 'give' in a spring tree saddle but this will not be excessive and the saddle should spring back into position easily. If there is no spring and the saddle bends easily or feels slack it indicates a weak or damaged tree. (There should be no 'give' in a rigid tree saddle.)

Then apply pressure inwards to both panels at the front arch. Any extra movement or grating sounds would indicate a broken tree. The cantle should feel rigid.

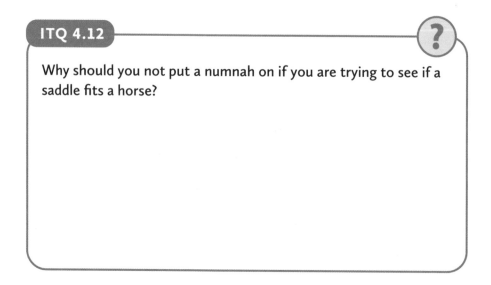

ITQ 4.12 ?

Why should you not put a numnah on if you are trying to see if a saddle fits a horse?

ITQ 4.13 ?

Give four points to observe about a well-fitting saddle:

1.

2.

3.

4.

ITQ 4.14 ?

Describe how to test a saddle for a damaged tree.

MARTINGALES AND BREASTPLATES

Martingales are artificial aids used to prevent the horse's head being raised so high that the rider has no control. They come into action once the head has been raised: they are not used to force the horse's head down.

Breastplates are used to prevent the saddle from slipping backwards, especially when the horse is exerting himself, for example when competing over jumps, or hunting.

Martingales

Running martingales
On a running martingale the reins run through two rings attached to straps which fasten around the girth. A neckstrap holds this in place. As the horse raises his head, he feels pressure on his mouth.

4.10 The running martingale

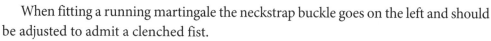

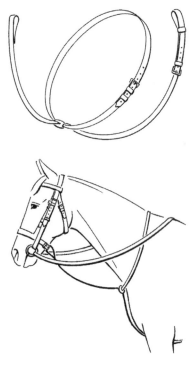

4.11 The standing martingale

Bib martingale

Irish martingale

4.12 The bib and Irish martingales

When fitting a running martingale the neckstrap buckle goes on the left and should be adjusted to admit a clenched fist.

To check the fitting of a running martingale, when the horse stands with his head in the normal position the martingale straps must be slack. It should come into action only when the horse raises his head beyond the point of control. Before passing the reins through the martingale rings, take both straps and hold the rings together towards the horse's withers – the rings should not touch the withers as this would make the fit too loose. Then pass the reins through the rings and re-buckle; standing beside the horse, and hold the reins up in the position they would be in if the rider were holding them on the horse. Check the fit – the straps should be slightly loose. Make adjustments on the buckle which lies between the forelegs. Always ensure that this buckle faces away from the skin to prevent chafing.

The neckstrap should be adjusted to admit the width of your hand. A rubber stopper must be used on the neckstrap to prevent it slipping along the main strap, which will affect its action. Rein stops are used on each rein to prevent the martingale rings running up too near the bit rings, which could panic a horse.

The **bib martingale** is a running martingale in which the two straps of leather on the martingale are 'filled in' with a piece of leather that prevents the horse catching hold of the martingale straps in his mouth.

Standing martingales

The standing martingale attaches directly to a cavesson noseband. There is no pressure on the mouth at all. It is used on horses prone to throwing their heads up suddenly and hitting the rider in the face. They can be useful if hunting a young and excitable horse.

A standing martingale should never be used on a drop noseband as the sudden pressure exerted on the lower part of the nasal bones could cause serious damage.

The neckstrap and strap reaching between the forelegs to the girth are fitted and adjusted as for a running martingale.

Irish martingale

Although called a martingale, this actually has no effect at all on the position of the horse's head. It is a 15cm (6in) length of leather with a ring at each end, through which pass the reins. Its function is to prevent the reins from flipping over the horse's head in the event of a fall or whilst galloping, e.g. whilst racing.

Breastplates

There are two types of breastplate in general use, both being employed to prevent the saddle from slipping backwards, particularly during times of exertion.

The Aintree breastplate comprises a webbing, elastic or leather strap that passes around the front of the horse's chest, held in position by two straps that attach to the girth on either side and a single adjustable strap that passes over the withers. The chest strap may be covered in sheepskin to prevent chafing.

The hunting breastplate consists of a leather strap that passes between the horse's forelegs, through which passes the girth. Attached to a ring at the breast

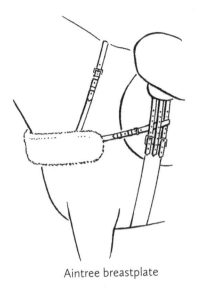
Aintree breastplate

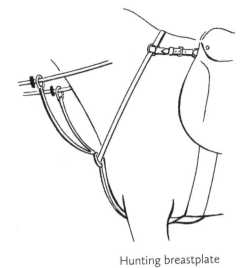
Hunting breastplate

4.13 Breastplates

is a V-shaped neckstrap that is attached by straps and buckles to the 'D' rings either side of the pommel. A martingale attachment can be added to a hunting breastplate.

PROTECTIVE BOOTS

Reasons for use

There are many different types of protective boot available, worn for one or more of the following reasons:

● To protect the lower leg from knocks and blows on the inside of a lower leg, caused by an opposite leg – i.e. brushing (brushing boots). Brushing is often caused through faulty action or tiredness.

● To protect the tendons from injury inflicted by the toe of the hind foot (tendon boots).

● To offer a degree of support to the tendons (tendon boots).

● To protect the bulbs of the heels from injury from the toe of the hind foot (overreach boots).

● To protect the front of the cannon bone from injury when jumping (cross-country boots).

● To protect the limbs when travelling (travelling boots).

● Knee boots offer protection against injury whilst hacking out or travelling.

- Hock boots protect against rubs when travelling and against capped hocks in the stable.

- Poultice boots are useful when dealing with a puncture wound of the foot, holding the poultice in place and helping to keep the foot clean.

- An **Equiboot** can be used to protect the foot in the event of a horse losing a shoe.

Types of boots

Brushing boots. Boots for everyday use are often made of synthetic materials, fastened with Velcro. Boots for competitive purposes may be made from leather and have leather straps and buckles. Brushing boots should be done up on the outside of the leg with the straps, whether leather or Velcro, facing towards the rear.

Horses who 'brush' should wear boots all round (on all four legs) when working. It is sensible to work all horses, especially valuable competition horses, in brushing boots to prevent injury and offer support.

Speedy-cut boots. High brushing is known as speedy-cutting, so called because this type of injury normally occurs when the horse is travelling at speed. Speedy-cut boots are longer than brushing boots.

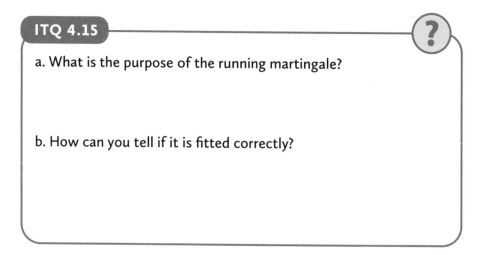

ITQ 4.15

a. What is the purpose of the running martingale?

b. How can you tell if it is fitted correctly?

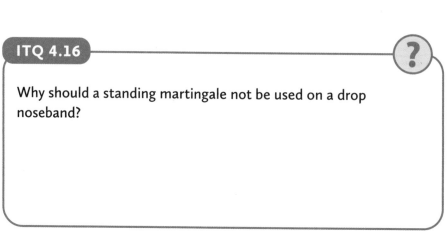

ITQ 4.16

Why should a standing martingale not be used on a drop noseband?

ITQ 4.17 ⟶ (**?**)

What is the difference between an Aintree and a hunting breastplate and when would you use each one?

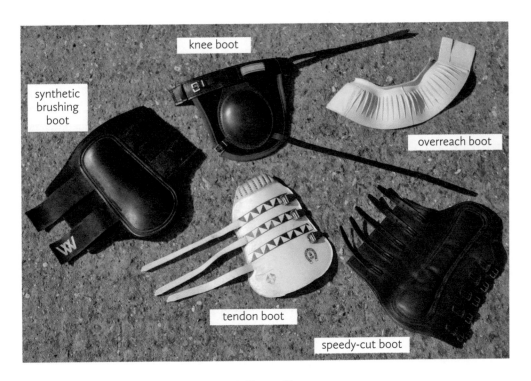

4.14 Types of boot

Tendon boots. These are open at the front but offer support and protection to the tendons. They are often used by showjumpers as the horse feels discomfort if he hits the pole but his tendons are protected. Tendon boots are normally only used on the forelegs.

Fetlock boots. These are made from the same materials as brushing boots but only cover the fetlock joint. They are often used by showjumpers as the horse can feel the discomfort of hitting a pole so is more likely to try to clear the fences, but his fetlocks are protected against brushing when turning.

Overreach boots. Overreaching may occur when a short-backed horse works with his hindquarters engaged, or when jumping or galloping. The toe of the hind foot strikes into the bulb of the heel of the forefoot, causing bruising and/or an open wound. Overreach boots are normally made of rubber or a padded synthetic material, with or without strap fastenings. The synthetic boots with Velcro fastenings are easy to put on and offer a greater degree of protection than the plain rubber boots.

Knee boots. The horse may injure his knees when walking up or down the lorry ramp, by stumbling when out hacking or by hitting a fence when jumping. So-called 'broken knees' are not bone fractures but injuries to the knee that can range from a superficial scratch to a deep puncture wound.

There are two main types of knee boot. The skeleton knee boot is used for exercise purposes. The travelling type of knee boot has an additional material edging.

Knee boots have two straps. The top strap is secured first, firmly enough to prevent the boot slipping down. The lower strap is fastened quite loosely to allow joint flexion. The buckles are always fastened on the outside, with the ends of the straps pointing forwards. When removing knee boots, always undo the lower strap first. If the top strap is unfastened first the boot may slip down and become entangled around the foot.

If a knee boot is worn for protection when jumping (normally when a horse has a minor wound on a knee), it is safer to have only one strap, the top one, fastened.

Hock boots. These boots are used for protection against rubbing when travelling. The straps are fastened in the same manner as knee boots.

Travelling boots. These thickly padded boots are normally long enough to protect the lower legs, including knees and hocks, when travelling. They are normally fastened with Velcro and are quick and easy to put on. If not fastened securely however, they can be prone to slipping down.

Equiboot. This is a very strong boot that fits exactly over the hoof. It can be adjusted at the heel to ensure a snug fit. The Equiboot can be used to protect the foot if it cannot be shod for any reason. It helps prevent a horse becoming footsore if he has lost a shoe. The Equiboot can also be used to hold a poultice in place.

ITQ 4.18   **?**

State three reasons for using protective boots:

1.

2.

3.

ITQ 4.20

How should the straps of a knee boot be fastened?

ITQ 4.20

What is the difference between a tendon boot and a brushing boot and why would each be used?

EXAM TIPS

When fitting boots it is easiest to fasten the middle strap first (if it has more than two) so that the boot is secured in position, allowing you to adjust the tension of the other straps easily.

Make sure that the boots fits well and will not pinch or move around, which could cause sores. In addition, using dirty boots will cause sores so ensure that you clean them regularly; brush off dry mud and wash to remove grease as required.

For competition purposes it is sensible to tape boot straps into position for added security.

CARE OF TACK

Checking tack for safety

Check the following regularly:

● The condition of all stitching. Any repairs must be carried out promptly to avoid an accident. Never use tack that is in need of repair or that is *very* old. A broken rein whilst cantering in an open space can be disastrous.

- On the saddle, keep a close eye on the stitching that holds the girth straps onto the webbing under the saddle flaps. Check the webbing for signs of wear.

- Leather girths can wear and, under periods of strain e.g. jumping, may break. Very old leather girths should be replaced. They definitely should not be used for showjumping or cross-country riding.

- The stirrup leathers. In addition to checking the stitching, bear in mind that if one rider uses the leathers all the time, they may start to show signs of wear where the leather is constantly bent. If the leathers become very worn they must be replaced. Wear is often made evident by the leathers stretching and becoming thinner in certain areas.

- All buckle holes, especially on stirrup leathers and girth straps, stretch eventually and can wear to such an extent that one hole runs into another. This seriously weakens the strap.

- If the stuffing in the saddle starts to feel lumpy and uneven, consult the saddler, who will pull out the old stuffing and re-flock the saddle. All saddles should be routinely re-flocked once a year.

- Make sure that you check all leather for signs of cracking or splitting regularly especially if it often gets very wet or muddy.

Care prior to storage

Prior to storage, tack should be checked for damage and wear, mended if appropriate, and thoroughly cleaned, oiled and soaped.

1 To clean tack thoroughly it should be dismantled.

2 Clean the leather with warm water from a sponge which has been well wrung to avoid over-wetting the leather. Make sure you remove all grease.

3 Apply a leather conditioning oil. Once the oil has soaked in, apply saddle soap from a dry sponge. To moisten, dip the soap bar in the water – do not immerse the sponge as this makes excessive lather which dulls the leather.

4 Now you have to reassemble the tack. When you are learning, this can be the interesting bit. You put it all back together again and find that you have one piece left over! To reassemble a bridle:

- Start with the headpiece and thread the browband onto it. Imagine how it looks on the horse as you do this. Think of where the ears come through and that the throatlash does up on the left. One common mistake is to have the headpiece the wrong way around. Now hang the headpiece on the cleaning hook.

● Next, attach the cheekpieces to the headpiece. If they have billets they go to the inside; buckles fasten on the outside. Remember to put them back on the correct holes. As they hold the bit in place, it is very important that they are in the correct position.

● Attach the bit to the cheekpieces, making sure it is the correct way up – i.e. it should hang in a smooth, rounded shape.

● Now attach the noseband. Make sure the noseband is the right way round (again, imagine how it would look on the horse). Thread the headpiece of the noseband under the right side of the browband, underneath the main bridle headpiece, down through the left side of the browband and buckle up on the correct hole.

● Attach the reins to the bit. Remember – billets to the inside, buckles to the outside. Pass the throatlash through the reins as previously described, fasten and do up the noseband before hanging up the bridle.

Storing tack

As previously mentioned, all tack should be kept in a dry environment. If the tack room is damp the tack will get mouldy, which leads to rotting of the leather and stitching. Spare tack should be cleaned thoroughly and well-soaped. It will need to be oiled occasionally to keep it supple. It is also necessary to ensure that mice cannot damage stored tack.

Bridles can be kept clean in storage by placing them in a bridle bag or old pillowcase. Saddles can be protected by a saddle cover, sheet or blanket.

ITQ 4.21   **?**

When cleaning tack, you should check for signs of wear. Give three areas that need to be checked regularly:

1.

2.

3.

Injuries caused by dirty or ill-fitting tack

Saddle sores

Symptoms

- Swelling on the back in the saddle area.

- The skin may be broken and sore.

Causes

- A horse who has been rested for a long period and just brought back to work will be in 'soft' condition, i.e. overweight, with slack muscles. At this stage the skin is prone to rubbing.

- Friction and uneven pressure caused by ill-fitting saddles and/or bad riding.

- Friction caused through lack of cleanliness, e.g. ungroomed coat or dirty numnah.

- Thin-skinned horses can be prone to rubbing.

Treatment

- Remove the cause.

- Stop all work under saddle, although the horse may be exercised in hand or on the lunge. Remember to adjust feeding as appropriate.

- Treat broken skin with warm salt water. This has mild antiseptic qualities and will also help to harden the skin.

- If the skin is broken, check that the horse is up to date with his tetanus vaccinations.

- Do not use a saddle until the horse is completely healed.

Prevention

- Always ensure that the horse is clean before tacking up.

- Use good-quality numnahs and make sure they are brushed and washed regularly.

- Saddles require regular checking by a saddler as the flock used to stuff them will shift and cause uneven pressure. Most saddles need to be re-flocked annually.

- When bringing a horse in 'soft' condition back into work, apply surgical spirit to the saddle and girth areas to harden the skin.

- After exercise, remove sweat marks by sponging and/or grooming

Girth galls

Girth galls are similar in every respect to saddle sores. These are found usually just behind the elbow, especially when nylon string girths are used. Thin-skinned horses are prone to galling.

Causes and treatment

As for saddle sores. If a horse is prone to galling, a sheepskin girth cover may be used.

Bit sores
Symptoms

- These vary from slight bruising to bleeding sores on the corners of the mouth.

- A horse with a sore mouth will not be receptive to rein aids.

Causes

- An ill-fitting or badly adjusted bit.

- Too severe a bit in use.

- Horse is very strong to ride and constantly pulling.

- Bad riding by a novice or ignorant rider.

Treatment

- Remove the cause.

- Rest the horse until the mouth is healed. Exercise in hand or on the lunge, without using a bridle. A lunge cavesson should give sufficient control.

- Exercise in a bitless bridle, e.g. a hackamore. (An inexperienced rider must not use a hackamore as its action is severe if used incorrectly).

- Apply warm salt water to the corners of the mouth.

- Once the mouth has healed, apply petroleum jelly to the corners whenever a bit is used. Use a gentle form of bit, e.g. rubber snaffle.

- Some products on sale for human mouth conditions have valuable healing properties and can be useful for horses.

- If the problem is caused by bad riding, educate the rider and encourage the use of a neckstrap. A good riding instructor should be sought.

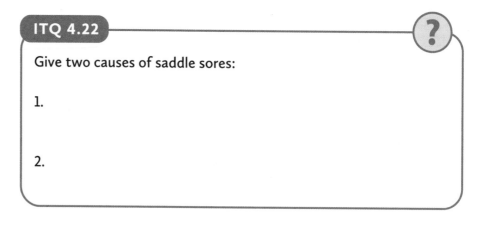

ITQ 4.22

Give two causes of saddle sores:

1.

2.

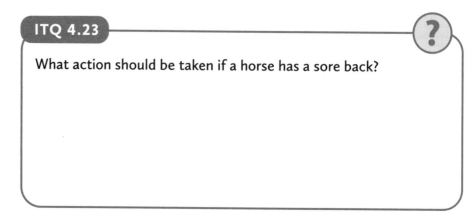

ITQ 4.23

What action should be taken if a horse has a sore back?

Boot rubs

Cause

Ill-fitting or dirty brushing boots or boots worn for a long period, e.g. for a whole day's hunting, can cause rub injuries.

Treatment and prevention

- Using a tube-grip (tubular) bandage beneath the boots can help prevent rubbing.

- Rubs should be cleaned, wound intrasite (hydro) gel applied and allowed to heal before fitting boots again.

5 Horse Anatomy

REQUIRED SKILLS/KNOWLEDGE	Learnt, revised, practised?	Confirmed
Know the horse's skeleton.		
• Be able to identify the horse's main bones.	☐	☐
Basic structure, function and potential problems of the horse's foot.		
• External parts of the horse's foot.	☐	☐
• Functions and importance of the parts of the foot.	☐	☐
• Problems associated with long feet.	☐	☐
Know the location of the horse's main internal organs.		
• Be able to indicate the location of internal organs in a horse.	☐	☐
Basic structure of the horse's digestive system.		
• The horse's digestive system.	☐	☐
• Function of the horse's digestive system.	☐	☐
• The importance of 'bulk' to the horse's system.	☐	☐

SKELETAL ANATOMY

The skeleton can be broadly divided into two parts:

Axial skeleton – the skull and spine

Appendicular skeleton – the limbs

The axial skeleton

The skull

Because the horse is a grazing animal he requires large, powerful jaws and teeth to enable the continual process of mastication. The **mandible**, or lower jawbone, is large enough to accommodate the molars easily. However, in order to house the jaws and teeth, the bones of the skull need to offer a wide and strong surface area – if this were achieved through bone deposition the head would weigh far too much. The skull is, therefore, widened and strengthened with air-filled cavities known as **sinuses**. Each side of the head accommodates several sinuses.

The spine

The spine is also referred to as the **vertebral column**. Its functions are:

- To provide strength for the suspension and propulsion of the bodyweight.

- To provide an attachment for the ribs, which protect the organs within the thoracic cavity.

- To protect the spinal cord.

The spine consists of a string of incompressible bony vertebrae which articulate with each other. Between each is a slightly compressible cartilaginous disc. There are, however, no discs in the spaces between the joints of the atlas and axis (the topmost two vertebrae). The inter-vertebral discs consist of dense fibrous tissue and act as shock-absorbers, allowing a certain amount of movement along the spine.

Each vertebra has **spinous processes** – bony extensions which facilitate the connection of muscles and ligaments.

The spinal column is divided, for reference, into the following groups of vertebrae.

Cervical (7). The first two cervical vertebrae are the **atlas** and **axis**. There are five other cervical vertebrae, all of which have reduced spinous processes to allow for the wide range of movement required by the neck.

Thoracic (18). The thoracic vertebrae have very pronounced spinous processes and are capable of only limited movement. The ribs extend from each of the thoracic vertebrae and encircle the chest, attaching to the sternum. There are eighteen pairs of ribs; the first eight pairs attach directly to the sternum – these are known as **'true' ribs**. The other ten pairs attach to the sternum by means of cartilaginous extensions and are known as **'false' ribs**.

The ribs are very elastic, allowing extensive expansion and contraction which is necessary during inhalation and expiration.

The sternum is made up of many bones linked by cartilage. It provides the site of attachment for some neck and pectoral muscles.

Lumbar (usually 6). The loin muscles attach to the lumbar vertebrae which have very rigid, well-defined transverse processes (flat bony extensions which project outwards) and are large and stout. The forward thrust of the hind legs is transferred to the body through the lumbar vertebrae.

Sacral. The five sacral vertebrae are fused, forming a single bone called the **sacrum**.

Coccygeal (15–20, usually 18). The coccygeal vertebrae form the tail. They are small and have very reduced processes as they are not subjected to any strong muscular tensions.

The appendicular skeleton

The forelimb

The forelimb of the horse supports two-thirds of the bodyweight when the horse is at rest and is subjected to concussive forces. Unlike humans, the horse has no clavicle (collarbone) to attach the limb to the trunk. Instead muscles and tendons attach the limb to the trunk in an arrangement called the **thoracic sling**. This allows the forelimb and trunk more mobility than a bony attachment and therefore increases the ability of the forelimb to absorb concussion.

The uppermost bone in the forelimb is the **scapula**, which slopes forward and downwards over the first six or seven ribs. The angle at which it does this plays a role in determining the length of stride of the horse. If the angle is too upright, this limits the potential advancement of the bones lower in the limb. The angle at which the scapula is set determines what is referred to in conformation as the 'slope of the shoulder'.

The lower end of the scapula articulates with the **humerus** to form the shoulder joint. This joint is contained within a joint capsule. Unlike other joints of the limb, the shoulder joint is not held in position by collateral ligaments (which join bone to bone), but by many strong muscles. The shoulder joint is very mobile in both the extent and direction of movement.

The humerus slopes downwards and backwards towards the elbow. The lower end of the humerus articulates with the **radius** and **ulna**.

The point of elbow is formed by the **olecranon** process of the ulna, which is positioned to the rear of the radius.

The lower end of the radius articulates with the **carpus** (knee). The carpus usually consists of seven bones (occasionally eight), lying in two rows one above the other with the **pisiform** or **accessory carpal bone** projecting at the rear.

The horse's **knee** (**carpus**) corresponds to the human wrist and is capable of similar types of movement. The lower bones of the knee articulate with the **large metacarpal** (**cannon bone**) and the **small metacarpal bones** (**splint bones**).

The large metacarpal is a long bone with a rounded shaft. The front surface is smooth and convex, the rear surface slightly flattened, with roughened edges on the outer and inner aspects for attachment of the two small metacarpal (splint) bones. The lower extremities end at the lower third of the large metacarpal in a small, bulbous point called the **button**.

The **first phalanx** or **long pastern** bone has a cylindrical shaft, the surfaces of which are roughened to accommodate ligamentous insertions. The upper end articulates with the large metacarpal bone to form the **fetlock joint**.

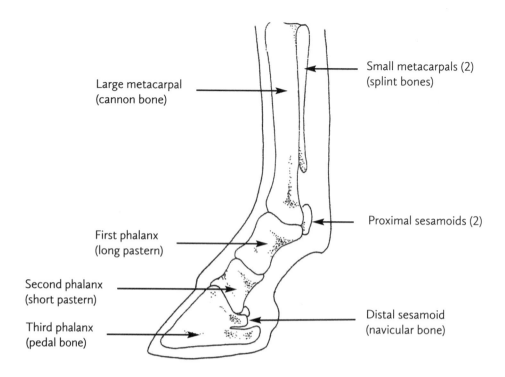

Large metacarpal
(cannon bone)

Small metacarpals (2)
(splint bones)

Proximal sesamoids (2)

First phalanx
(long pastern)

Second phalanx
(short pastern)

Third phalanx
(pedal bone)

Distal sesamoid
(navicular bone)

5.1 The bones of the lower limb

At the rear of the fetlock joint is a pair of small bones, the **sesamoids**. The lower surface of the first phalanx articulates with the **short pastern bone**, forming the **pastern joint**. The short pastern is a cube-shaped bone, also referred to as the **second phalanx**.

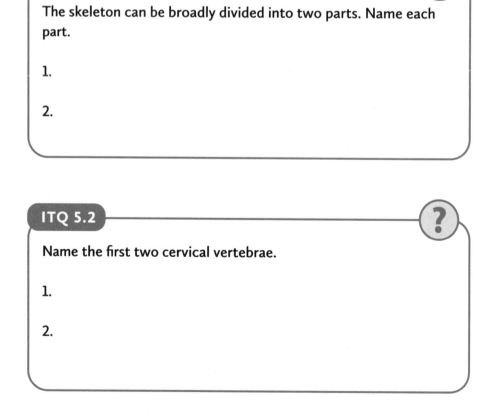

ITQ 5.1 ?

The skeleton can be broadly divided into two parts. Name each part.

1.

2.

ITQ 5.2 ?

Name the first two cervical vertebrae.

1.

2.

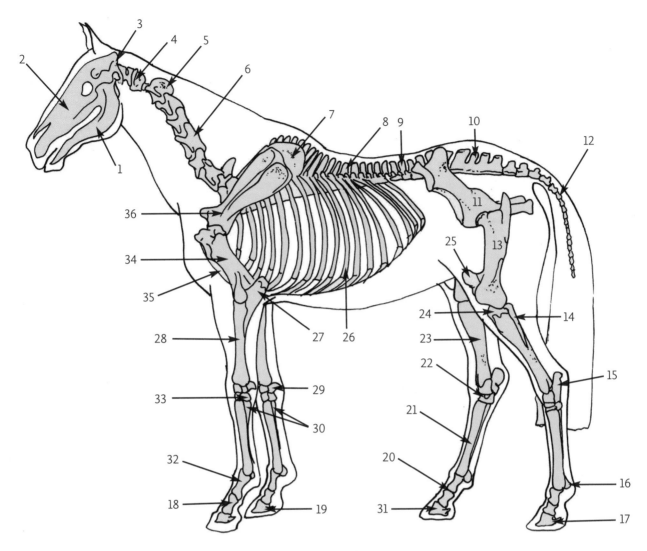

5.2 The skeleton

1. Mandible (lower jaw)
2. Skull
3. Occipital bone
4. Atlas
5. Axis
6. Cervical vertebrae (7)
7. Cartilage of prolongation
8. Thoracic vertebrae (18)
9. Lumbar vertebrae (6)
10. Sacral vertebrae (5)
11. Pelvis (ilium, ischium and pubis)
12. Coccygeal vertebrae (15–20)
13. Femur
14. Fibula

15. Os calcis
16. Sesamoid bones
17. Navicular bone
18. Short pastern bone (second phalanx)
19. Coffin or pedal joint
20. Fetlock joint
21. Cannon bone
22. Tarsus (hock joint)
23. Tibia
24. Stifle joint
25. Patella
26. Ribs (18)
27. Ulna
28. Radius

29. Pisiform
30. Splint bones
31. Pedal bone (third phalanx)
32. Long pastern bone (first phalanx)
33. Carpus (knee)
34. Humerus
35. Sternum
36. Scapula (shoulder-blade)

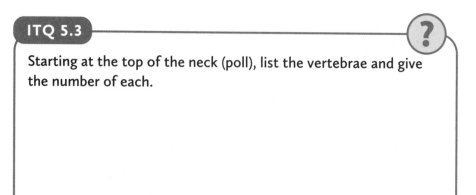

ITQ 5.3 **?**

Starting at the top of the neck (poll), list the vertebrae and give the number of each.

ITQ 5.4 **?**

a. How does the forelimb attach to the trunk?

b. What are the advantages of this attachment?

The foot

The lower end of the short pastern meets the **pedal bone** to form the **coffin** or **pedal joint**. The pedal bone is also known as the **third phalanx** or **coffin bone** and is crescent-shaped, corresponding with the shape of the hoof. Attached to the upper borders of the wings of the pedal bone are the large, elastic **lateral cartilages**. These extend above the coronet and may be felt in that region.

The whole of the laminal surface of the pedal bone is attached to the **sensitive laminae**. The **common digital extensor tendon** attaches to the extensor process of the pedal bone.

To the rear of the coffin joint is the small **navicular bone** (sometimes referred to as the **distal sesamoid** bone). The lower surface of the navicular bone is very smooth, being covered in cartilage over which the **deep digital flexor tendon** glides.

Between the deep digital flexor tendon and the navicular bone is a fluid-filled sac – the **navicular bursa**. This allows free movement and reduces friction as the tendon passes over the navicular bone. After passing over the navicular bursa, the deep digital flexor tendon attaches to the rear aspect of the pedal bone.

Other structures of the foot are discussed in the following section.

The pelvis and hind limb

The pelvis is sometimes called the pelvic girdle. It is made up of the fused sacral vertebrae and two hip bones (**os coxai**). The hind limb attaches to the pelvic girdle in a depression called the **acetabulum**, into which the ball-like head of the femur fits to form the **hip joint**.

The **femur** or **thigh bone** slopes down and forward to meet the **tibia** at the stifle. At the front of the stifle joint is a sesamoid bone called the **patella**, which corresponds to the human kneecap.

Beside the tibia is the smaller **fibula** which is approximately 10cm (4in) long. The tibia slopes down and back towards the **hock** which contains six bones and corresponds to the human ankle. The **tuber calcis** (point of hock) projects upwards and backwards.

The structure below the hock is similar to that of the forelimb, with the cannon and splint bones being known as the **large** and **small metatarsals**.

STRUCTURES OF THE FOOT

The bones of the foot and their relationship to major tendons and ligaments have been discussed in the previous section. Here, we look at other structures that constitute the foot.

The hoof wall

The outer, protective layer of the foot, the hoof wall, originates from the horn-secreting tissues of the **coronary cushion**, a fibro-cartilaginous structure composed of many tiny papillae. These papillae produce the specialised skin cells which form the horn tubules.

The horn grows from around the coronary cushion at a rate of approximately 6mm (¼in) per month. It takes approximately 9–12 months to grow from coronet to toe and 6 months from coronet to heel.

As it grows, the horn becomes compressed, harder and tougher (keratinised). The horn tends to be tougher and thicker at the toe, more pliable at the heel. Overall, the horn should be tough but not brittle, with a slightly elastic quality. Under normal circumstances, horn contains approximately 25 per cent water.

Above the coronary cushion, lying within the perioplic groove, is the **perioplic ring**; a smaller cushion of fine papillae which secrete a waterproof, varnish-like horn (the **periople**) which covers the wall, helping to prevent excessive evaporation of moisture from within.

If the wall is allowed to grow excessively long it causes the foot to become unbalanced. As the toe grows long the horse's weight is transferred onto the heels, exerting greater pressure on the navicular bone within the foot, over which the deep digital flexor tendon passes. Over time this can lead to problems and it is thought this may be a contributory factor in the development of navicular syndrome.

This change in angle also exerts extra strain on the tendons which pass down the back of the leg, which can lead to tendon strain.

As the wall grows excessively the hoof can be seen to splay laterally and very often the horn will crack. If left, sections of the hoof around the ground surface may break away from the foot, which can cause foot pain and makes the foot susceptible to dirt which can track up into the white line causing an infection within the foot.

The horny sole

The sole is a plate of hard horn approximately 2cm (⁴⁄₅in) thick. This horn is secreted by papillae from within the sensitive sole and contains approximately 30 per cent water. The sole flakes away in a natural shedding process (exfoliation). The main functions of the horny sole are to assist in weight carrying and to protect the inner, sensitive structures.

On the ground surface of the sole, the union between the sole and the wall is marked by a narrow band of soft waxy horn called the **white line**.

The frog

The insensitive frog is a wedge-shaped mass of elastic horn. It is made up of the same type of horn as the wall, but contains more glutinous inter-tubular horn and approximately 40 per cent water, making it the most elastic and pliable structure of the foot.

To either side of the frog and in the centre of its bearing surface are fairly deep clefts, which allow for expansion of the foot. The frog performs several important functions, each of which can only be carried out successfully if the frog is in contact with the ground. If the frog doesn't come into contact with the ground it may become atrophied (diminished) as a result of disuse.

The functions of the frog are:

- To protect sensitive underlying structures.

- To assist in weight carrying; if the frog is not bearing weight, more pressure is borne by the walls of the hoof.

- To prevent slipping – the rubbery texture and depression formed by the clefts provide grip.

- To protect against concussion. As the foot comes down, the heel touches the ground first, therefore taking the bulk of the weight. This jarring effect is lessened by the rubbery compression of a healthy frog.

- To promote a healthy blood supply. The insensitive frog becomes compressed which, in turn, causes pressure on the sensitive frog and **digital cushion** – a wedge-shaped fibro-elastic pad which fills the hollow behind the heels and is of a firm but yielding consistency. Frog pressure compresses the digital cushion which, in turn, causes the expansion of the lateral cartilages. This forces the lateral cartilages against the horny wall, which flattens out and empties the blood vessels between the cartilages and wall. Once the pressure is relieved (when the foot is lifted off the ground), the blood vessels refill. This process thus aids the circulation of blood within the foot.

The laminae

The hoof is attached to the pedal bone very securely by an interlocking (dovetailing) of hundreds of leaf-like structures known as laminae, of which there are two types.

The sensitive laminae are fleshy, vascular leaves, attached to the **periosteum** of the laminal surface of the pedal bone. They extend downwards from immediately under the coronary cushion to the lower edge of the pedal bone, at which point a fringe of papillae secrete the waxy horn of which the white line is composed

The horny laminae are thin, flat plates of horn which grow outward from the interior (laminal) surface of the wall and interlock with the sensitive laminae.

The hundreds of laminae provide a very large surface area which helps to distribute the weight of the horse to the hoof wall more evenly, which eases stress on the pedal bone.

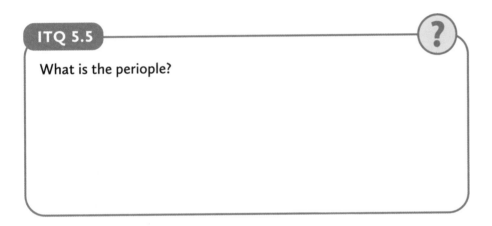

ITQ 5.5 ?

What is the periople?

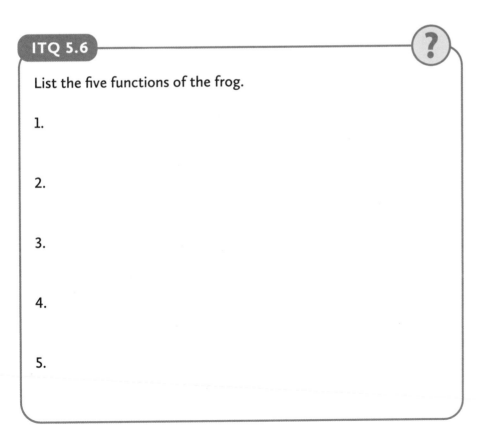

ITQ 5.6 ?

List the five functions of the frog.

1.

2.

3.

4.

5.

THE DIGESTIVE TRACT

The gut of a carnivore (meat-eater) is relatively short, but the gut of a herbivore (plant/grass-eater) is long because it deals with cellulose, which is relatively difficult to digest and therefore needs to be held in the digestive tract for longer.

The horse's digestive tract consists of the **foregut** – mouth, pharynx, oesophagus, stomach and small intestine, and the **hindgut (large intestine)** – caecum, large colon, small colon, rectum and anus.

The foregut

The mouth

Lips	The upper lip is very strong and mobile and is used to sort and grasp the food.
Incisors	These are the cutting teeth at the front of the jaw used to bite the food.
Molars	These are the grinding teeth at the back of the jaw which chew the food.
Salivary glands	These are arranged in pairs and produce saliva which warms, wets and lubricates the food to aid its movement down the digestive tract. Approximately 10–12 litres (around 2½ gallons) is produced daily.
Tongue	This forms the food into a **bolus** (ball-shaped mass) and passes the bolus to the back of the mouth.

The pharynx (throat)

This is the cavity behind the mouth through which food passes on its way to the oesophagus. It passes over the opening of the windpipe (trachea) which is protected by the **epiglottis**. This is a small cartilage at the root of the tongue which covers the opening to the windpipe (trachea). The windpipe leads to the lungs and the epiglottis is depressed during swallowing to prevent food or water entering it.

The oesophagus (gullet)

The oesophagus is a tube approximately 1.2–1.5m (4–5ft) long which connects the throat to the stomach. It passes down the back of the trachea, down the left-hand side of the neck. It passes through the chest between the lungs, through the **diaphragm** (a sheet of muscle which separates the chest from the abdomen), into the abdominal cavity and to the stomach. No digestion occurs within the oesophagus.

The stomach

When empty the stomach is relatively small, approximately the size of a rugby ball, but it can expand to contain 9–15 litres (2–3.25 gallons). Food is allowed into the stomach by a small ring muscle called the **cardiac sphincter**.

As food arrives in the stomach it stimulates the release of gastric juice; 10–30 litres (2¼–6½ gallons) are produced daily. The horse's stomach is designed to remain partially full at all times; most food passes out of the stomach within 45 minutes, whilst some remains for approximately 2 hours.

The food leaves the stomach, regulated by another ring muscle, the **pyloric sphincter**, to enter the first section of the small intestine. At this stage the food is known as **chyme**.

Note: when feeding horses on a day-to-day basis, we should always bear in mind that the horse's stomach is so small in relation to his overall size. It is tempting to feed too much in one feed. It is better to feed to slightly below appetite, taking into account the volume capacity of the stomach. Divide the horse's daily ration into as many small feeds as is practical.

The small intestine

This is the major site for the breakdown of concentrated food such as starch and protein, and for the absorption of nutrients. The small intestine lies in coils and moves quite freely in the abdomen, except for its attachment at the stomach and caecum. The lining of the intestine is covered with small hair-like **villi** which give a huge surface area to aid absorption.

Food is passed through the intestines by involuntary muscular contractions called **peristalsis**. The gut wall consists of a layer of longitudinal muscle and a layer of circular muscle. These layers work against each other (antagonistically) to push the food in one direction.

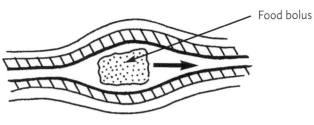
Food bolus

5.3 Peristalsis

There are three parts to the small intestine.

The duodenum

This is the first part of the small intestine. The duodenum is approximately 1m (3ft 3in) long and forms an S-shaped bend. Into it flows **bile**, secreted by the liver and **pancreatic juices**, secreted by the pancreas.

The jejunum

This second part of the small intestine is approximately 20m (66ft) long. Here, amino acids, vitamins, minerals and glucose are absorbed into the bloodstream. Fatty acids and glycerol are taken up by a separate system called the **lymphatic system** as minute globules. These globules are transported to the vascular system which distributes the fat around the body.

The ileum

The ileum is the final part of the small intestine and is approximately 2m (6ft 6in) long.

The duodenum, jejunum and ileum together have a volume capacity of approximately 50 litres (11 gallons).

Mesentery tissue loosely supports the small intestines and supplies them with blood vessels, lymphatics and nerves.

ITQ 5.7   **?**

Why does the horse's digestive tract need to be relatively long?

ITQ 5.8   **?**

a. Approximately what size is the horse's stomach?

b. How is food regulated in and out of the stomach?

ITQ 5.9   **?**

What is peristalsis?

The hindgut (large intestine)

Following on from the small intestine is the large intestine. This is the major site for the fermentation of roughage. The large intestine is held in place only by its bulk and, because of flexures where the gut narrows and changes direction, it is prone to blockages which result in the horse suffering from colic.

The caecum

The caecum is the first part of the large intestine. Food reaches the caecum approximately 3 hours after a meal and remains in the large intestine for 36–48 hours. The caecum is capable of holding 35 litres (approx. 8 gallons). Food coming into the caecum is controlled by a valve. The caecum then holds food, passing it on a 'top-up' basis to the next section of the large intestine, the large colon.

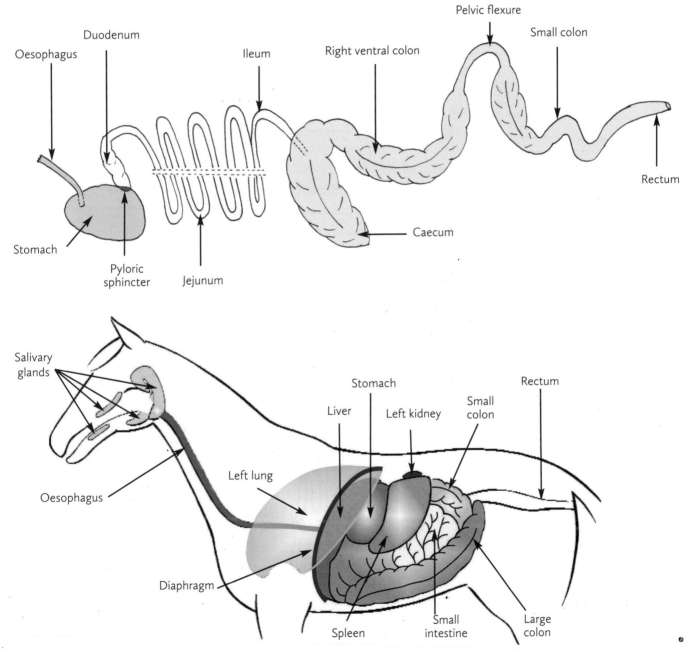

5.4 The digestive tract

The digestion of roughage begins in the caecum through the process of **fermentation**. This process is activated by a population of bacteria and protozoa specific to particular types of feedstuff.

Cellulose is an insoluble carbohydrate which is fermented in the large intestine by micro-organisms, which synthesise essential vitamins. Cellulose provides **fibre** (also called **roughage**) – an important component of the horse's diet. Fibre aids digestion and ensures that the horse's digestive tract functions properly. It has to be remembered that the horse's digestive tract is designed to break down and ferment large quantities of roughage.

As grass and hay contain cellulose they provide a good source of fibre. Very new, young grass is not very high in fibre and this can cause the droppings of a horse out on new grass to be loose. The stabled horse's cellulose requirements are met when hay is fed. As plants get older their cells lignify (turn woody). As the amount of lignin increases, the cells become more resistant to breakdown, becoming tough and indigestible. For this reason, hay must be cut at the right time – if the grass is left too long before cutting, the stems will be woody and indigestible.

The large colon

The second section of the large intestine is the large colon. It is 3–4m (9ft 9in–13ft) long and holds approximately 82 litres (18 gallons). There are bacteria in the large colon which continue the fermentation of cellulose.

The small colon

The third and final part of the large intestine has a much reduced diameter and is 3–4m (9ft 9in–13ft) long. It is capable of holding only 14 litres (3 gallons). The small colon lies intermingled with the jejunum and can move quite freely, making it

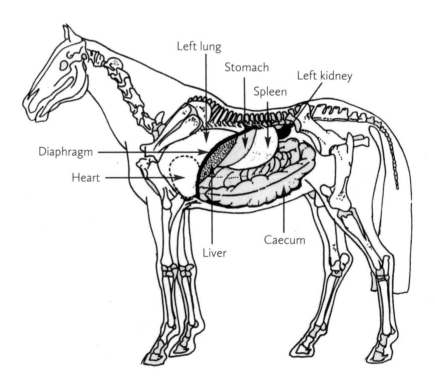

5.5 Location of the main organs

susceptible to twisting. Again, this can cause serious colic.

Water and nutrients are extracted through the walls of the small colon. Further water is extracted in the rectum, where the waste materials are formed into faeces to be expelled through the anus.

Note: the design of the digestive tract renders the horse susceptible to problems as a result of too much concentrate feed. The horse cannot digest and utilise excessive amounts of carbohydrate, which can cause problems such as laminitis and azoturia. Because of the flexures in the large colon the horse is prone to blockages, which cause colic.

ITQ 5.10

Starting with the stomach, list each organ of the digestive tract in the correct order and write one thing that you remember about each. You might remember its size and/or volume capacity, or you might remember that a certain nutrient is digested and absorbed in a particular section.

1. STOMACH:

2.

3.

4.

5.

6.

7. SMALL COLON:

ITQ 5.11

a. Which parts of the digestive tract make up the foregut?

b. Which parts make up the hindgut?

ITQ 5.12

a. Why is fibre important in the horse's diet?

b. How is fibre digested?

6 Horse Health

REQUIRED SKILLS/KNOWLEDGE	Learnt, revised, practised?	Confirmed
Be able to assess a horse's health, welfare and condition.		
• Normal temperature, pulse and respiration rates.	☐	☐
• Be aware of how the horse's stance and bodily functions indicate his state of health and well-being.	☐	☐
• Know the signs of poor health in a horse.	☐	☐
• Know the signs of unsoundness in a horse.	☐	☐
• Recognise the signs of a horse having problems with his teeth.	☐	☐
Be able to recognise and treat minor wounds.		
• Know the various types of minor wounds.	☐	☐
• Describe the treatment of minor wounds.	☐	☐
• Know when a vet may need to be called.	☐	☐
Care for sick horses.		
• Be familiar with the principles of sick nursing.	☐	☐
Know the importance of keeping horse records.		
• Understand the reasons for keeping health records.	☐	☐
Understand why worming is important.		
• Know the signs of worm infestation in the horse.	☐	☐
• Know how a worming programme is devised.	☐	☐

SIGNS OF GOOD HEALTH

In your Stage 2 exam you will be asked to look at a horse and point out signs that indicate good health. Describe his general overall attitude and demeanour, as this is the first thing you will notice. Then, starting at the head, work methodically through the body. The following are key points to consider.

Overall signs

Attitude and demeanour. He should have an alert outlook. When fit and well, most horses appear bright, are alert and show interest in their surroundings. They react to certain stimuli, e.g. feed time, passing horses, loud noises, and generally have an interested, yet relaxed attitude.

Condition. A horse's condition, i.e. how much weight he is carrying, can be indicative of his health. A healthy horse will be carrying the right amount of weight, i.e. have a good covering of flesh without being too fat.

Eyes and nostrils. The eyes must be bright and, like the nostrils, free of discharge, particularly that of a thick, sticky consistency. Occasionally horses have a slight clear, watery discharge – if no other symptoms are present, this can be considered as normal.

Mucous membranes. These are the membranes of the gums and eyes. The gums should be moist, slippery to the touch and salmon pink in colour. If checking the membranes, you must untie the horse to prevent him pulling back as you attempt to turn the lower eyelid down or open his lips to observe his gums.

Skin and coat. The skin should feel supple and quite loose. As you run your hand over the skin you should see small 'ripples' appear. The coat should have a smooth and naturally glossy appearance.

Limbs and posture. The horse should be happy to stand weight-bearing on all four limbs; he may rest a hind leg, but never a foreleg. The limbs should feel cool and be free from heat, pain and swelling.

When out of the stable he must be sound, taking even, free steps. The walls of the hooves should feel uniformly cool, be free from excessive cracks and should be well trimmed/shod. The clefts of the frog should be clean and dry without an offensive smell or black discharge.

Excretion. Droppings should be passed regularly and will vary in colour and consistency according to the diet. A stabled horse eating hay and short feed will pass yellow-brown droppings, whilst the droppings of a grass-kept horse will be dark green-brown. The droppings should be fairly firm, breaking apart on hitting the ground, and be free of any offensive smell.

Micturition (urination/staling). Horses micturate approximately four to six times per day, passing between 5–15 litres (approx. 9–26 pints) of urine.

Most horses wait until they are standing over deep bedding or grass before staling as they don't like to do so on concrete or in a lorry without straw or shavings down. They will often wait until they return to their stable or field. Horses adopt a typical posture when staling – they stand with their hind legs separated, leaning forwards slightly. Geldings normally extend their forelegs forwards as well and some horses make 'grunting' sounds as they stale.

The urine should be pale yellow to amber in colour and free of any offensive smell.

Appetite. Most horses have a very healthy appetite and clear up their feeds immediately, however some are slow feeders, inclined to be a bit fussy about what they eat.

If a usually 'greedy' horse does not finish his feed it could be a sign that something is wrong. 'Slow' feeding can be caused by overfacing the horse with large feeds. (Always remember to feed 'little and often'.) A slow feeder may dislike the food or something that has been added to it, e.g. not all horses enjoy cubes or garlic additives.

Temperature, pulse and respiration (TPR)

The normal rates for a healthy adult horse at rest are:

- Temperature – 38 °C (100.5 °F)

- Pulse – 25–42 beats per minute

- Respiration – 8–16 breaths per minute

Although commonly cited as TPR, it is preferable to record the respiratory rate first as this is an unobtrusive process which will not upset the horse, thereby causing an increased heart rate. Taking the temperature should be left until last as this can upset a nervous type.

To gauge what is normal for each individual horse, take the TPR first thing each morning for several days and write down the readings.

To observe respiration

1 The horse must be standing still, at rest.

2 Watch the rise and fall of the flanks. Each complete rise and fall is one breath.

3 Count either the rise or fall for one minute.

The normal rate of respiration for an adult horse at rest is between 8 and 16 breaths per minute.

To take the pulse (heart) rate

1 Lightly press two fingers against the transverse facial artery, which is found slightly to the rear of and below the eye, or on the sub-mandibular artery, on the inside edge of the lower jaw, where it passes over the bone fairly near the surface, or:

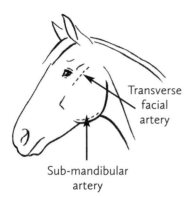

Transverse facial artery

Sub-mandibular artery

6.1 Sites for taking the pulse

2 Using a stethoscope – press the stethoscope against the horse's girth just behind the left elbow and listen for the heartbeat. You will hear a 'lubb-dub, lubb-dub, ...' sound. Each 'lubb-dub' represents one heartbeat.

Count the pulse rate/heartbeat for 1 minute or for 30 seconds and multiply by two. The pulse rate of an adult horse at rest is between 25 and 42 beats per minute.

To take the temperature

1 If the horse is unknown to you he should be untied and held. This is to prevent him pulling back and breaking the weak link should he become upset by the procedure.

2 If using a mercury thermometer, shake it down so that it reads several degrees lower than normal. If using a digital thermometer, turn it on. Lubricate the end with petroleum jelly. Stand behind the horse, slightly to one side.

3 Hold the horse's tail to one side, making sure no tail hairs are in the way of the thermometer. Insert to halfway and hold at a slight angle to press the thermometer against the side of the rectum.

4 If using a mercury thermometer, hold in position for 1 minute. The digits on a digital thermometer will stop flashing or it will 'beep' when the maximum temperature has been recorded.

5 Withdraw and read the thermometer. Always wipe it clean and disinfect it before returning it to its case. Disinfectant wipes are a convenient way of doing this.

ITQ 6.1   ?

How should the coat and skin of a healthy horse appear?

ITQ 6.2   ?

Describe how the mucous membranes of the gums should appear.

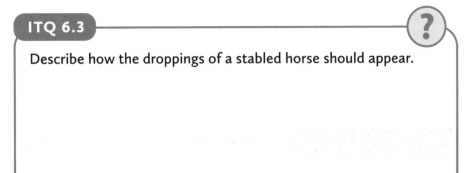

ITQ 6.3 **?**

Describe how the droppings of a stabled horse should appear.

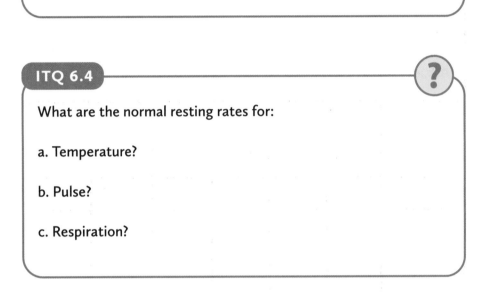

ITQ 6.4 **?**

What are the normal resting rates for:

a. Temperature?

b. Pulse?

c. Respiration?

You will develop an eye for health and condition as you spend more time with horses. The most important consideration is to be aware of what is normal for each particular horse. Regularly check the limbs, TPR etc., so you are familiar with the norm – this way any changes will be more easily recognised.

SIGNS OF ILL-HEALTH

We now go on to discuss the signs of ill-health. A horse may show only one or two of the following signs – it is up to you to be observant and notice the sign(s) in the first instance and then take appropriate action.

If you do notice one or two signs of ill-health you should:

- Look for additional signs which will help identify the problem.

- Consult an experienced person who can offer professional help.

- Decide whether or not to call the vet.

- Prevent the condition from worsening whilst waiting for the vet (with the help of your experienced person).

- If you decide the vet is not needed:
  — identify the cause
  — treat the problem
  — take steps to prevent it from occurring again.

IN-TEXT ACTIVITY

Select a horse known to you and record his temperature, pulse and respiratory rates on consecutive days. Record the details below.

Ask an experienced person on your yard to assist you.

	Temperature (°F and/or °C)		Pulse (beats per min)		Respiration (breaths per min)	
	Day 1	Day 2	Day 1	Day 2	Day 1	Day 2
Horse's Name:						

Common signs

Disinterested, dull attitude

Standing in the corner of the stable with the head low is one of the first signs to indicate that all is not right.

Possible causes

- The horse *could* simply be tired and having a rest! Keep a close eye on him though.

- A viral or bacterial infection could be starting.

Loss of appetite

If the horse fails to clear up a feed and is not interested in his hay or water, you should be on the lookout for further symptoms.

Possible causes

- He may not like an additive, e.g. garlic, or a wormer.

- A horse new to a yard may take a day or two to settle in and start eating properly.

- A viral or bacterial infection could be starting.

- The horse may be starting to have abdominal pain (colic).

Dull and staring coat

Possible causes

- The horse may be cold.

- Worm infestation.

- Nutritional deficiency.

- General lack of condition.

Tight skin

Dehydration causes the skin to lose its elasticity and feel 'tight'. Dehydration is a serious condition and, if suspected, needs to be investigated thoroughly.

Sweating

Possible causes

- Excitement.

- Pain.

- The horse may be too warm, e.g. if he's wearing too many rugs in mild weather or has just been exercised.

- The stable may be stuffy and poorly ventilated.

Having ruled out obvious reasons for sweating, look out for other signs, especially **colic signs**. These include:

- Pawing at the ground.

- Looking round at the flanks.

- Kicking at the belly.

- Repeatedly lying down and getting up.

- Rolling.

- Lying flat out in the stable.

- Increased pulse and respiratory rates.

- Loss of appetite.

ITQ 6.5 ?

Give two reasons why a horse may not eat his feed:

1.

2.

Lack of condition

This is fairly easy to recognise. When speaking of condition it is usually the horse's weight and general appearance that are being referred to.

A horse in poor condition usually has a dull coat, does not carry enough flesh, and may even have projecting hips, shoulders and ribs if he is very thin.

Possible causes

Horses don't normally lose condition overnight so poor condition indicates an ongoing problem which needs to be dealt with. The more common causes include:

- Poor diet – insufficient food.

- Sharp teeth, which prevent the horse from chewing his food properly.

- Worm infestation.

- Overwork.

- Cold – e.g. thin-skinned horse kept out with inadequate shelter.

A rapid loss of condition indicates a serious problem and the vet should be consulted.

Abnormal discharge from eyes and/or nostrils

Possible causes

- Discharge from the eyes and nostrils indicates an infection such as a cold or influenza, especially if accompanied by a 'wet' sounding cough.

- Discharge from the eyes only, especially if the lids and/or membranes are inflamed, indicates a foreign body such as a hay seed, or an infectious condition such as conjunctivitis.

- If the horse is allergic to the dust found in hay and straw he may have a thick yellow (mucous) nasal discharge accompanied by a dry cough.

Abnormal mucous membranes

Possible causes

If the membranes of the eye and gums are:

Pale coloured – anaemia.
Yellow (jaundiced) – liver complaint.
Tacky and dry – dehydration.
Dark red/purple – toxaemia, shock.

Abnormal droppings

Possible causes

- Too hard – constipation.

- Too soft/loose – worm infestation, excitement, too much rich grass, sharp teeth preventing the horse from chewing his food properly.

- Diarrhoea – infection e.g. salmonella, or poisoning.

- No droppings – constipation or impaction (blockage).

Abnormal urine/urination

Possible causes

- Thick and cloudy and/or bloodstained – kidney disease.

- Smell of violets and dark-coloured – rhabdomyolysis (azoturia).

- Repeated efforts to urinate without producing any urine – kidney problems, cystitis.

Abnormal limbs

Possible causes

- Cold swellings are often a consequence of poor circulation caused by lack of exercise. Once the horse has been turned out or exercised this type of swelling often goes down.

- Hot swellings may be a result of impaired circulation, infection or injury, e.g. a sprain. The swelling may or may not be painful, and the horse may be lame. The vet should be consulted.

- It is normal to rest a hind leg, but never a foreleg. A pottery, stilted action indicates laminitis. The laminitic horse will also stand with the weight back on his heels and be reluctant to move. He may shift his weight from one forefoot to the other.

- Heat in one or more hooves may indicate a problem such as pus in the foot (very common) or laminitis.

Abnormalities of TPR

Possible causes of abnormal temperature

- A rise of 1 or 2 degrees indicates pain, e.g. colic or injury.

- A rise of more than 2 degrees indicates a more serious infection.

- Hypothermia will cause a reduction in body temperature.

Remember to take into account whether recording the temperature in Celsius or Fahrenheit – a rise of 1 degree Celsius is of greater consequence than a rise of 1 degree Fahrenheit.

Possible causes of abnormal pulse rate

- A rapid pulse of 43–50 beats per minute indicates pain.

- A very weak pulse indicates that the heart is failing, e.g. when a horse is in shock.

Possible causes of increased respiratory rate

- Pain.

- Laboured breathing and respiratory distress indicates damage to the lungs, e.g. chronic obstructive pulmonary disease.

When investigating TPR abnormalities, take into account that a horse who has just worked strenuously will have an increased temperature, pulse and breathing rates.

Wounds

Any break in the skin, i.e. a wound, needs to be assessed and treated. Simple wounds can be cleaned and, if necessary, protected. Check that the horse is vaccinated against tetanus. More complicated wounds may need to be stitched or stapled, requiring veterinary attention.

The heel region should be checked for cracking and mud fever in wet conditions, particularly if the horse is turned out in a muddy paddock.

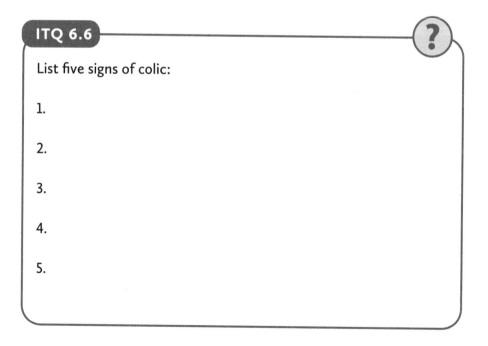

ITQ 6.6   **?**

List five signs of colic:

1.

2.

3.

4.

5.

ITQ 6.7

How should the urine of a healthy horse appear?

ITQ 6.8 ?

What may cause the droppings to be very loose?

ITQ 6.9 ?

Give four causes of poor condition:

1.

2.

3.

4.

ITQ 6.10 ?

What ailment causes the horse to move with a pottery, stilted action?

LAMENESS

Lameness is unfortunately fairly common in horses and ponies because of the wear and tear imposed on their limbs, combined with the demands of roadwork and competitive riding.

When trying to detect lameness it is first necessary to be able to recognise when a horse is sound.

The sound horse

A sound horse will stand with his weight evenly distributed over all four legs. He may rest a hind leg, but should never rest a foreleg. When walking, the horse's head nods slightly in rhythm with the walk. He should take even, level and purposeful strides. In trot, the head should be still. Again, in a sound horse, the strides will be even, loose and level. When observing the horse moving away from you the hips will rise and fall evenly.

The limbs should feel cool and be free from any puffiness and swellings. The walls of the hooves should be cold or cool – all four hooves should feel the same.

Detecting lameness when ridden

When riding, lameness may be felt as the horse taking uneven or shortened steps and/or limping. If this happens when you are out riding, dismount and pick out the hooves – look for stones wedged in the foot. Remove any stones and lead the horse up to see if he is still unsound. If he is sound you can remount and ride home. If, however, he still feels lame or there are no signs of stones jammed in the foot, then the horse must be led home. If home is far away it would be necessary to get someone to bring out a trailer or lorry and give him a lift back.

Once home you must try to decide exactly which leg he is lame upon.

Leading up to detect lameness

1. Pick the feet out and check that there are no stones wedged in the foot. Also check the condition of the shoes at this point, as a slipped shoe would be uncomfortable and any movement of the nails may put pressure on the sensitive structures within the foot, causing lameness.

2. Put a bridle on the horse and ensure that your assistant wears gloves. The bridle gives extra control and gloves will prevent burns should the horse decide to pull away.

3. A whip should be carried to encourage the horse forwards.

4 Make sure that the yard gate is closed. This will stop the horse escaping, should he pull away from the handler.

5 Look at the way the horse stands. The pastern of a lame leg may appear more upright, or the horse may stand with the affected leg extended forward and the toe 'pointing'.

6 Have the horse led on a level, hard surface, not a stony drive.

7 You must watch him walk towards and away from you on a loose rein.

8 If he is very lame it will be apparent at the walk. If the lame leg is not obvious at the walk, it will be necessary to see the horse in trot. Have the horse trot on briskly. If the lameness is in a foreleg, his head will come towards the ground (nod) as the sound foreleg comes in contact with the ground. He will try to keep the weight off the lame leg, so will raise his head every time the lame leg comes to the ground.

9 If both forefeet are affected, for instance in the case of laminitis, the horse will take shortened, shuffling steps (also described as 'pottery' steps).

10 If the lameness is in a hind leg he may appear to drag the toe of the affected leg. The hip of the affected side may appear to rise upwards as the lame leg comes to the ground, again as the horse tries to keep the weight off the lame leg.

11 Make sure that you watch the horse moving from the side so that you can note any shortened strides, irregular footfalls or abnormalities in the way the horse lifts and places each foot.

Locating the seat of lameness

Having decided which leg the horse is lame upon, you now have to find out exactly which spot is affected, and the cause.

1 Always start at the foot – 90 per cent of problems causing unsoundness originate in the foot. Pick out the hoof and scrub the sole. You are looking for **wedged stones** and/or signs of **bruising** or a **puncture wound**.

2 Feel the walls of the hooves to compare warmth. Ideally, hooves should feel cool, although on a hot day they may feel warmer than normal. Provided all four hooves feel the same, this is normal. Excessive or uneven heat is an indication that something is wrong. It's a good idea to know what is normal for your horse's hooves. Feel them regularly whilst attending to his feet when you know that he is sound.

3 You will not feel any swelling around the hoof because the hoof wall is unyielding and cannot swell. Tap the wall lightly with a hammer to see if the horse flinches.

4 Another useful aid is the **hoof tester**. This looks like the farrier's pincers and is normally used by a vet to apply pressure on the sole and wall. If the horse feels pain upon this pressure he will flinch. This may indicate that infection is present, (often referred to as **pus in the foot**).

5 If the lameness does not appear to be in the foot, feel the rest of the leg for any **cuts, swelling** and **heat**. Compare both legs (i.e. both fore or both hind) to see if there is any difference between them.

In some cases of lameness there are no obvious signs. Your course of action must then be to:

1 Stop work immediately and put the horse onto a non-heating diet.

2 Arrange for the vet to come and see the horse. It may be necessary for the vet to **nerve-block** the area. This involves injecting local anaesthetic into the nerves supplying specific areas of the foot and lower leg. This desensitises the area, allowing the vet to find out more precisely which area is affected – when the affected area is nerve-blocked the horse will trot up sound.

3 The vet will then be likely to suggest taking **radiographs (X-rays) or ultrasound scans** of the affected area. X-rays are useful if a joint or bone is affected whereas ultrasound shows up problems in soft tissue such as tendons and ligaments.

ITQ 6.11 ?

Describe how the hooves of a healthy, sound horse should feel.

ITQ 6.12 ?

What should you do if a horse feels lame whilst out hacking?

ITQ 6.13

When trotting a horse up, what signs indicate lameness in a foreleg?

ITQ 6.14

What signs indicate lameness in a hind leg?

ITQ 6.15

a. What it meant by a horse taking 'pottery' steps?

b. What ailment causes horses to move like this?

ITQ 6.16

Why is it important to watch the horse moving from the side?

ITQ 6.17 ?

When trying to find the seat of lameness, what should you look for:

a. When examining the hooves?

b. When examining the limbs?

IN-TEXT ACTIVITY

The best way to identify a soundness problem is to know what is normal for each horse.

Using two horses known to you, examine their legs and make a note of the following:

Hoof walls. Do they feel cold, warm or hot? Are all four hooves the same temperature?

Lower limbs. Do the tendons and fetlock joints feel cold and clean? Is there any sign of warmth or puffiness? Are there any bony enlargements (lumps)? Are there any soft swellings?

Talk to the owner of these horses and ask if there are any specific things to look for, e.g. old injury scars, lumps or signs of wear and tear.

WOUNDS

Types of wound

Wounds are classified as **open** or **closed.**

Open wounds

- **Incised wound** – a clean cut caused by a sharp object such as glass or metal. An incised wound may need stitching and, if deep, underlying structures (such as muscles or tendons) may be damaged. With the correct treatment incised wounds tend to heal quickly.

- **Lacerated or tear wound** – a rough-edged wound often caused by barbed wire or a projecting nail. There are often flaps of skin and the wound may be contaminated with dirt. These wounds may take longer to heal than an incised wound and there is often some skin or flesh missing.

- **Puncture wound** – a deep wound with a small point of entry caused by a nail or thorn. The wound may become infected as the object causing the puncture may introduce dirt and bacteria into the wound. Puncture wounds provide the ideal environment for tetanus bacteria to reproduce. It is therefore important to ascertain whether a horse who has sustained a puncture wound is vaccinated against tetanus; if not he will require an anti-tetanus injection from the vet.

- **Abrasions** – these are superficial graze-type wounds that may result from ill-fitting tack or rugs, or from falling on a hard surface.

Closed wounds

- **Contused wound** – bruising caused by a kick or blow, fall or overreach. Bleeding occurs beneath the skin. This may also be accompanied by fluid-filled swelling.

- **Tendon injury** – fibres in the tendons of the lower leg may be torn or damaged, causing inflammation.

Wound treatment

Sources of bleeding
Bleeding may be from **arteries, veins** or **capillaries.**

- **Arterial bleeding.** If an artery is damaged the blood will be bright red as it contains oxygen. It is pumped under pressure by the heart so will escape in spurts.

- **Venous bleeding.** Blood from a vein will be darker in colour than arterial blood as it is deoxygenated (most of its oxygen has been deposited in the tissues). The blood flow will be slow and continual.

- **Capillary bleeding.** Slight wounds such as abrasions may only bleed lightly. Bleeding from capillaries normally stops very quickly without further treatment.

Stemming bleeding

Bleeding must be controlled to prevent excessive loss of blood.

Slight bleeding

Slight bleeding can be stemmed with gentle cold hosing. When a wound bleeds slightly it removes particles of debris which helps to clean the wound. Slight bleeding normally congeals and clots naturally fairly quickly.

Serious bleeding

Pressure must be applied to stem serious bleeding. A tourniquet should not be used as it may cause complications and actually make the bleeding worse.

- Keep the horse still and reassure him. Ideally he should be wearing a headcollar or bridle.

- If the injury is not too large, press the edges of the wound together firmly with your thumbs and keep that pressure up for a long time. The pressure will help to stem the bleeding.

- If the wound is on the leg, press the edges together firmly and hold. Once the bleeding has slowed you will need to make a **pressure pad**. If you are not near your yard improvise with an item of clothing. Tie firmly in place making sure that it does not slip.

- If you are near the yard or have a first aid kit with you, you will be able to make a pressure pad from a clean tea towel and bandage firmly over the wound. If the blood seeps through, don't remove the bandage. If you were to remove the bandage you would be likely to remove any clot forming and restart the bleeding. Apply another pad over the top of the first and leave in place until the vet arrives.

- Call the vet immediately or send someone to do so.

- Once the bleeding has stopped the vet will remove the pad.

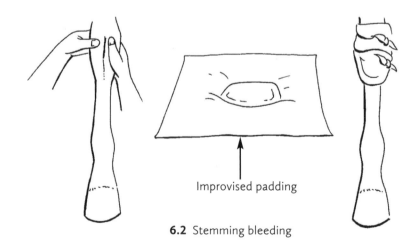

Improvised padding

6.2 Stemming bleeding

ITQ 6.18 ?

List four types of open wound:

1.

2.

3.

4.

ITQ 6.19 ?

Why is it important that a horse who has sustained a puncture wound is vaccinated against tetanus?

ITQ 6.20 ?

a. Describe arterial bleeding:

b. Describe venous bleeding:

Cleaning wounds

Before attempting to clean a wound, put a headcollar on the horse and either get an assistant to hold him or tie him up safely.

Wash your hands – it is important that your hands are clean whenever cleaning or examining a wound so bacteria are not introduced into the wound.

Gentle **hosing** is an effective method of washing a wound and surrounding coat. This cleans out any dirt and, because the water is cold, the blood vessels constrict (tighten and close up) which helps to stop the bleeding. Don't use high pressure because particles of dirt may be pushed deeper into the wound and high pressure can cause damage to surviving tissue. When hosing, ensure that you position the

ITQ 6.21

Describe two ways to apply pressure to stem bleeding:

1.

2.

hose above the wound so as to flush particles out and downward.

If the wound is not infected or heavily contaminated, it can be flushed with **saline solution**. Saline has a mild antiseptic effect and can be used to clean wounds. Dissolve a teaspoon of salt into approximately 0.6 litre (1 pint) of warm, previously boiled water. A plastic syringe (without the needle attached!) can be used to squirt the saline into the wound. This helps prevent bacterial infection and doesn't introduce new bacteria into the wound.

Alternatively, Gamgee swabs can be used. Dip a swab into the saline solution. Wipe the wound from the centre outwards and throw away the swab. Never start to swab the wound from the outside edge towards the centre – this would push dirt and bacteria from the coat into the wound.

Continue this procedure until the wound is completely clean.

If the wound is infected or heavily contaminated it can be cleaned with an **antiseptic wash** such as **Hibiscrub (chlorhexidene)**. Once the wound has been hosed the wound can be flushed through with a dilute solution (2 per cent Hibiscrub). It is important to ensure that the solution is dilute because strong antiseptic can damage healthy/surviving tissue surrounding the area, which will increase healing time.

If the wound does not need to be sutured (stitched) you should then apply an **intrasite gel,** also known as **hydrogel**. These gels promote healing by maintaining a moist wound environment, preventing infection and helping to keep the wound clean. Do not cover the wound in wound powder as this has the opposite effect of the hydrogels.

Suturing

If the wound is open and gaping it will require stitching (suturing) or stapling. The vet will only be able to do this if there is sufficient loose skin to draw the edges of the wound together. Suturing is usually most effective when completed within a short time of the injury occurring (less than 4 hours). Sutures are normally left in place for approximately 10 days.

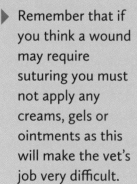

SAFETY TIP

▶ Remember that if you think a wound may require suturing you must not apply any creams, gels or ointments as this will make the vet's job very difficult.

ITQ 6.22

What percentage solution of antiseptic would you use for an infected/contaminated wound and why would you ensure this solution strength?

Dressings

Wounds may need to be bandaged for the following reasons:

- To hold a dressing in place to keep the wound clean and provide a moist (not wet) environment for wound healing.

- To immobilise the wound to aid healing.

- To apply pressure to control and reduce swelling.

Follow the vet's advice about the use of dressings. If the wound needs to be covered to keep it clean, use a non-adhesive dressing. The dressing should be sterile or at least very clean.

Animalintex poultices are made from gauze and wool impregnated with boracic powder and can be used as a dry dressing. Gamgee or cotton wool should be used over melolin or Animalintex as padding to even out the pressure from the bandage and absorb any discharge. Cotton wool should never be applied directly to a wound as it will stick and clog the wound.

Advanced/active dressings are those which contain active ingredients such as silver, charcoal, collagen, etc; there are a number on the market aimed at speeding up healing time of specific types of wound. Specialist advice should always be sought before using one of these dressings to ensure it is appropriate for the wound conditions.

Bandaging

When bandaging to hold a dressing in place, elasticated adhesive bandages are very useful as they don't slip.

There are several important considerations when bandaging:

- As with ordinary bandages, the bandage and padding must be flat, not lumpy or wrinkled as this will cause pressure points.

- Bandage in the same direction that the padding overlaps, e.g. if the padding overlaps left over right, wrap the bandage around the limb left to right. This prevents the padding from becoming ridged and uneven.

- Start bandaging in the middle, working first down and then up. This makes the bandage more secure, helping to prevent it from slipping. It is also thought that bandaging upwards helps prevent fluid filling in the limb.

- The whole of the lower limb should be bandaged as any unbandaged area would be prone to filling.

- Ensure that about 2.5cm (1in) of padding is left exposed at the top and bottom of the bandage to prevent pressure sores and restriction of circulation.

- Each wrap of the bandage should overlap the previous turn by half a width of the bandage to ensure that pressure is evenly distributed.

- Never bandage too tightly as the circulation may be impaired.

- Make sure that you bandage the sound limb for support.

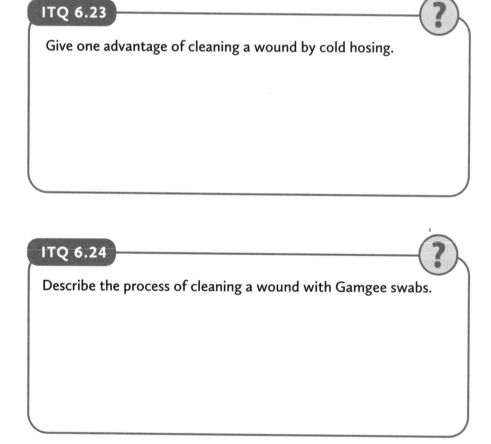

ITQ 6.23 ?

Give one advantage of cleaning a wound by cold hosing.

ITQ 6.24 ?

Describe the process of cleaning a wound with Gamgee swabs.

General notes on wound treatment

- Upon discovering that a horse has injured himself your immediate action must be to remove the cause. For example, this may mean that if he is tangled up in wire fencing you must free him to prevent further injury. Should a horse get caught up in fencing he may panic and make matters worse – it's important that you don't panic. If you find a horse tangled up in the fencing call for help and try to keep the horse calm. Use wire cutters to cut the fencing – if it is barbed wire you will need to wear gloves to protect your hands.

Note: barbed wire is very dangerous and should never be used as fencing for horses and ponies as it can cause terrible injuries.

- Never use sponges to clean wounds as they harbour bacteria which lead to the spread of infection and cause contamination of a wound.

- Ideally all water used to clean wounds must be boiled first to sterilise it, and allowed to cool.

- Never use strong antiseptics or disinfectants on a wound. These kill the living skin cells resulting in the production of scar tissue known as **proud flesh**, which causes an ugly, lumpy scar.

- When cold hosing remember to pack the heels with petroleum jelly to prevent cracking and soreness. Dry the heels carefully afterwards.

- If the horse needs time off work because of the wound, especially if he has to go onto box rest, his diet must be adjusted. He could be fed non-heating cubes mixed with dampened chaff. A constant supply of hay and fresh water is necessary.

Summary of wound treatment

Step 1 Remove the cause and prevent further injury.

Step 2 Stop the bleeding.

Step 3 If necessary, call the vet.

Step 4 Clean the wound.

Step 5 Dress the wound with intrasite gel (hydrogel). (Don't dress the wound if the vet has been called – the vet will need the wound clean and bare in order to stitch it if necessary).

Step 6 Protect the wound if necessary with a non-adhesive dressing. Use Gamgee or cotton wool as padding. Do not bandage too tightly.

Step 7 Stop work and adjust the diet, i.e. put the horse onto a non-heating diet.

Don't forget …

- Is the horse vaccinated against tetanus?

- Does the wound need stitching?

- If in any doubt – call the vet and follow advice!

SAFETY TIP

▶ It is useful to have a pack of irrigation fluid (saline solution) in your first aid kit as this is great for flushing out a wound. The packs are sterile and easy to use and store.

PRINCIPLES OF SICK NURSING

The stable regime

Generally, when a horse is sick, he will spend most of the time stabled to allow you to monitor his condition and maintain a high level of care. In this section, we will look at appropriate stable regime for the sick horse.

Light and ventilation

- To ensure a constant flow of fresh air, maintain the respiratory health of the horse and keep the horse at a comfortable temperature, the stable must be well ventilated. Keep the top door open to allow fresh air in. Ideally there should also be a window on the same side of the door that opens inwards to encourage the air to lift upwards. A ventilation cowl in the roof allows warm, stale air to escape as it is replaced by cool, fresh air.

- Proper ventilation is important, however the stable must be free of draughts or the horse will feel cold and may catch a chill.

- In most conditions it is desirable for the stable to be naturally light. However, it may be necessary to keep a horse who is suffering from an eye injury or disease such as periodic opthalmia in a darkened stable.

- The stable must be peaceful to allow him to rest quietly. Keep noise and activity around the sick horse's stable to a minimum. Ideally, try to give the horse a good view from his stable, especially if he is to be on box rest for some time, as this will help to relieve boredom.

Bedding

- The bedding must be clean, dry and dust-free. If the horse is well enough, lead him into a spare stable while you muck his own one out. Pay great attention to hygiene in the stable, using a disinfectant to wash down the floor at least once a week. Also pay attention to the hygiene in the spare stable, making sure that it is kept clean. Bank up the sides of the bed well to exclude any draughts and to help prevent the horse from becoming cast when he lies down. Make sure that you turn the bedding in the banks and replace it regularly to ensure that it does not become stale and dusty.

- It may be necessary to use a non-edible bedding such as paper to prevent the horse from eating (straw) bedding and suffering from an impacted colic. If the horse has a leg injury, the bedding must not be too deep as it will drag on the limb as the horse moves around. A thin layer of paper or shavings on rubber matting would be suitable.

Warmth

- In cold weather the horse must be kept warm through the use of additional clothing rather than by closing the top door and window. Well-fitting rugs must be used as needed.

- Layers of lightweight sheets are useful as they can be adjusted easily. If the horse is prone to breaking out in a sweat, place an anti-sweat or cooler sheet beneath his stable rug to help the air to circulate; alternatively a thermal rug can be used. In very cold conditions a neck hood may be worn.

- Stable bandages applied over Gamgee also help to keep the horse warm. These should be removed every 12 hours (or as specified by the vet if bandaged for support) and the legs hand-massaged to promote circulation. Massage also helps to prevent the legs from being marked by the bandages (although this would only happen if the bandages were too tight and/or applied unevenly). Roll up the bandages and re-apply if they are clean, or replace them with fresh bandages if soiled.

- In extremely cold weather or when a horse is very sick, infra-red heat lamps/panels may be used. These are suspended above the horse, e.g. from a beam. Great care must be taken, particularly with heat lamps, as there is a fire risk. All wires must be safely out of the horse's reach and a circuit-breaker plug used.

To check your horse for warmth, look for the following signs:

- **Body heat** – put your hand underneath the horse's rug to feel how warm he is. He should feel comfortably warm – not hot and damp with sweat. Lift the rug(s) and check his flanks to see if he is sweating.

- **Ears** – should feel dry and warm, not cold or damp. If they feel very cold, use a towel and gently rub and pull the ears to help the circulation.

- **Coat** – will be dull and staring if he is cold.

- **Shivering** – if very cold, the horse will shiver and look 'tucked up' and miserable.

ITQ 6.25 (?)

Why should the top stable door always be left open?

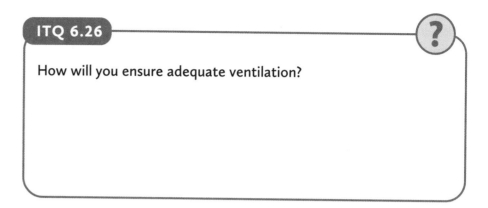

ITQ 6.26

How will you ensure adequate ventilation?

Feeding

Very often illness will result in a loss of appetite. If the horse is not eating or drinking you must consult the vet as dehydration becomes a serious threat if the horse's water intake is reduced.

The sick horse must go immediately onto a non-heating diet, i.e. low carbohydrate and protein. If he is confined to the stable and still fed his normal working diet, many problems would occur. These problems include:

- Equine rhabdomyolysis (azoturia)
- Lymphangitis
- Laminitis
- Weight gain and bad behaviour
- Colic

Forage

Colic can occur as a result of impaction from eating the bedding, combined with the lack of exercise which slows down gut function. Feed good-quality soft meadow hay – this is easily digested, will keep the horse occupied and will not 'hot him up'. Soaking the hay makes it softer and therefore easier to digest, whilst steaming is a great method to use in order to reduce both nutrient leakage (compared with soaking) and dust/spore inhalation.

Put the hay in a net with small holes – it will take longer for the horse to pull the hay through, so helping to occupy him.

If he has a dust allergy, shake all hay and soak for 10 minutes before feeding. If feeding a haylage product, choose a high-fibre, non-heating type.

Other feed

- Warm bran mashes are non-heating, palatable to an 'off-colour' horse and are easily digested. Add limestone flour to boost calcium levels (remember that bran has a high level of phosphorus which inhibits the horse's uptake of calcium). If a laxative effect is needed, add a tablespoon of Epsom salts. However, not all horses like the taste of Epsom salts.

- A more nutritionally balanced alternative to bran mashes would be a mash made from non-heating horse and pony cubes. These can be soaked in warm water to provide a soft, easily digested feed. This method also ensures that you are not changing the horse's diet suddenly, which could add to the risk of colic.

- A nourishing gruel can be made by adding boiling water to oatmeal. Allow to cool and offer it to the horse. Glucose can be added to provide energy. This sort of feeding is usually only necessary if the horse is suffering from a debilitating condition which prevents him from swallowing, e.g. strangles.

- If a horse is not keen to eat, try offering a tasty treat such as sliced apples or carrots. Some horses enjoy molasses and freshly cut (not mown) grass. Putting dry feed in a horse ball and allowing the horse to 'graze' on it can sometimes initiate some interest as well.

- If the horse refuses to eat his food, remove it from the stable. Never leave uneaten food in the manger as it soon turns rancid and attracts flies and vermin. Offer very small quantities of food to tempt him – he may eat if hand fed.

Water

- Use water buckets for the sick horse so you can monitor the amount he drinks. Switch off the automatic water supply in his stable but do make sure the horse has seen and will use the water buckets. If the horse refuses to use the buckets but will use the automatic drinker then obviously you will have to stick with the drinker.

- Ensure that there is a constant supply of clean, fresh 'chilled' water. ('*Chilled*' water has had a drop of hot water added *to take the chill off*). A drink of icy cold water would make a sick horse feel uncomfortable and could lead to abdominal pain.

- Change the water frequently, especially if the horse has a nasal discharge that will taint it.

- Add a small amount of glucose to the drinking water to give the horse an instant source of energy and nourishment. Alternatively, electrolytes can be added to the feed or water if needed. If using electrolytes in the water, always have one bucket of plain water available to the horse so he can choose. Horses have to get used to the taste of electrolytes and not every horse will drink water with them added.

ITQ 6.27   **?**

Give three signs indicating that a horse is cold:

1.

2.

3.

ITQ 6.28

Describe how you will bed the stable for:

a. A horse on box rest who is prone to eating his bedding.

b. A horse on box rest with a lower limb injury.

(Give the reasons for your choice of bedding.)

ITQ 6.29

What feeding considerations must be implemented for the horse on box rest?

ITQ 6.30

What problems may arise if the horse's diet is not altered when on box rest?

Grooming

- Pick out the feet twice daily to prevent thrush.

- Whether or not to brush the horse over each day depends upon how sick he is. Keep grooming to a minimum – a quick brush over with the body brush is good for circulation and hygiene. Check rugs for slipping and chafing. Massage the legs to improve circulation.

- Wipe the eyes, nostrils and dock. This can be done with absorbent kitchen roll or with separate clean, damp sponges. Sponges however, provide a breeding ground for bacteria so if they are used each horse should have his own sponges and these must be regularly boiled in a disinfectant solution to kill bacteria. The advantage of the kitchen roll is that each piece is disposed of after use, preventing a build-up of bacteria. Alternatively, if the ailment is contagious, such as strangles, wipe the eyes and nostrils with cotton wool swabs and dispose of the swabs carefully after use.

- Always wash your hands before and after handling a sick horse.

Box rest

Box rest is the term used to describe the process of keeping the horse permanently stabled, normally without any form of exercise. Depending upon the severity of the injury or disease and on the vet's instructions, it may be possible to lead the horse out in hand for a few minutes daily for a pick at some grass and a gentle walk.

Conditions requiring box rest include:

- Post-operative colic surgery.

- Fractures.

- Tendon injury.

- Serious wounds requiring immobilisation to promote healing.

- Seriously debilitating diseases.

- Infectious diseases.

The vet will instruct you as to whether total box rest is necessary or not. In the case of most wounds, depending on their site, a period of box rest is beneficial to aid healing. The following points must be considered.

- Adjust the diet immediately. Cut out all heating, energy feeds and feed small quantities of non-heating feedstuffs. As mentioned earlier, failure to adjust the diet will lead to problems such laminitis, equine rhabdomyolysis (azoturia), weight gain and, once box rest is over, explosive behaviour.

- Feed plenty of meadow hay to satisfy the appetite and prevent boredom. Horses who are not working are able to live on maintenance rations, i.e. 100 per cent forage.

- If there is any reason to feed anything other than forage, horse and pony cubes can be soaked to provide a feed of soft consistency that is nutritionally balanced and non-heating.

- Bed down on non-edible bedding if the horse eats straw. The lack of movement, combined with eating bedding, can lead to an impacted colic. This is especially important after colic surgery as the horse's gut may be susceptible to problems.

- Keep the bedding clean and (taking into account the nature of any injury) pick out the hooves twice daily if possible to prevent thrush.

- Monitor the bandages and dressings frequently and change as necessary.

- Make sure the top and bottom bolts are always fastened securely to prevent the box-resting horse from escaping. The yard gates must always be shut so if he should escape he cannot go far.

- Provide a salt lick and, if appropriate, some sort of horse 'toy' if the box rest is to be prolonged. Leaving a radio playing nearby for few hours gives the horse something to listen to.

- When you do lead the horse out for the first time use a bridle and attach a lunge line or long rope to give full control. A Chifney may be needed on a very spirited type. It is imperative that you do not let go of the horse as all the benefits of box rest will be undone very quickly. Wear gloves and a crash cap for your own protection.

- Provided the horse has been previously used to one, a horse-walker provides a safe means of walking the horse out.

- As the horse's condition improves, the walking in hand can be gradually built up to help use up excess energy and help promote circulation and improve muscle tone. Towards the end of the convalescing period, if the horse is of a sensible disposition, he can be trotted in hand and then lunged quietly. This will increase the chances of the horse staying calmer when turned out for the first time. If the horse starts to misbehave on the lunge, halt him and resume walking in hand. When lungeing, bear in mind that the horse will be in soft, unfit condition so must not be overworked or allowed to charge about. If he is overstressed you may well end up with new injuries to deal with.

- When a horse is first turned out after box rest, put him in the smallest paddock available on his own. Make sure horses in nearby fields do not 'wind him up' by galloping around. A small turnout 'cage' is ideal as the horse cannot build up any great speed and thereby injure himself. It is also impossible for the horse to jump out of a cage (although only specialist yards tend to have them).

- When the horse is first turned out he will be more likely to stay calm and eat grass if he is a little hungry. Only give a small feed and minimal hay the morning he is due to be turned out.

- As the horse will be unused to grass, increase the amount of time spent out gradually, especially if spring grass is available. This will allow the horse's digestive tract time to adjust and should help reduce the risk of colic.

- Discuss with the vet the benefits of mildly sedating the horse for his first turnout to prevent him from galloping around.

Barrier nursing

The method of nursing isolated horses to prevent the spread of infection is termed **barrier nursing**. Quarantine and isolation refer to the separation and segregation of infected or potentially infective horses from those presumed to be free of infection. The term quarantine is normally used in relation to horses who are to be kept separated before travelling abroad and/or upon arrival at a new yard. In terms of import and export, quarantine regulations vary between countries. Yards receiving new horses – especially horses who have come from the sales or whose health status is unknown – should quarantine all new horses for approximately 10 days before allowing them to mix with others, in case they are incubating an infectious disease.

Horses known or suspected to have an infectious disease should be isolated, as should horses who have had diarrhoea within the previous 24 hours or enlargement of the lymph nodes around the head. Viral infections such as rhinopneumonitis and influenza, and bacterial infections such as strangles, can spread through a group of horses causing an epidemic. In serious cases, movement of horses on and off the premises must stop. If more than one horse is infected they must be isolated as a small group.

Any animals who have been in contact with the infected horses are referred to as **'in-contacts'** and should be isolated as a small group (away from the infected group).

The isolation box/yard

Every commercial yard should have at least one stable specially set aside for isolation purposes. Large concerns may have an isolation yard equipped to deal with several horses. The yard should be clearly signed as an isolation facility with access restricted to authorised persons only.

No other horses must be able to contact an isolated horse, although ideally the horse should be able to see others, as he may become distressed if completely separated. The isolation box/yard should be sited as far away from the main yard as possible, ideally no closer than 80m (90 yards) to the main yard. It should face away from the stables, with the prevailing wind blowing from the main yard towards the isolation boxes. There should be road access to the isolation boxes so horses can be unloaded or loaded close to the isolation area without having to walk past other horses.

The isolation yard should also have a building to contain all the equipment needed. This has to be large enough to contain overalls, washing facilities, medication cupboard, feed, hay, grooming equipment, bedding and mucking out equipment.

Isolation boxes should be constructed to allow for easy and thorough disinfection after use. They should be made of brick rather than wood, as harmful organisms remain in wood for a longer time. Ideally the brickwork should be rendered and painted with rubberised paint so that it can be kept as clean as possible. If possible there should be a water supply close to the box, so that cleaning the box after use can be carried out as easily as possible. There should be as little stable furniture as possible in the box, only a water bowl and tie ring, to prevent the build-up of harmful organisms on surfaces.

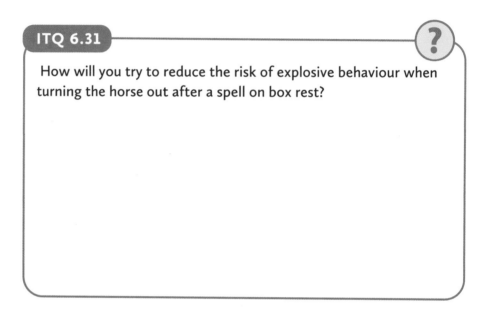

ITQ 6.31

?

How will you try to reduce the risk of explosive behaviour when turning the horse out after a spell on box rest?

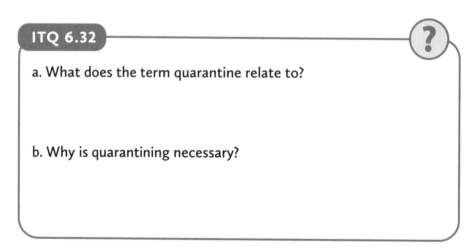

ITQ 6.32

?

a. What does the term quarantine relate to?

b. Why is quarantining necessary?

Equipment

Each horse in isolation must have his own equipment such as mucking out tools, grooming kit, buckets and rugs. These must never be used on any other horses. All items should be labelled to avoid confusion. A good way of doing this is to put a small dab of brightly coloured paint or electrical (bandage) tape on everything, each particular colour relating to an individual horse.

There should also be a separate muck heap which may be burnt to destroy the soiled bedding. The grooming kit must be washed regularly in hot water and disinfectant.

All equipment must be washed frequently and, after it is finished with, it must be washed and disinfected before being stored away.

The handler

Ideally, one person should have the sole responsibility of caring for one isolated horse. This lessens the chances of spreading the disease around the yard. If this is not possible, whoever is going to look after the sick horse must leave him until last. Overalls should be worn and the handler's head should be covered. The handler's boots must be dipped in a disinfectant boot dip before and after handling. Disposable boot covers and head covers should be provided.

Latex gloves should be worn and the handler's hands and arms scrubbed in hot soapy water after handling. A waste disposal bin should be placed outside the stable for disposable protective clothing.

WHEN TO CALL THE VET

Keep the vet's telephone number displayed near every phone to minimise delay in an emergency. Call the vet out for any of the following situations.

- **Suspected colic.** Call the vet out if the horse shows mild signs of colic for 20 minutes or more, or immediately if the horse shows violent colic signs. The vet will give painkilling and muscle relaxant injections as even a mild case of colic can soon worsen; a horse in great pain will roll and thrash about, risking further injury and life-threatening complications such as a twisted gut, which requires surgery.

- **Wounds.** If a wound:
  - Is very deep
  - Is complicated, e.g. on a joint
  - Is infected
  - Requires stitching
  - Is bleeding profusely
  - Is spurting blood (indicating arterial bleeding)
  - Has punctured the sole of the foot

  The vet will also be needed if there is any doubt about the horse's tetanus vaccinations. A quick-acting tetanus anti-toxin will be needed.

- **Lameness.** If a horse is very lame and not weight-bearing call the vet immediately. (Also call the vet if the horse has been mildly lame for a day or two and you cannot determine the reason.)

- **Laminitis.** As well as being in great pain, a horse or pony suffering from laminitis will be in danger of irreparable life-threatening damage occurring within the hoof.

- **Suspected fractures.** Accidents can happen whilst horses are turned out to grass or being ridden.

- **Repeated coughing.** The horse may or may not have a purulent discharge from one or both nostrils.

- **Abnormal temperature.** An increase from normal of more than 1 °F.

- **Signs of ill-health described earlier.** In particular, watch for loss of appetite and a dull attitude. These could be early warning signs of infection.

Other than this, a general guide is to call the vet when your horse is showing any of the signs of ill-health and you are unable to determine why, or administer the necessary treatments. It is always better to play safe if in any doubt, and call the vet out. A vet would far rather come out and deal with a minor ailment, than have to attend to a problem that has been left and worsened, possibly causing the horse to suffer in the meantime.

Preparation for a visit by the vet

The horse should not be worked if showing signs of ill-health.
Whenever the vet is to visit your yard try to ensure that:

- If possible, the horse is in a dry, well-lit loose box.

- There is warm water, soap and towel available for the vet to wash hands before and after treatment.

- If it could be relevant, any droppings the horse has passed are kept in a skip. This may help the vet to make a diagnosis.

- A record is kept of all relevant information, including any food the horse has eaten within the last week or so, as well as any other signs of abnormalities. It is also important to record and inform the vet of any new horses to the premises in case they have brought diseases with them.

KEEPING RECORDS RELATING TO HEALTH

Records and references

1. Keep recorded in a book the dates and all other relevant details of your horse's visits for shoeing, vaccinations, teeth rasping, worming and treatment for any minor ailments or cuts he may have suffered. You will then always know when your horse is due for one of his important 'health checks'.

2. You should also ensure that important telephone numbers are always on display near the telephone. These should include:
The vet.

The farrier.

Owner's contact details if the horse is on livery.

Emergency services.

The owner of the yard.

3 If a horse becomes sick, a daily record of the following should be kept:

Visits by the vet – with diagnosis and treatment.

The horse's condition, including clinical signs, temperature, pulse and respiratory rates.

Treatments administered by you.

Food and water intake.

Whether droppings and urine are normal.

Always be observant; note any changes which occur so that you can give the vet all relevant information.

Insurance

Depending on the nature of a disease or injury, the owner of the horse may have to inform the insurance company as soon as the horse becomes sick or injured. It is important to read the policy as failure to disclose information can invalidate certain types of insurance claim.

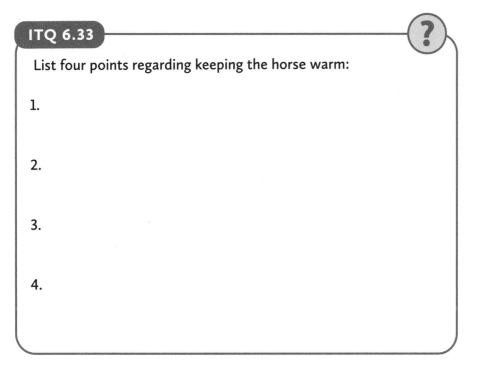

ITQ 6.33   **?**

List four points regarding keeping the horse warm:

1.

2.

3.

4.

WORMING

All horses harbour internal parasites, known more commonly as worms. It is important that worm infestations are controlled. If worms are not controlled they can do irreparable damage to the intestines and major blood vessels.

Signs of heavy worm burden

Signs that a horse may be suffering from a heavy worm burden include:

- Dull and staring coat.

- General lack of condition, weight loss and depression.

- Anaemia – mucous membranes will be too pale.

- Diarrhoea and colic.

- Distended stomach.

- Loss of appetite.

NB: *even a horse who looks perfectly well and healthy will be harbouring some worms and must still be wormed.*

Potential damage by parasitic worms

Different species of worms have different life-cycles and may damage their hosts in various ways. These include:

- Damage to the lining of the digestive tract, which impairs the absorption of nutrients.

- Further damage to the gut linings by reducing or stopping blood flow. Food cannot pass normally through the dead portion, which results in colic.

- The larval stages of some worms travel through the walls of the intestine, enter the small arterioles (blood vessels) then migrate through the arteries moving against the flow of blood. Some travel to the heart, causing valve damage, inflammation, and weakening. Such damage is irreparable and may prove fatal.

- The adult worms cause anaemia as a consequence of blood sucking. Ulceration, colic and diarrhoea may also occur.

Control of worm infestation

This aspect of horse care may be divided into two areas:

Paddock management. Grazing should be kept clean through regular picking up of droppings (at least twice a week in the summer, once a week in a cold winter or twice a week in a mild winter), allowing grazing to rest and recover, appropriate stocking levels, cross-grazing (grazing by sheep) and topping of long grass.

Chemical control using drugs (anthelmintics). Using the horse's bodyweight as guidance, the correct dose must be administered.

Basic considerations

- All new horses whose worming history is unknown must be wormed on arrival at the yard.

- Brood mares must be treated regularly, but note that some drugs are not suitable for pregnant mares. The pasture must also be clean. Between 4 and 6 weeks of age, foals must be wormed and then treated every 4 weeks until 8 months old. From that age they must be wormed on a regular programme for the rest of their life.

- Weanlings are particularly at risk from small redworm disease at the end of a hot, dry summer. They should be dosed with fenbendazole, mebendazole, oxybendazole or moxidectin in mid-October and then be turned out on clean pasture that has not been grazed by horses for at least 5 months.

- Horses at grass must all be wormed at the same time.

- Stabled horses must be wormed regularly because they will have picked up worm larvae during a spell at grass. Therefore they may still have a worm burden and be suffering damage from migrating larvae.

Worming intervals
The interval between worming depends on certain factors.

- **The type of drug.** Ivermectin compounds should be used every 8–10 weeks. Moxidectin should be administered every 13 weeks. Pyrantel compounds need to be used every 4–8 weeks.

- **The age of the horse.** Weanlings and youngstock need frequent worming as the worm eggs reappear after a shorter period.

- **Stocking density.** Ideally there should not be more than one horse per acre (0.4ha). If there are more, the rate at which horses become infested increases.

- **Worming programme on the yard.** All horses sharing grazing should be wormed at the same time.

● **Results of faecal egg counts.** To avoid worming unnecessarily, and to ensure the correct type of drug is used, each horse's worm burden can be estimated by performing a worm egg count in a sample of droppings. If an excellent paddock management regime has been followed and the egg count is low, it may not be necessary to administer anthelmintics. A small sample of dung is examined in the laboratory to find out how many worm eggs are present. A count of less than 200 eggs per gram (e.p.g) is considered a low count. Between 200 and 1,200 e.p.g. is a medium count. Above that level the count is considered high. An initial test will determine the level of adult, egg-laying, parasites present – it will not show immature or encysted worms or tapeworms, so this must be taken into account.

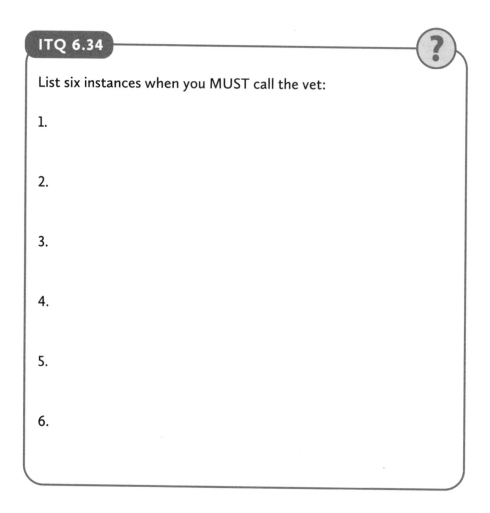

ITQ 6.34 ?

List six instances when you MUST call the vet:

1.

2.

3.

4.

5.

6.

CARE OF THE TEETH

The horse's molars should be inspected for sharp edges approximately every 6 months. Sharp edges need to be rasped down by a vet or equine dentist approximately once a year, although this is variable and some horses may need more frequent attention. Some horses may need to be sedated to allow the vet or dentist to work safely and effectively.

The cheek teeth of the upper jaw are set wider apart than those in the lower jaw.

The circular grinding action when the horse chews causes the inside edges of the lower molars and the outside edges of the upper molars to become sharp, sometimes with hooks developing.

A horse with sharp teeth will not be able to chew his food properly, which may cause food to fall out of his mouth (quidding) or cause the food to pass partially undigested through his system. In extreme cases severe discomfort may deter the horse from even trying to eat his food, which will lead to hunger and loss of condition. Ulcers can develop on the inside of the cheeks and on the edge of the tongue, which will prevent the horse from eating properly and cause discomfort when the horse is working with a bit in his mouth. In such cases, the horse may toss his head, ignore the rein aids, refuse to turn and generally appear uncomfortable in his mouth when ridden.

Also, as horses get older their teeth may become loose, making it difficult to chew properly. Look out for quidding and loss of condition and consult your vet or equine dentist.

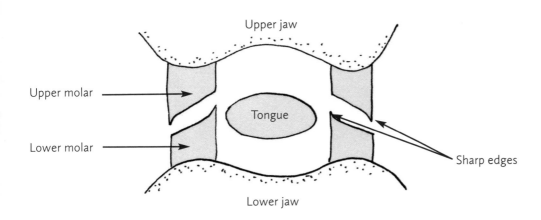

6.3 Molars, showing sharp edges

ITQ 6.35 ?

Give three examples of internal damage caused by worms:

1.

2.

3.

ITQ 6.36 ?

Give three points stating how the burden of internal parasites can be reduced and controlled:

1.

2.

3.

ITQ 6.37 ?

What is a faecal egg count and why is it used?

ITQ 6.38 ?

List three signs that indicate that a horse has problems with his teeth:

1.

2.

3.

7 Clipping and Trimming

REQUIRED SKILLS/KNOWLEDGE	Learnt, revised, practised?	Confirmed
Reasons for clipping and related welfare issues.		
• Why and when horses may be clipped.	☐	☐
• Have an understanding of the welfare implications of clipping.	☐	☐
• Know the different types of clip.	☐	☐
Be able to assemble and maintain clippers.		
• Know how to assemble clippers.	☐	☐
• Know what to check before clipping.	☐	☐
• Describe the maintenance of clippers during and after clipping.	☐	☐
• Be aware of the potential dangers of clipping and how to minimise them.	☐	☐
Know why and how to pull manes and tails.		
• How, why and when to trim and pull a mane.	☐	☐
• How, why and when to pull a tail.	☐	☐
Know why and how to trim horses.		
• How, why and when to trim a tail.	☐	☐
• How, why and when to trim other parts of the horse's body.	☐	☐
• Know when it would not be appropriate to trim a horse.	☐	☐
• Different methods of trimming.	☐	☐

CLIPPING

Reasons for clipping

1. In the winter months horses grow a thick, greasy coat for warmth. This thick coat will make the horse sweat up when he works, causing him to feel very uncomfortable – he will be unable to work to the best of his ability.

2. Clipping prevents a loss of condition resulting from excessive sweating.

3. Clipping reduces the risk of the horse catching a chill – an unclipped horse who is wet with sweat is in danger of getting cold and catching a chill. Often, after drying off, the horse will break out in a cold, patchy sweat which can cause chilling – this is known as **'breaking out'**.

4. It is much easier to groom a clipped or partially clipped horse, so it is labour-saving.

Types of clip

Full clip. The whole coat is clipped, including the hair of the head and legs. This is a little drastic for the average horse and is really only necessary for horses in very hard work.

Hunter clip. The whole coat is clipped except for the legs and saddle patch. The hair on the legs offers protection from thorns when out hacking; the hair on the saddle patch protects the back from rubbing. This clip is suitable for horses in hard work.

Blanket clip. The neck and belly are clipped, leaving a blanket-shaped area unclipped. This type of clip keeps the horse's back warm, which is ideal as it is important that the loins, beneath which lie the kidneys, are not allowed to get cold as a chill may result.

Trace clip. This clip derives its name from the days of harness horses who were clipped level with the traces of the carriage harness. Depending on how much hair is removed it is known as a **high** or **low trace clip** and is suitable for horses and ponies in medium work. If a horse lives out in a turnout rug he may have a low trace clip – although a careful eye must be kept on him to ensure that he does not feel cold.

Chaser clip. A line is drawn from the poll to the stifle joint and everything below that line is clipped except the legs.

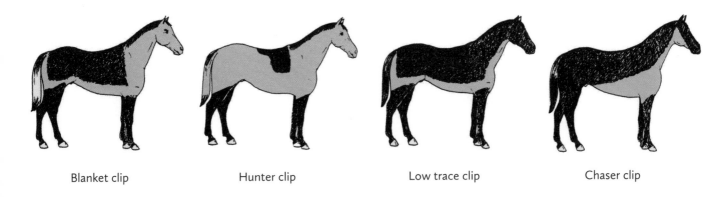

| Blanket clip | Hunter clip | Low trace clip | Chaser clip |

7.1 Types of clip

When to clip

Horses usually have a thick coat from around the beginning of October, so this is normally the time to give the first clip. One or two additional clips may be needed throughout the winter until February/March (and some competition horses are clipped in the summer to aid cooling). As the weather gets warmer, so the horse will start to shed his coat. It is not practical to clip while the coat is changing.

Preparation for clipping

1 The coat must be very clean and as free of grease as possible. A dirty coat will soon blunt the clipper blades. For the few days before clipping, the coat should be groomed very thoroughly.

2 Get the horse used to wearing a rug by rugging up for a week prior to clipping. This also helps ensure that the coat is clean.

3 The clippers must be in good working order, well oiled and the blades sharpened. You must never try to clip with blunt blades as these tear at the coat and cause discomfort. Some horses are difficult to clip as they remember previous uncomfortable experiences.

Equipment needed

- Clippers in safe working order, oiled with sharp blades.

- Spare blades.

- Residual current device (circuit-breaker plug).

- Extension lead if necessary.

- Overalls and rubber-soled boots.

- Old blanket to keep the horse warm.

- Brush to clean clippers.

- Grooming kit.

- Blade cleaning fluid.

- Clipper oil.

- Block to stand on if clipping a tall horse.

- In some situations, e.g. if the horse is likely to be sensitive or unpredictable, it would be sensible to wear a crash cap.

Clipping procedure

1. If clipping in the horse's stable, remove all unnecessary items, such as water buckets, feed bowls and empty haynets.

2. It is important to have good light – either electric or natural.

3. The floor must be clean and non-slip. Ideally the clipping box floor should be covered with rubber matting to prevent slipping and to provide insulation against electric shocks. If a special clipping box is not available, bank the bedding into one corner to prevent it from becoming soiled by the clippings.

4. The clipper blades must be attached to the machine and all moving parts oiled. The blades are tightened down by means of a tension screw – it takes some practice to get the tension on the clipper blades right. Tighten the tension screw until you feel some resistance – then make another 1½ turns. The blades should sound as though they are gliding over each other and not rattling. They should then cut through the hair easily without pulling or chewing.

5. The clippers will probably have to be plugged into an extension lead. The extension lead should be plugged into a special safety plug – a **residual current device** or **circuit-breaker**. This will instantly cut off the electrical supply in the event of an accident or electrical fault, which could help to stop either the horse or handler from getting an electric shock. Extension leads must not remain coiled whilst in use as heat is generated within the wire, which will melt the outer cable and cause an electrical fault. Before use, check the extension lead for splits and wearing.

6. The wires must never trail on the floor where they could be trodden on or tripped over. One or two loops of string attached to the wall can be useful as the wires can be passed through these to keep them off the floor. If it is raining, care must be taken that plugs are not allowed to get wet.

7. Having groomed the horse thoroughly, keep him warm with an old blanket. This will stop his stable rug from becoming spoilt with the hair clippings. These clippings go everywhere and do not brush out very easily. For this reason you

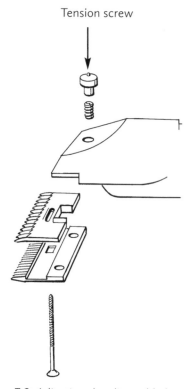

Tension screw

7.2 Adjusting the clipper blades

should wear overalls and old clothes when clipping. Put a tail bandage on the horse to protect the top of the tail.

8 As an extra precaution against electric shock, rubber-soled boots should be worn to provide insulation.

9 Make sure that the horse never has the opportunity to chew or stand on the wires.

10 Have an assistant if the horse is nervous or badly behaved.

11 Allow plenty of time. Clipping should not be rushed, particularly by an inexperienced person.

SAFETY TIPS ⚠

▶ Electricity presents the greatest danger when clipping. Remember:

Use a circuit-breaker plug.

Keep wires out of the horse's way so he cannot chew or stand on them.

Unroll the extension lead to prevent it overheating.

Use a stable with rubber flooring to improve insulation.

ITQ 7.1 ?

Give four reasons for clipping:

1.

2.

3.

4.

How to clip

1 If necessary, mark out the area to be clipped with chalk or wet soap. A numnah or blanket can be used accordingly to give the right shape.

2 Switch on the clippers and let the horse get used to the noise. A nervous horse will need to be held by an assistant. A calm one will probably stand quietly and eat from his haynet. However, while his head and neck are clipped the horse will have to stop eating from the net.

3 Some horses resent the clipping procedure, often because they have previously been burned or nicked through careless clipping. Horses who are very difficult to clip may need to be twitched or sedated.

Old-fashioned twitches consist of a loop of soft rope threaded through a hole near the end of a wooden pole. The loop is passed over the horse's top lip and twisted until a pressure is exerted. Modern or 'humane' twitches are made of rounded metal and have a 'nutcracker' action which is held on the top lip.

It has been proposed that the twitch acts in the same way as acupuncture in that the pressure causes the release of the body's natural analgesics, known as

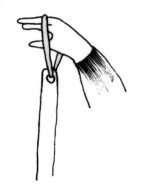

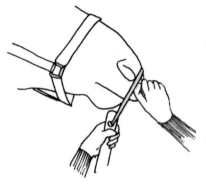

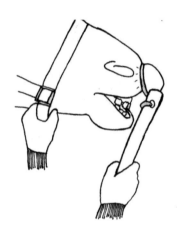

7.3 The twitch

endorphins. As the endorphins circulate throughout the body, the horse becomes more relaxed. There is, however, no scientific evidence to support this theory and it is now believed that the reason the horse remains still whilst twitched is more likely to be because twitching hurts.

Some horses react badly to the application of the twitch and can become very difficult/dangerous, in which case the twitch cannot be used.

If a horse is very upset by the clipping procedure it is safest for everyone if he is sedated by the vet. Whilst this increases costs it can prevent serious injury. Some sedatives can cause the horse to sweat after a while so this must be taken into account when clipping. The vet will advise on the most appropriate form of sedation.

4 Start to clip at the shoulders and neck, using the clippers against the lie of the hair. Hold the clippers flat and use fairly long strokes. An experienced person should be in charge of the clipping procedure. An inexperienced person can be taught using a quiet horse under supervision.

5 Great care must be taken when clipping the head as there are projecting bones to clip around. Untie the lead-rope in case the horse pulls back.

6 Allow plenty of time when clipping to ensure a neat finish. Never clip too near to the base of the mane or tail. With the exception of a full clip, the clippers must not be used on the legs.

7 In order to clip around the elbow and between the forelegs it will be necessary to have an assistant to hold one foreleg forwards. The assistant must hold the leg securely by the fetlock and knee. Take care on the sensitive areas – if the horse tries to kick, the assistant can hold up a foreleg. Some horses do, however, manage to stand on two legs.

8 Once the clippers have been running for a while the blades will get hot. Stop the machine, clean off all hair clippings and oil the moving mechanisms. Spray the blades with cleaning fluid with the motor running. Cleaning fluid removes any build-up of grease, keeping the blades sharper, and acts as a coolant which prevents the blades from getting too hot. If the blades do get hot, leave them for a while to cool. Never use very hot blades as you will burn the horse. Taking care not to burn yourself, check the temperature of the blades with your hand. First hold the blades close to your palm – can you feel heat from the blades? If you feel great heat as your hand gets closer, *do not* touch the blades or you will burn yourself – do not use them on the horse either. Allow them to cool then try again – once you can touch the blades comfortably with the back of your hand, they are cool enough to use on the horse.

Horses always remember bad experiences, so if you use blunt, hot blades which pull at his hair and burn him, the horse will soon begin to object very strongly to being clipped.

9 Keep the horse warm throughout the clipping procedure otherwise he will get cold, bored and start to fidget. Once he is clipped, give him a thorough groom to remove all hair clippings, then rug up. If it is particularly cold use extra blankets beneath the stable rug. Your horse will now rely on rugs for warmth, so never turn

him out on a cold, damp day without a well-fitting turnout rug. Feel his ears and look out for a staring coat and shivering as signs that he is cold.

⑩ Having finished clipping you must remove the clipper blades, clean, oil and return them to their plastic sleeves. Remove all the hair from the clipping machine and oil all the moving parts. Store the clippers and extension lead in a safe, dry place.

⑪ The blades will need to be sharpened and the motor serviced periodically. Every year the clippers and extension lead should be checked by a qualified electrician for faults.

IN-TEXT ACTIVITY

1. Find out about the types of clipping machines owned by friends or your local yard.
2. Under supervision, attach and adjust the blades.
3. Make a note of the ease of fitting and adjustment, weight and noise level for each type of clipping machine. Try to see at least three different types.
4. If access to different types of clipping machines is difficult, tack shops and trade stands at exhibitions and shows are useful places to look.

Type of clippers	Comments on blade fitting and adjusting	Noise level when running	Weight and ease of handling

EXAM TIPS

Handle a variety of clipping machines and practise dismantling and reassembling the blades.

Make sure you practise clipping quiet horses and make sure you are confident how to adjust the blade tensions.

TRIMMING

The process of tidying up a horse and improving appearance is called **trimming.** This includes pulling the mane, possibly pulling the tail and trimming up with scissors. The areas to be trimmed with scissors include:

● The headpiece area – approximately 2.5cm (1in) is trimmed from the mane just behind the ears to allow the headpiece to fit comfortably.

● The external ear hair. Hold the ear closed and trim the external hair neatly.

ITQ 7.2

a. What is a circuit-breaker?

b. Why must the extension lead be uncoiled when in use?

ITQ 7.3

Give three ways of reducing the risk of electric shock when clipping:

1.

2.

3.

ITQ 7.4

a Explain how a 'twitch' works.

b. What is the more humane way of restraining a horse who is difficult to clip?

ITQ 7.5

When clipping, how can you make sure the blades work effectively and prevent over-heating?

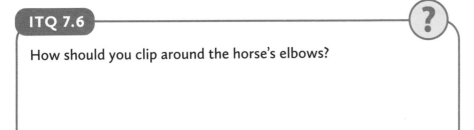

ITQ 7.6

How should you clip around the horse's elbows?

- The withers. Closely trim the mane which lies beneath the numnah.

- The feathers. Use a plastic comb to comb through the long hair around the fetlocks and, cutting against the direction of growth, trim the hair which protrudes through the teeth of the comb. Continue this process until the area is neatly trimmed. The long hair which grows over the hoof from the coronet can also be trimmed.

- The bottom of the tail. This should be cut so that the bottom of the tail hangs 10cm (4in) below the point of hock when the horse is moving. To judge this, place your hand beneath the tail to give the effect of raising it. Then measure approximately 10cm (4in) below the point of hock and cut the tail straight across.

- Show horses are trimmed extensively. The whiskers are removed and the hair from inside the ears is also often removed. However, this should be avoided as a general practice since the horse needs the internal ear hair to prevent foreign bodies entering the ear, and the whiskers are used as sensory feelers. Never use scissors to trim the mane or the top of the tail. *Never* trim Arabs or Mountain and Moorland breeds if they are to be shown in competition.

Pulling the mane

1. Exercise the horse first to ensure that the pores of the skin are open. It would be very painful if you were to pull the mane on a cold day without having exercised him first. Brush the mane over onto the offside (right) of the neck.

2. Using a mane comb, take hold of a few of the longest hairs and back-comb, keeping hold of the few long hairs. Wind these once around the comb and pull downwards without yanking. The hairs should come out easily. If they do not, you have probably taken too much, which will be uncomfortable for the horse. After each pull, comb the hair down flat and repeat the process.

3. When thinning the mane, always take the hairs from underneath the mane – never from the top of the mane, as they would end up standing upright. Move along the mane, keeping it as level as possible.

4. Never pull too much in one go as the horse's neck will get sore – spread the process out over several days. Once the mane is thinned sufficiently, shorten it by pulling the longer hairs.

5 Once the mane is pulled and lying over neatly, damp it down with a water brush.

6 If the horse objects to having his mane pulled it is possible to buy a specially adapted comb and razor. This allows you to shorten the hair without actually pulling it.

Pulling the tail

1 Brush out the tail carefully and remember only to pull on a warm day, after exercise.

2 Never pull the tail of a grass-kept horse as this will deprive him of protection against the elements.

3 Start on the underneath of the dock bone and gently pull a few hairs only from each side. Gradually work onto the sides of the dock bone.

4 Take great care not to make the tail sore – do a little each day rather than pulling the whole tail in one day.

5 To keep a pulled tail looking neat and tidy, damp down with the water brush, then put on a tail bandage and leave on for 3–4 hours. Never leave a tail bandage on overnight as it could restrict the blood vessels in the dock bone.

6 A 'switch' tail is the term used to describe a tail which is extensively pulled, with the end allowed to grow to a natural point. A 'bang' tail is pulled, with the end cut straight across.

7 As with the mane, the humane alternative to tail pulling is to use a specially designed comb which incorporates a blade. With practice, a neat finish can be achieved.

ITQ 7.7   ?

List five areas that can be trimmed with scissors:

1.

2.

3.

4.

5.

⑧ Principles of Shoeing

REQUIRED SKILLS/KNOWLEDGE	Learnt, revised, practised?	Confirmed
The procedure for shoeing, including use of farrier's tools.		
• Be able to discuss the reasons for shoeing horses.	☐	☐
• Describe the method for shoeing a horse.	☐	☐
• Be able to recognise a well-shod foot.	☐	☐
• Farrier's tools and their use.	☐	☐
Know how to remove a damaged shoe in an emergency.		
• Describe how to remove a loose and/or twisted shoe in an emergency.	☐	☐

WHY AND WHEN HORSES NEED SHOEING

In the wild, a horse's hooves wear down at a similar rate to the growth of the wall, so the feet never become too long or too worn. Domesticated horses and ponies are required to work on hard ground or tarmac roads for fairly long periods. If unshod, the hooves would soon wear down and the horse would become footsore and lame.

As a rough guide, horses need to be shod every **five to seven weeks**. It must not be left any longer than this, and sometimes you will find that a horse needs shoeing more frequently. Horses and ponies who do not go on the roads and are only in light work may be left unshod, however, they still need to have their hooves trimmed regularly as the hoof wall constantly grows downwards at a steady rate.

Signs that a horse needs shoeing

A horse needs shoeing when:

- Between five and seven weeks have elapsed since he was last shod.

- A shoe is loose or has slipped inwards.

- The clenches (nail tips) have risen from the hoof wall.

- A shoe has been cast (lost).

- The toe has grown over the shoe.

- The shoe has become excessively worn.

- The horn has cracked badly. This will reduce the security of the shoe, which may then become wrenched off.

If shoes are left on too long:
- The toes will grow long and the feet will be out of balance.
- The shoes will become loose and may slip under the feet and press on the soles.
- The horse may stand on the nails as a shoe slips.
- The hoof wall is likely to crack and split.

Signs that an unshod horse needs his feet trimmed

An unshod horse needs to have his feet trimmed:

- Approximately every five to seven weeks, dependent upon the rate of growth and natural wear.

- Whenever the toes appear too long. If the toe grows too long it will unbalance the foot, which increases the force exerted onto the navicular bone and causes excessive strain to be exerted upon the tendons.

If trimming is not carried out regularly the hoof will grow out of shape and split.

Always book the farrier well in advance. Farriers are normally very busy and need at least two weeks notice of a booking.

PREPARATION FOR SHOEING

- The farrier must be told in advance if you require a special type of shoe (see below). You must also tell the farrier if you require stud holes in the shoes as these are put in when the shoe is on the anvil.

- The horse should be in the yard with clean, dry legs and feet. It is not acceptable to bring him in from the field as the farrier arrives and present the horse with wet, muddy legs.

- Ideally a non-slip, dry and well-lit area on hard standing (no bedding) should be provided. In poor weather this needs to be under cover.

- The horse should be used to having his feet picked out. Prepare a young horse by tapping around his feet with a hammer to get him used to the banging action.

- Stay on the yard to hold the horse if necessary. If the horse is quiet and well-behaved he can be tied up. If he is young and/or difficult to shoe, put a bridle on him and hold him.

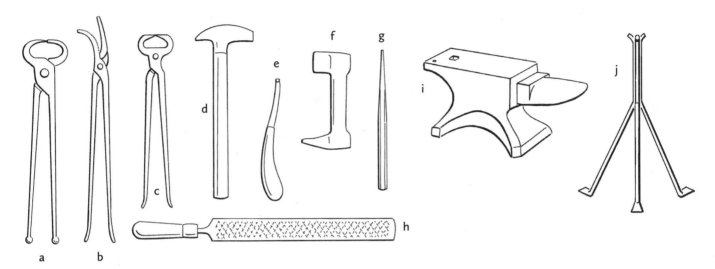

a. Pincers	d. Driving hammer	g. Pritchel	j. Foot stand
b. Clenching tongs	e. Drawing knife	h. Rasp	
c. hoof cutters	f. Buffer	i. Anvil	

8.1 The farrier's tools

Assessing types of shoe

There are various patterns of shoe for specialised purposes and a number of remedial patterns – some of which are custom-made by farriers specialising in remedial shoeing. For the purpose of the Stage 2 exam you need to learn about the most commonly used type, i.e the **hunter shoe.**

Hunter shoes
Most horses and ponies wear hunter shoes as they are more practical in most normal circumstances than other patterns. The iron is not flat – it is concave to help prevent the shoe from being sucked off in sticky going. The surface of the shoe which touches the ground is **fullered**, i.e. a groove is made, into which the nail heads rest. This groove will often fill with grit and small stones, which help to provide a better grip.

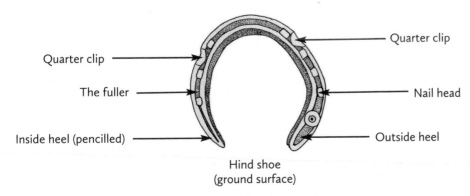

Hind shoe
(ground surface)

8.2 Parts of the hunter shoe

ITQ 8.1 ?

List three signs indicating that a horse needs to be shod:

1.

2.

3.

ITQ 8.2 ?

How often should a horse be shod?

The heels of the front shoe may be **pencilled**. This means it becomes finer at the ends to help prevent the hind foot striking the heel and possibly wrenching the shoe off. The inside heel of the hind shoe may be pencilled to reduce the risk of brushing.

METHODS OF SHOEING

Shoeing may be carried out **hot** or **cold**. Hot shoeing is the process whereby the shoes are made red-hot in a forge and then fitted and shaped whilst hot.

A forge is needed for hot shoeing. Most farriers have a portable forge and will come out to you. If your farrier doesn't have a portable forge, you will have to take your horse to the farrier.

A forge is not needed for cold shoeing – the shoeing process is the same as for hot, but the shoes are fitted cold.

The hot shoeing process

1 **Removal.** The first stage involves removing the old shoes. The horse's forefoot and lower limb are supported by being held between the farrier's legs; this keeps the farrier's hands free. The hind leg is supported on the farrier's thigh. The

clenches are 'knocked up' with the **buffer** and **driving hammer**. The flat end of the buffer is placed under the clench and, when struck by the hammer, prises the clench up and straightens it. When all the clenches have been knocked up the shoe is levered off with the **pincers**. The pincers are used starting at the heels, working towards the toe with a downward pulling action. Some farriers pull the nails out before removing the shoe.

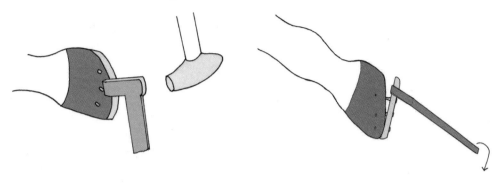

8.3 Removing the shoe

2. **Preparation (also referred to as dressing the foot).** Excess horn is cut away with the **hoof cutters** and **drawing knife**. Ragged bits of the frog are trimmed. The **rasp** is then used to give a level bearing surface upon which the shoe will rest. The drawing knife is used to make a notch in the wall for the toe clip (forefoot) or quarter clips (hind foot) to rest in.

3. **Forging.** This is the process of making a new shoe, although many farriers buy in ready-made shoes. It is important that the correct weight of iron and size of shoe are used to suit each individual horse or pony.

   The shoe is put in the forge and made red-hot. It is then removed using the **fire tongs** and placed on the **anvil**. The farrier will use the **shoe tongs** to hold the shoe and the **turning hammer** to shape it as needed, and will then knock the **pritchel** into one of the nail holes and use this to carry the shoe to the horse.

4. **Fitting.** Whilst the shoe is red-hot it is fitted onto the foot. This burns the horn and gives the farrier an indication as to what alterations are necessary. This does not hurt the horse as the outer horn is insensitive.

   The shoe is once again held on the anvil and hammered until it is exactly the right shape for the horse's foot.

5. **Nailing on.** When the farrier is happy with the fit of the shoe it is immersed in cold water to cool it. Shoeing nails are then used to hold the shoe in place. This is a very skilled job as the nails must never press on or puncture the sensitive laminae. A mistake made whilst nailing on could make a horse lame.

   The point of the nail comes out through the wall and is known as a **clench**. It is twisted off with the claw end of the driving hammer.

6. **Finishing off.** When nailing on is complete the horse stands with his foot on a metal **tripod**. The rasp is used to make a bed for the clenches, which are then either hammered down neatly until level with the wall of the hoof, or pulled down tightly with the **clenching tongs**.

EXAM TIP

In your exam you will be asked to demonstrate safe shoe removal via simulation. Protect your thighs with a stable rubber. If one is not available explain why it is needed and request one.

The clenches should be the correct distance up the wall (approximately one-third of the way up the wall) and appear fairly level. If the clenches are too low the shoe may be wrenched off easily. This is known as **fine nailing**. **Coarse nailing** is when the clenches are too high up the wall. Here lies a danger of the nails pressing on the sensitive laminae within the foot.

The front shoe has a **toe clip** and the hind shoe, **quarter clips**, embedded into shallow grooves to help prevent the shoes from slipping. A toe clip in the hind foot would increase the risk of injury if the horse overreached, which is why hind shoes have two quarter clips instead.

Finally, the rasp is lightly run around the foot where it meets the shoe to ensure a neat finish.

Removes/refits

If a horse has not been out on the road very much, the shoes may not be very worn. In this case the shoes may be removed, the feet trimmed, prepared and the old shoes put back on. This process is called **removes** or **refits.**

ITQ 8.3

a. Which tools are used to knock up the clenches when removing the old shoes?

b. Which tool is used to lever the shoe off?

ITQ 8.4

a. What is fine nailing?

b. What is coarse nailing?

c. What problems may occur as a result of fine and coarse nailing?

POINTS TO LOOK FOR IN A NEWLY SHOD FOOT

To assess whether a horse has been well shod, look for the following points:

1. The shoe must be made to fit the foot and not vice versa. Cutting the toe back too much it is known as **dumping** and can adversely affect the balance of the foot.

2. The foot must be evenly reduced in size at the toe and heel, inside and outside of the foot.

3. The correct type of shoe and weight of iron must be used according to the size of the horse and the work he is required to do. A small pony would have a lighter iron than a large hunter.

4. The rasp must not be used excessively on the hoof wall. This would remove the protective periople and may lead to drying out of the wall.

5. There should not be excessive use of the knife on the sole or frog. The frog should ideally be in contact with the ground – it cannot perform its functions if it does not touch the ground.

6. The correct number of nails has been used. There are normally seven, three on the inside and four on the outside. (This may vary if the farrier has had to deal with certain foot problems.)

7. The correct size of nail must be used. The nail head should be neither too large nor too small.

8. The clenches must be even and approximately one-third of the way up the wall.

9. No daylight must show between the foot and the shoe.

10. The groove for the toes and quarter clips must be neat. The clips must be neatly embedded in.

11. The heels must not be too short or too long.

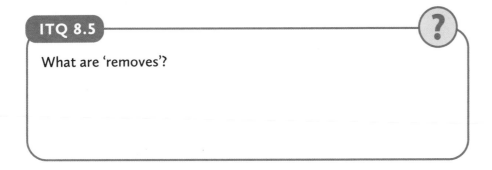

ITQ 8.5

What are 'removes'?

ITQ 8.6

Why should the rasp not be used excessively on the hoof wall?

ITQ 8.7

Which points indicate that the shoe fits the horse's foot?

ITQ 8.8

What problems can occur if the toe of an unshod horse grows excessively long?

⑨ Watering and Feeding

REQUIRED SKILLS/KNOWLEDGE	Learnt, revised, practised?	Confirmed
The rules of watering.		
• The rules of watering.	☐	☐
• Understand the reasons behind these rules.	☐	☐
• Know the various methods of providing water for horses.	☐	☐
The rules of feeding.		
• The rules of feeding.	☐	☐
• Understand the reasons behind these rules.	☐	☐
Feedstuffs, their preparation and suitability.		
• Be able to recognise feed samples, assess them for quality and describe their method of preparation.	☐	☐
• Know which feedstuffs have a 'heating' or fattening effect on horses.	☐	☐
• Identify feedstuffs suitable for different types of horses/ponies.	☐	☐
Feeding bulk food.		
• Know why hay is soaked.	☐	☐
• Be familiar with alternatives to hay and their nutritional differences.	☐	☐
Producing feed charts.		
• Understand why a feed chart is essential.	☐	☐
• Understand ways to devise a feed chart.	☐	☐

FEEDSTUFFS

General categories

Feedstuffs may be divided into the following categories:

Cereals (also known as 'straights' or 'concentrates'). These include grain such as oats, barley and maize. The cereals are often prepared in such a way as to improve digestibility. This includes boiling, rolling, bruising, flaking or a heat treatment called **micronising**.

Protein feeds. These are either of animal origin such as dried milk or, more commonly in horse feed, of plant origin such as beans, peas and linseed.

Bulk feeds. Foods such as bran, sugar beet pulp, grass meal and chaff add bulk (roughage/fibre) to the diet and aid digestion.

Compound feeds (together with cereals these are also know as 'concentrates'). These include the extensive and ever-expanding range of cubes and coarse mixes. They are prepared to include the necessary balance of nutrients for each specific area, e.g. resting horses, competition horses, breeding stock, etc. They are often labour-saving as they are pre-mixed and reduce the need to store many bins of straight feeds.

Forages. These include grass, hay and haylage. The amount of nutrition grass provides varies according to the time of year, level of upkeep the grazing receives, grass species in the sward and the number of horses grazing it. Likewise, the quality of dry forage varies depending upon the upkeep of the land, time of cut, method of cutting and baling and storage methods.

In addition to the bulk feeds, forages provide fibre (also known as roughage) which is essential for healthy gut function. The fibre is provided in the form of **cellulose** – a fermentable carbohydrate that the horse digests in his hind gut.

The feed pyramid opposite represents the quantities in which each type of feed should be fed to the horse.

Cereals

Cereals, by comparison with other feeds that we give our horses, are high in quick-releasing energy sources, which include sugars and starch. These energy sources can have the effect of making the horse excitable – some people refer to this as the 'heating effect'. Many people believe that oats are the main culprit of causing horses to be excitable but actually they have a lower energy level weight for weight than any of the other cereals. Oats are actually the grain which is lowest in starch, but the starch in them is said to be more digestible than the starch contained in other cereals

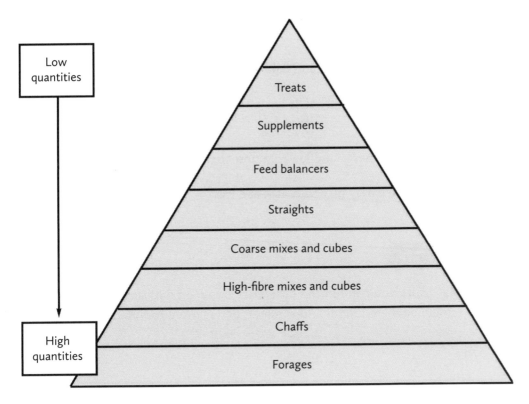

9.1 Feed pyramid

and so this might be partly responsible for the excitable effect that oats have on some horses.

As a rule of thumb, cereals need to be fed to horses using a considered approach, remembering that the horse is not designed to eat cereals. The majority of horses in light and medium work could easily be fed a diet free from cereals and still have plenty of energy to carry out the work required of them. Cereals can form a useful part of the diet of a working horse provided that they are not fed in too large a quantity, as this is likely to cause behavioural issues in some horses.

Oats

For the reasons outlined above oats are best fed to horses in hard work only. Oats are normally **rolled** or **bruised** to aid digestibility – this is achieved as the processing breaks the hard, indigestible outer husk. Oats can also be fed in their **naked** form, meaning that the outer husk is not present and the energy in them is much more available to the horse.

> **EXAM TIP**
>
> Oats are higher in fibre than barley, wheat and maize because of their fibrous outer husk. Naked oats (husk removed) are much higher in energy and lower in fibre weight for weight than traditional oats and therefore less 'safe' as a feedstuff.

9.2 Rolled oats

9.3 Whole barley

9.4 Micronised barley

Barley

- Barley can be bought cooked and flaked, or micronised.

- This is a fattening feedstuff as it has a high carbohydrate content and excess carbohydrate will be stored by the horse as fat.

- Barley is higher in energy and lower in fibre than oats.

- Whole uncooked barley may be boiled and fed.

> **EXAM TIP**
>
> Make sure you can tell the difference between oats and barley; oats are longer and slimmer, barley more rounded.

Maize

- Because of its high carbohydrate content, maize is unsuitable for many horses and ponies unless they are in very hard work.

- Maize, like barley, is a fattening feedstuff.

- It is fed cooked and flaked or micronised.

> **EXAM TIP**
>
> Maize is sometimes referred to as corn, especially in the USA.

Protein feeds

Beans and peas

These may be fed crushed, split, steamed and flaked or micronised to a horse requiring increased protein levels and are commonly added to coarse mixes.

Linseed

Linseed, the seed of the flax plant, is very high in oils and protein. The small, flat, brown seeds are poisonous to horses in their raw form and so must be cooked and processed before being fed. Linseed can be fed to horses in the form of linseed jelly, tea, cake or oil.

9.6 Flaked maize

9.5 Whole maize

Soya

Whole soya beans are high in oils and protein but must be cooked through toasting or micronising before feeding. Soya bean meal is much lower in oil as the oil is removed during the preparatory process.

9.7 Bran

Bulk feeds

Bran

- Bran is the by-product of wheat milling and has a low energy value. Because the milling process is far more efficient than it was years ago, bran is now commonly more dusty than it once used to be and contains flakes that are much smaller.

- It contains a high level of fibre but is otherwise low in nutritional value.

- Bran should always be fed dampened, as dry bran can cause the horse to choke.

- It is not suitable to feed in large quantities as it contains too much phosphorous and not enough calcium. The effect of this leads to impaired bone growth which could cause significant problems in the young, growing horse.

To make a bran mash

A bran mash is beneficial when a horse is unwell or suffering from colic as it is easily digested and has a slight laxative effect. It is also a useful feed to give when the horse is having a rest day as it is non-heating and low in energy. The main nutritional disadvantage of bran mashes is the poor calcium:phosphorus ratio. As mentioned above, bran is high in phosphorus, low in calcium.

1. Add enough boiling water to the bran to make the mixture moist and crumbly, not wet and sloppy.

2. 1kg (2¼lb) is usually a good amount for a 13hh pony; 1.25kg (2¾lb) would be sufficient for a 15hh horse. Boiled barley or linseed may be added to make a nutritious mash.

3. Add 30g (approx. 1oz) of limestone flour to boost the calcium level.

4. Cover the bucket with a heavy sack or blanket and allow the bran to cool a little. It will also cook a little under the blanket.

5. To increase the laxative effect, add 50g (1¾oz) of Epsom salts.

6. Once the mash has cooled, but is still warm, feed it to the horse. If he is unwell and will not eat it, don't leave the bucket in the stable for hours. Remove it and try the horse again later with a fresh mash.

EXAM TIPS

Both sugar beet pulp and alfalfa are high in calcium so can be added to a bran mash to help correct the calcium:phosphorous imbalance.

Whilst you need to know about bran, it is not commonly fed – avoid mentioning it if talking about suitable feedstuffs in your exam.

EXAM TIP

Traditionally a bran mash was thought to be a warm, 'comforting' feed for a horse after a hard day's work and during his day off. It is actually just as 'comforting' (and more nutritious) to offer the horse his usual feed type (ration size adjusted to compensate for a day off) with some warm water added to make a mash. This works especially well with compound cubes. In this way the horse's digestive system does not have to compensate for a rapid change in diet.

9.8 Sugar beet cubes

Sugar beet pulp

- Sugar beet pulp is the by-product of the extraction of sugar from sugar beet. Limestone is added during the extraction process, making sugar beet pulp high in calcium.

- Sugar beet comes in dried form and is either shredded or in 'cubes'.

- On no account must it be fed dry. It must always be well soaked – shredded beet for at least 12 hours, beet cubes for at least 24 hours. This is to prevent the pulp swelling up inside the horse's digestive tract and causing colic.

- It is now possible to buy sugar beet that only requires soaking for 10 minutes and this can be very convenient, especially if one forgets to soak the shreds or cubes in time for the next feed!

- Pulp is a good fibre feed and is non-heating when fed in its unmolassed form, so is therefore safe to feed to all horses.

- Horses with a higher energy requirement can be fed molassed sugar beet pulp, which contains more sugar and therefore provides more energy than the same amount of unmolassed pulp.

9.9 Sugar beet flakes

EXAM TIP

Make sure you can tell the difference between sugar beet cubes and horse and pony cubes. Sugar beet cubes are usually smaller and darker than other types of cubes.

9.10 Soaked sugar beet

Grass meal

- This is non-heating and often comes in the form of pellets; it is included in many coarse mixes.

- Grass meal is nutritious and useful to feed in winter when there is no feed value in the paddock grass.

Chaff

- The old-fashioned type of chaff was simply chopped hay and straw.

- Chaff can now be purchased with additives such as molasses, limestone flour, garlic, vitamins and minerals.

- Feeding alfalfa chaff is now very popular. Alfalfa is a legume crop which provides higher protein and is nutritionally a better 'mixer' than bran. It aids digestion and helps to prevent a horse bolting his food.

- Unmolassed varieties can safely be fed to all horses and ponies dampened in with the short feed.

- Chaff can be added to the feed to 'bulk' it out and satisfy the horse's appetite. This is useful when the horse receives only a small ration.

> **EXAM TIP**
>
> Try to look at lots of different types of chaff and learn what each type looks like. There are large variations in nutrient content between chaffs, which you should try to be aware of when planning a feed ration.

Compound feeds

Cubes

There is a range of different types of cube, all very similar in appearance, hence it is difficult to identify individual types of cubes. The information on the feed sack will describe the content of each type of cube.

Water must always be available to a horse eating cubes, as they are dry. This is an important point to remember as choking and colic may result if water is not available.

Complete cubes

- Complete cubes are very high in fibre as they contain the forage ration as well as the short feed.

- Complete cubes may be fed to replace the hay ration if a horse suffers from a very bad dust allergy, although it is possible to buy dust-extracted, vacuum-packed hay or haylage which is more interesting for the horse.

Horse and pony cubes

- These have a good balance of all the necessary vitamins, minerals, proteins and carbohydrates that a horse in light to medium work requires. The majority of their content is derived from fibre sources.

9.11 Cubes – they're not necessarily cubic!

- They are specially designed to be non-heating, so may be safely fed to most horses or ponies.

- It is quite safe to feed nothing but horse and pony cubes, although some horses may become bored and go off them.

Stud cubes

Stud cubes are high-protein cubes designed to meet the needs of brood mares, foals, stallions and youngstock.

Racehorse/event cubes

These are high in carbohydrates and meet the energy needs of high-performance competition horses. They are composed of a combination of milled cereals, protein sources and oils packed into uniform cubes.

Coarse mixes

9.12 Coarse mix

- These comprise a highly palatable mixture of cereals and bulk feeds with added vitamins and minerals.

- High-protein coarse mixes will contain split beans, peas and protein cubes in addition to the cubes, barley, oats, grass meal, molasses and linseed cake contained in the lower-protein mixtures.

- Coarse mixes are designed to make up the whole concentrate ration to be fed with the normal quantities of hay. It is possible to mix a coarse mix with other feedstuffs such as chaff and pulp, if desired, however it must be borne in mind that doing this might unbalance an otherwise balanced concentrate ration and so is probably best avoided.

- As with cubes, coarse mixes are prepared to meet the differing needs of all types of horse and pony. There is a complete range starting with non-heating, low-energy mixes, through to high-energy competition mixes.

> **EXAM TIP**
>
> Practise identifying the various feedstuffs present in coarse mixes. Once you have identified the feedstuffs you should be able to state fairly accurately the intended use for the mix. For example, a mix with high levels of barley and oats is likely to be a competition mix; one including high cereal content and high protein content will be a racehorse mix. A high-fibre, low-cereal mix will incline towards the non-heating, low-energy (cool mix, pasture mix) type feed.

ITQ 9.1 ?

List the three main cereals fed to horses:

1.

2.

3.

ITQ 9.2 ?

Bran contains high levels of which mineral?

ITQ 9.3 ?

How should dried sugar beet pulp cubes be prepared before being fed?

ITQ 9.4 ?

What are the advantages of feeding chaff?

ITQ 9.5

A horse in your yard is known to be of an excitable nature. What feeds will you try to avoid feeding him and how would you ensure that he receives adequate energy for the medium work he is in?

ITQ 9.6

A horse in your yard is overweight. What feeds will you avoid feeding and how could you alter the amount of feed he is fed to effect weight loss?

ITQ 9.7

You have an event horse in your yard who competes regularly throughout the season. What types of feedstuffs would be suitable for this horse to provide his nutritional requirements?

IN-TEXT ACTIVITY

Using magazines/advertising/feed suppliers as sources of information, select four feed manufacturers and obtain the following information:

Manufacturer's name	Name of non-heating cubes	Cost per 20kg bag	Name of high-energy/ competition cubes	Cost per 20kg bag
1.				
2.				
3.				
4.				

Forages

We have discussed the feedstuffs which make up the 'short feed' or 'concentrate' part of the horse's daily ration. Forage (traditionally in the form of hay) should make up the larger part of the ration, especially when the horse spends long periods stabled.

Hay

Hay, the most important feedstuff for horses (especially when fresh grass is not available), is grass that has been cut and dried. It varies in quality, depending on the types of grasses, the weather when the hay lay on the fields, its age and how well it has been stored.

Meadow hay is taken from pasture normally used for grazing and is generally softer than **seed hay,** which is a specially sown crop containing fewer grass varieties. Meadow hay tends to include a greater variety of grasses. The nutritive quality of hay depends upon the variety of grasses used and the weather conditions during the haymaking process. Generally, an early cut of ryegrass (seed) hay has higher protein and energy levels than mixed grass meadow hay, with alfalfa (lucerne) hay higher still. However, any crop, no matter how good the grasses, will lose nutritional value if it gets soaked after cutting or is cut late in the season. Hence the weather plays an important role in determining the feed value and quality of every hay crop.

Poor-quality hay should never be fed, but even good hay contains a significant amount of dust. Some horses are allergic to the dust found in hay. The dust allergy affects the respiratory system and causes the horse to cough. With these horses it will be necessary to soak the hay for approximately 20 minutes before feeding. This makes the dust particles stick to the hay, which then prevents the dust from being inhaled.

Hay should not be soaked overnight as then the nutrients are washed out, reducing the hay's feed value. Poor quality, dusty hay should never be fed – soaking will do nothing to enhance its feed value or palatability. The only circumstance in which you might consider feeding hay that has been soaked for significantly longer than 20 minutes is if you are feeding a very overweight or laminitic horse or pony and you want them to eat a hay ration that contains few nutrients. In these cases soaking hay for long periods (whilst being careful to change the soak water regularly) can be very useful and will keep the horse or pony occupied and happy without overfeeding nutrients.

Hay can also be steamed prior to feeding and this method of preparing it is becoming more popular. Steaming hay effectively sterilises it by killing the spores that are naturally present in it, whilst soaking it does not have this effect. There are a number of commercial steamers available on the market but you can also make your own using a large, sealable container and a heating element from a kettle or wallpaper stripper. The length of time required to steam hay effectively varies from 40–60 minutes depending on the type of steam that you have. The advantage of steamers is that you use far less water and don't have the same problem with getting rid of the waste soak water associated with soaking hay.

If a horse is *very* allergic to hay, he will need to be fed **haylage** or **vacuum-packed (bagged) hay**. These are dust-free alternatives to normal hay. As they have had the dust extracted, they are expensive compared to normal hay.

Qualities of good hay

- The first thing you will notice is the way the hay smells. It should have a good **'nose'**. This means it should smell sweet and pleasant, never musty.

- The bales must be dry – if they have been stacked whilst damp they will soon start to rot. In addition, moulds may be formed which may cause damage to the horse's respiratory tract when ingested.

- When you cut the strings the bale should fall loosely apart.

- The hay should be greenish-light brown in colour, depending on the grasses used. Meadow hay is normally greener than seed hay.

- There should be a good selection of grasses in the bale.

- It must be completely free from poisonous plants, especially ragwort. Buttercups are harmless in hay.

- The hay must be free from weeds. A few thistles will do no harm, but too many thistles should be avoided.

- It must not be dusty or mouldy – if mouldy hay is fed the horse will soon start coughing as he will inhale mould and dust spores.

- Mouldy hay can also cause colic.

When discussing (or actually feeding) haylage remember:

- When feeding weight for weight you need to feed up to 40 per cent more haylage than you would hay because of its high water content; however it is higher in sugar than hay so can cause weight gain. It is not advisable to feed haylage to an overweight or laminitic pony.

- Check bales for spoilage and always ask to see a nutritional analysis of the cut of haylage you are buying.

- Ensure that you use the bale within 4 days of opening as moulds begin to grow when the bag is opened.

Haylage

Haylage is grass cut between heading and flowering, left to partially dry before being baled and wrapped in plastic. It retains a high moisture content (usually between 30–40 per cent). The wrapped haylage must remain airtight to prevent moulds forming and causing it to be spoilt. Mouldy haylage can cause respiratory problems and colic.

Qualities of good haylage

- The bag must not be punctured as this causes the haylage to rot.

- Haylage smells different from hay because of the fermentation process. However, it must smell clean, not unpleasantly pungent or over-fermented.

- It must be free of mould.

Silage

This is highly nutritious forage preserved by 'pickling' the grass in the wrapped bale. It is not recommended as feed for horses as it is too high in protein and energy for most and carries a higher risk of botulism.

Storage points for forage

- Hay and haylage are expensive. These products must always be stored in a dry place and waste must be avoided (although not at the risk of feeding unsuitable samples).

- Hay/haylage may be fed from a haynet to prevent wastage, although haynets in a field can be hazardous. When used, haynets should be secured correctly.

- Feeding from the floor is a natural position for the horse.

Practise identifying different hay and haylage samples. As well as looking at samples you must always smell them too.

ITQ 9.8

?

What is the difference between meadow hay and seed hay?

ITQ 9.9

?

List three qualities of good hay:

1.

2.

3.

ITQ 9.10

?

How would you soak hay, and how long for?

ITQ 9.11

?

Give one disadvantage and one advantage of:

SOAKING HAY
Disadvantage:

Advantage:

STEAMING HAY
Disadvantage:

Advantage:

ITQ 9.12

What forage would you feed to a horse with an allergy to hay?
Explain your choice.

THE RULES OF FEEDING AND WATERING

When we talk about feeding horses there are certain well-established rules that must be followed. These rules are known as **'The Rules of Feeding'** and must be learnt by everyone involved with horses. Using these rules as the basis for feeding horses will help keep the horse in good health and help you avoid making mistakes which could lead to colic or other problems associated with diet. Regular (preferably *ad lib*) access to clean, fresh water is essential to the horse's well-being and appropriate provision of such water can be considered in conjunction with feeding.

1 **Feed little and often.** Relative to his size, a horse has a small stomach. It is approximately the size of a rugby ball and has a capacity of between 9 and 15 litres (about 2–3.25 gallons). In the wild a horse grazes on and off all day so that his stomach is always about two-thirds full; the horse's stomach is most efficient if it remains about two-thirds full all of the time.

It is, therefore, more natural to give the horse two or three smaller feeds a day – ideally of a maximum 2–2.5kg (approx. 4½–5½lb) each as well as a constant supply of forage, rather than one large concentrate feed and two or three haynets, especially if the horse is stabled.

2 **Feed at regular times each day.** Horses are creatures of habit and soon learn when to expect their next meal. Each day you should try to feed at more or less the same time so a routine is developed.

3 **Feed plenty of bulk (roughage/fibre).** As a horse's natural diet is grass, his digestive system is designed to ferment and digest large quantities of roughage. Hay is dried grass so provides the necessary roughage, helping the digestive system to work properly. Eating hay also helps to alleviate boredom in the stabled horse and the action of chewing stimulates the horse to produce saliva, which helps to prevent problems further down the digestive tract. The additional fluid held within the digestive tract during roughage digestion acts like a reservoir for the horse's bodily systems.

4. **Feed only good quality food and hay.** All food should be fresh, free from mould and/or dust and have a pleasant smell. Some feedstuffs can be stored longer than others, e.g. horse and pony cubes last well, but bran absorbs moisture from the atmosphere so does not keep for long. As mentioned earlier, dusty or mouldy hay will cause health problems in horses and should be thrown away.

5. **If water is not always available, water before feeding.** Horses should have clean, fresh water available to them at all times. If however, you have been riding, e.g. at a show or schooling, you will need to offer the horse a drink well before you feed. This is to prevent him taking a long drink immediately after eating, which could wash most of the food through his stomach before the digestive process started.

6. **Introduce changes gradually.** Horses get used to particular types of food and, if their diet is changed suddenly, they may not be able to digest the new food properly.

   In the event of a sudden change there may not be the correct conditions in the horse's digestive tract to digest the new feedstuff. Therefore, always try to add a little of the new food at a time, gradually building up the amounts given. Sudden changes in feedstuff and grazing quality can lead to colic.

7. **Allow 1½ hours after a feed before exercising.** Once a horse has eaten he requires approximately 1½ hours for the food to leave his stomach. If he is exercised strenuously soon after eating, it could cause colic as the circulatory system (heart and blood vessels) directs blood away from the digestive tract to the muscles needed for work. In addition, a full stomach leaves less room for lung expansion and will apply pressure to the diaphragm during exercise.

   It is quite safe to ride your horse *before* he has been fed. If you ride first, allow him to cool off, get his breathing back to normal and have a drink before he eats.

8. **Feed something succulent every day.** If your horse lives out at grass he will be eating something succulent every day – grass. If he is stabled most of the time, or it is winter and there is no grass, you should feed something succulent such as carrots, apples or parsnips. These must be **sliced** – never diced or cubed as a horse could easily choke on a square piece of carrot or apple.

   Succulents aid digestion and add variety to the diet. They can be a very useful addition to the diet of a horse on box rest or one off his feed.

9. **Always keep feeding equipment clean.** Feed scoops, buckets and mangers must be scrubbed and rinsed out regularly in order to keep them clean. Bad hygiene can lead to rotten food building up, which not only smells bad but can cause harmful bacteria to develop. Ideally, each horse should have his own feed and water buckets.

10. **Feed according to work, type, age, size, temperament and time of year.** This is probably one of the most important rules of feeding so we shall break it down into the different headings, as each one is important. More harm is caused through overfeeding than any other type of mismanagement problem. Overfeeding can make the horse fat, badly behaved and cause laminitis.

(a) **Feed according to workload.** If a horse is not working he will require food purely to keep him alive and looking well. This is referred to as maintenance rations. In the summer, good grass will provide the maintenance ration. If the horse does not have access to good grass, lots of good-quality meadow hay should be sufficient.

A horse in work will need extra energy – if a working horse is not given extra food he may lose weight. However, if he is not working very hard, he will not require lots of extra food.

(b) **Feed according to type and temperament.** An excitable horse will need non-heating (low-carbohydrate) food, whereas a lazy cob type may benefit from higher-energy foods.

Thoroughbreds tend to need more food to keep their condition than natives. Some Thoroughbreds can be highly strung and excitable so need non-heating feeds.

Small ponies do not cope with heating feedstuffs at all well. They become too 'fizzy' for their young riders and are very prone to developing laminitis.

(c) **Feed according to age.** A young, growing horse up to the age of 4 years needs a balance of vitamins, minerals and protein to ensure good bone and tissue growth.

An old horse of, say, 20 years or more may need plenty of bulk (hay) and quite fattening foods to prevent him from losing weight. Many of the manufacturers produce mixes specially designed to meet the nutritional needs of the older horse.

(d) **Feed according to size and bodyweight.** Obviously you would not feed a small pony the same amount as a big horse. Usually the smaller the pony, the less he has to eat, depending on his type, temperament and work done. The amount to feed is calculated according to the weight of the horse or pony.

Within this book we will not be looking at detailed ration calculation; we'll start to look at some samples of daily rations to give you the idea of how much food a horse or pony needs in a day (see next section).

(e) **Feed according to the time of year.** This applies to horses who spend time out at grass. The grass has no feed value during the winter months so additional hay will be needed. Grass-kept horses need extra hay and food in winter to help keep them warm – the process of digesting hay generates body heat.

Once the grass starts to grow in the spring no extra hay will be needed whilst the horse is in the field. If the grass is very lush and/or the horse is prone to laminitis, it will be necessary to restrict his access to the grass either by stabling or dividing the field.

ITQ 9.13

Why should horses be given two or three smaller feeds per day, rather than one large feed?

ITQ 9.14

Give three reasons why horses need plenty of hay in their diet:

1.

2.

3.

ITQ 9.15

Why should changes in diet be introduced gradually?

ITQ 9.16

Why should you allow 1½ hours after feeding before you exercise your horse?

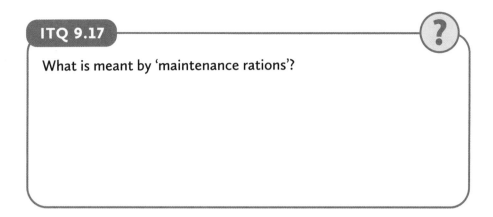

ITQ 9.17

What is meant by 'maintenance rations'?

ITQ 9.18

Which nutrients are needed in high levels when feeding young, growing horses?

Sample feed rations

Useful measurements:
1 kg = 2.2 lb
1 lb = 0.45 kg

The average section of hay weighs approximately 1.8 kg (4 lb).
When filled level, a normal 1,500 ml (2½ pint) feed scoop holds the following:

1.35kg (3lb) cubes
0.56kg (1¼lb) flaked barley
1.35kg (3lb) soaked sugar beet pulp
0.33kg (0.75lb) chaff
0.67kg (1½lb) coarse mix
1.35kg (3lb) carrots
0.45kg (1lb) bran

The following feed charts have been devised for horses and ponies turned out all day and stabled at night. They are in light work – in your exam light work is defined as 'daily walk, trot, canter where the horse is not stressed'.

Assume that they are all around 8 years old, of calm disposition and maintain condition well. There are many types of feedstuffs to choose from – while those used in the following sample rations are suitable there may be other similar feeds which are equally suitable.

All weights shown are **dry weights** and whilst many feeds may be fed dry, it improves mastication and aids digestion if the feeds are well dampened. Many owners like to feed sugar beet pulp as it dampens the feed, provides a non-heating energy and fibre source, keeps weight on and is suitable for all horses and ponies.

When calculating the ration to include sugar beet, weigh the beet *dry* (unsoaked). Do not take into account the weight of the water in which the pulp has been soaked or cooked, as the water does not contain any significant nutrients – these are derived from the dry feed.

Ponies and hardier types of horses are much less likely to require large amounts of feed as they have evolved to live in harsher environments and on less food than finer horses – this should always be borne in mind when planning diets as overfeeding can be very dangerous.

The examples that follow are based on ponies and horses who are being fed a set amount of hay and concentrate feeds. Rations are often worked out in these terms and are based on a forage: concentrate ratio – in simple terms the more work the horse or pony is doing, the higher the percentage of concentrates he can safely receive. Horses and ponies in light work or on a maintenance ration can often remain very healthy and looking well eating only fibre. The percentage of concentrate feed in a ration should never be greater than 65 per cent.

It is becoming more common for nutritionists and vets to recommend feeding horses *ad lib* forage and to disregard the older system of using a forage:concentrate ratio. This can be very useful for the vast majority of horses as it is much more harmonious with their bodies and mimics the way they would feed in the wild. Feeding forage in this way can also save money in the long run as it is likely that the horse will need less expensive hard feed if he has access to a constant supply of good-quality forage. However, in your exam you will be required to estimate total quantity and therefore it is useful for us to provide examples which include a definitive amount of forage.

Stabled 13hh pony

13hh pony	Metric	Imperial
Concentrates	0.9kg	2lb
Hay	3.6kg	8lb
Daily total	**4.5kg**	**10lb**

This could be split equally into two feeds:

	MORNING AND EVENING FEEDS	
	Metric	Imperial
Horse and Pony cubes	0.22kg	½lb
Chaff	0.115kg	¼lb
*Sugar beet	0.115kg	¼lb
Amount per feed	0.45kg	1lb
Daily total of 2 feeds	**0.9kg**	**2lb**

With hay fed as follows:

Morning hay	–	–
Evening hay	3.6kg	8lb
Daily total hay	**3.6kg**	**8lb**
Total daily amount fed	**4.5kg**	**10lb**

Important points to remember

● *The weight of the sugar beet shown is the dry weight – you do not include the weight of water in your calculations because water, although essential for life, does not contain a significant amount of nutrients. (Water contains a few trace minerals but no protein, carbohydrates or lipids). Sugar beet **must always be thoroughly soaked** before feeding.

● In the stabled pony example ration the pony has not been given any hay in the morning because he has been turned out to grass during the day. If there was snow on the ground, hay could be given in the morning and slightly more hay given at night.

● If the pony was kept constantly in the stable (not recommended) the ration would be split into three feeds a day.

● In summer this pony's ration would be reduced according to the quality of the grass he has access to whilst turned out. If constantly stabled, the ration would remain unaltered. A 13hh pony should be quite able to carry out light work with no extra feed.

● Remember to work either in kilos (kg) or pounds (lb) – don't mix the two or you will get very confused! When you add up the columns to check the totals, make sure you add *either* the measurements shown in kilos or pounds – don't add up a mixture of the two.

● Never feed ponies diets that are high in cereals or high-energy coarse mixes as they can cause laminitis, obesity and bad behaviour.

14hh pony

● Late autumn/winter.

● Light work so a ratio of 80 per cent forage to 20 per cent concentrates has been used.

● Good doer – keeps condition well.

● Stabled at night and out at grass all day – no feed value in grass.

14hh pony	Metric	Imperial
Concentrates	1.36kg	3lb
Hay	6.8kg	15lb
Daily total	**8.16kg**	**18lb**

	MORNING AND EVENING FEEDS	
	Metric	Imperial
Horse and Pony cubes	0.45kg	1lb
Chaff	0.115kg	¼lb
*Sugar beet	0.115kg	¼lb
Amount per feed	0.68kg	1½lb
Daily total of 2 feeds	**1.36kg**	**3lb**

Morning hay	2.3kg	5lb
Evening hay	4.5kg	10lb
Daily total hay	**6.8kg**	**15lb**
Total daily amount fed	**8.16kg**	**18lb**

Important points to remember

- In this ration some of the hay has been put out in the field in the morning.

- If the pony needs more energy the Horse and Pony cubes could be replaced with coarse mix.

- Sugar beet shown as dry weight (before soaking).

- In summer this pony's ration would be reduced according to the quality of the grass he has access to whilst turned out. If constantly stabled, the ration would remain unaltered. A 14hh pony should be quite able to carry out light work with no extra feed.

15hh horse

- Late autumn/winter.

- Medium work, so ratio of 60 per cent hay to 40 per cent concentrates.

- Good doer – keeps condition well.

- Stabled at night and out at grass all day – no feed value in grass.

15hh pony	Metric	Imperial
Concentrates Hay	4.1kg 6.8kg	9lb 15lb
Daily total	**10.9kg**	**24lb**

	MORNING AND EVENING FEEDS Metric	Imperial
Coarse mix	1.61kg	3½lb
Chaff	0.22kg	½lb
*Sugar beet	0.22kg	½lb
Amount per feed	2.05kg	4½lb
Daily total of 2 feeds	**4.1kg**	**9lb**

Morning hay	1.8kg	4lb
Evening hay	5kg	11lb
Daily total hay	6.8kg	15lb
Total daily amount fed	**10.9kg**	**24lb**

Important points to remember

● The energy level of the coarse mix can be chosen to suit the type of horse. A lazier sort might need a higher level of energy than a 'fizzy' sort of horse. If the horse is very lively it is better to replace the majority of coarse mix with more fibre in the form of either chaff and sugar beet or hay.

● Sugar beet shown as dry weight (before soaking).

Summary of the important points to consider when working out how much to feed a horse

● Time of year – is there any feed value in the grass?

● Is the horse turned out or stabled?

● What work is he doing? Hacking, eventing, showjumping, dressage or resting?

● His ability to maintain condition; some horses lose condition easily whilst others put weight on, on very little feed.

- Temperament – is he calm or 'fizzy'?

- Type: cobby or Thoroughbred? Light, medium or heavyweight?

- Age – very young or old?

- Is the horse susceptible to conditions such as laminitis?

Can you think of any more?

-

-

EXAM TIPS

Keep your calculations as simple as possible when planning and revising how much to feed in a ration.

Avoid talking about complicated rations containing too many different feed stuffs as you will be more likely to get yourself confused in an exam – keep it simple!

Always work to the nearest whole unit.

IN-TEXT ACTIVITY

Using your local yard, friends, feedstore, feed manufacturers, etc., collect and label small samples (30–60g/1–2oz) of the following feedstuffs:

a. A non-heating coarse mix

b. Horse and Pony cubes

c. Dry sugar beet pulp nuts and/or shredded beet pulp

e. Oats

f. Barley

g. Bran

MULTIPLE CHOICE QUESTIONS ?

Tick the correct answer(s)
There may be more than one correct answer

ITQ 9.19

Fibre is needed for?
a. Good digestion
b. Replacement of body tissue
c. Energy
d. Healthy hooves

ITQ 9.20

Carbohydrate in the diet provides?
a. Bone strength
b. Amino acids
c. Energy
d. Oil

ITQ 9.21

Which of the following are bulk feeds?
a. Chaff
b. Horse and Pony cubes
c. Sugar beet pulp
d. Linseed

ITQ 9.22

Oats are rolled to?
a. Make them more palatable
b. Aid their digestion
c. Make them smell fresher
d. Make them last longer in storage

Watering and feeding at grass

Watering

A constant supply of clean, fresh water is essential. Whichever method of providing water is used, it should be checked regularly to ensure cleanliness.

Troughs

The self-filling type of trough is ideal. This must have rounded edges to prevent injury. If a tap is used it must be enclosed within a wooden box to prevent the horse injuring himself on it. The trough must be emptied and scrubbed out regularly to prevent the inside becoming green and slimy as algae forms.

Pipes should be well lagged – although in the winter they may still freeze. In freezing conditions the ice will need to be broken and removed at least three times a day and the trough must then be filled with buckets of water.

The area around the trough may become wet and muddy in the winter, so some form of hard standing such as shingle on concrete should ideally be used.

Buckets

Provided you do not have to carry the filled buckets too far, this is an easy method of providing water in the field. The buckets may be stood in two old car tyres to stop them from being kicked over. Buckets must be scrubbed out regularly and filled with clean, fresh water daily.

Streams

Before allowing horses to drink from a stream you must check that it:

- Is not polluted.

- Has a safe approach, i.e. firm and not steep.

- Has a stony base, not a sandy one. Horses can develop colic through drinking water which contains sand.

- Is fenced at your boundaries to prevent horses wandering up and downstream.

If the stream does not meet all of the above requirements, it must be safely fenced off and water provided in another way.

Ponds

The water in a pond is stagnant and so must never be used as a water supply for horses. Ponds should be fenced off as they can be dangerous – horses may get stuck in the mud, and foals, in particular, are prone to drowning in ponds.

Notes on seasonal feeding and watering

Spring
Feeding
Don't cut back hard feed suddenly. Try to reduce feed gradually and maintain as high a forage ration as required by work, stabling and grazing conditions. If you have laminitic ponies, watch out for flushes of spring grass.

If bringing a horse into work make sure that you do not introduce large amounts of concentrates rapidly and try to ensure that grazing still makes up a large proportion of his diet.

Watering
Make sure there is a good supply of clean water at all times. Repair any damage caused by a hard winter.

Summer
Feeding
During a very dry summer the grass may not grow well – attention must be paid to the horses' condition as they will not gain enough from the grass and may need additional feed and/or hay. If, on the other hand, grass is plentiful the horses may get fat and need access to grass restricted. Monitor grazing condition regularly and alter feeding as required.

Watering
The water trough must be checked frequently as horses will drink more in hot weather. Long hours of sunlight encourage algae growth so very regular cleaning is required. In addition, horses working hard during summer months will sweat a lot and may require additional electrolytes before/after work and travel.

Autumn
Feeding
Depending on the weather, the grass is not normally as abundant and starts to lose its feed value. Later in the autumn you must start feeding hay to supplement the diet and prevent the horses from losing condition.

Watch out for an autumn flush of grass, dependent on weather conditions, which could cause a bout of laminitis or alter behaviour in your horses.

When you need to introduce (or increase) concentrates, do so gradually.

Ensure that you are prepared for winter with a good stock of high-quality forage.

Watering
Watch out that fallen leaves do not block and foul the water trough. As it starts to get colder at nights, thin-skinned horses may need to be rugged up.

Winter
Feeding
By the time winter arrives the grass has a much reduced feed value – for most of the winter it may be frozen and covered in snow, or completely poached. Your

horses must receive plenty of hay and, if you are riding them regularly, short feed as well, e.g. sugar beet pulp, chaff and perhaps a low-energy coarse mix or cubes. For horses in little or no work you must ensure they are receiving an adequate supply of micronutrients (vitamins and minerals) perhaps in the form of a lick or supplement.

When feeding horses in the field, the following must be considered:

- If you have more than one horse in a field, keep them well apart at feed time to prevent bullying and fighting. It may be necessary to remove either the most timid horse or the bully to ensure that each receives the correct amount of food.

- Feed bowls should be of a design that cannot be kicked over.

- Always put out more piles of hay than the number of horses – this way every horse should have access to some hay even if they are chased off the first pile by others.

- Haynets are best avoided in fields – haynets hang lower when empty – this can be dangerous as a horse may get a foot caught. Horses who play-fight can get caught up, even in nets that are safely tied up.

Watering

In the winter the water troughs and pipes will freeze so it is important that you check these three times a day, break the ice and remove it from the trough, or carry water buckets to the field. Placing a ball in a water trough can help prevent it from freezing completely and make life easier when you come to break the ice. Horses working hard in winter will still require lost electrolyte replacement.

ITQ 9.23   **?**

Why should a stream not be used as the water supply if it has a sandy base?

ITQ 9.24   **?**

Why are ponds unsuitable as a water supply for horses?

ITQ 9.25

a. What is the main danger when using haynets in a field?

b. What is the other, safer method of giving hay to horses in a field?

ITQ 9.26

How will you ensure that horses have a constant supply of water in icy weather?

Feeding old and sick horses

Old horses

Once a horse gets to the age of 15 or 16 years he is often said to be 'aged', even though the vast majority of horses this age are still very fit and healthy and are still in full work. Many horses won't need a significant change in their diet until they reach their late teens or twenties but this does vary from individual to individual and some horses might need additional nutritional support earlier than others.

As horses age some of their nutritional requirements alter, meaning that greater quantities of some vitamins and minerals are needed in order for them to maintain optimal condition. This is because the digestive tracts of older horses are less efficient at absorbing vitamins and minerals than the digestive tracts of younger horses.

The teeth of older horses can become very long and show significant signs of decay. A horse with a very 'old' mouth will be less able to chew his food easily prior to swallowing it and, if fed on a diet of very long fibre and hard concentrate feeds, he will be unable to get the full benefit of his diet. This is because horses rely on their teeth to break down the food mechanically before it reaches their lower digestive tract, in order that the lower part of the digestive tract can complete the process of digestion effectively. If mastication in the mouth is limited, the lower part of the digestive tract is unable to process some elements of the diet (particularly long fibre and cereals) and these pass through the horse relatively undigested. In these circumstances it is best to give an old horse a soft diet which requires little chewing before it is swallowed – cubes can be soaked to produce a feed of soft consistency which will be well digested. It will also be useful to feed soaked hay and, if the horse has very poor teeth, replace a proportion of the hay ration with short fibre like chaff as this will be more easily chewed and digested.

Older horses who still have good teeth and no problems chewing won't necessarily need soaked feeds. However, you will still need to take into account that an older horse might need additional quantities of some vitamins and minerals. Many feed companies make diets specifically designed for older horses which take all of these circumstances into account and provide a balanced diet – they are easy to obtain and provide a problem-free solution to feeding the older horse. However, healthy older horses in good physical condition can be fed a very similar diet as any adult horse which can be supplemented with a broad-spectrum vitamin and mineral supplements to take into account their increased requirements for these substances.

As safeguards when feeding older horses, ensure that their dentition is checked regularly and that any issues arising are dealt with promptly to prevent loss of condition. Also, monitor condition constantly and try to alter feeding as soon as you notice any change. Investigate any loss of appetite immediately and rectify the problem.

Sick horses

In order to avoid the digestive disturbances associated with rapid changes in diet, and depending on the nature of the illness, sick horses should be fed a diet close to the one that they normally receive when healthy. There is, however, one important change that does need to be made as soon as a horse is confined on box rest. Depending on his condition, a horse who is to be confined should be fed a lower-energy (non-heating) diet, i.e. low starch. This means cutting out much, if not all, of the cereal content of the horse's diet. If confined to the stable and still fed his normal working diet many problems could occur. These include:

- Equine rhabdomyolysis syndrome (azoturia)

- Lymphangitis

- Laminitis

- Weight gain and bad behaviour

Impaction colic can occur from eating straw bedding combined with the lack of exercise. Dust-extracted shavings or paper can be used as bedding to prevent the horse from eating it.

Feeding good-quality meadow hay or high-fibre haylage will keep the horse occupied, aid digestion and will not 'hot him up'. Meadow hay is easier to digest than seed hay.

Some advocate feeding hay from a net with small holes as it will take longer for the horse to pull the hay through, so helping to occupy him. There are, however, disadvantages to using haynets; the horse is eating in an unnatural position as the incisors do not align with each other when the head is raised. This affects the chewing action and the way in which the teeth wear. Having the head low, as when eating from the ground, encourages the clearance of bacteria and fluid from the lungs. This clearance is greatly reduced if the horse has his head raised for long periods. If practical, grazing in hand is beneficial to the horse for this reason, as well as providing a good source of forage.

All hay should be as dust-free as possible, especially if the horse has a dust allergy. Hay should be steamed for 40–60 minutes or soaked for 20 minutes before feeding. If feeding a haylage product, choose a high-fibre, non-heating type. Fibre can also be provided through feeding alfalfa (a highly nutritious hay made from lucerne) or chopped hay. There are many types of chopped hay products, some of which have vitamin and mineral additives that can be beneficial to the sick horse. Chopped hay is also easier than long hay to chew and digest.

Horses recovering from colic surgery can be fed small handfuls of picked (not mown) grass. Once the horse is able to leave his stable he can be led in hand for a pick of grass.

Warm bran mashes are non-heating, palatable to an 'off colour' horse and easily digested. Add limestone flour to boost calcium levels. If a laxative effect is needed, add a tablespoon of Epsom salts. (Although bear in mind that not all horses like the taste of Epsom salts.) Alternatively, soak non-heating cubes in hot water to make a nutritionally balanced mash. Feed manufacturers produce compound feeds specifically for the recuperating horse so it is easy to feed a balanced and safe diet.

If a horse is not keen to eat, try offering a tasty treat such as sliced apples or carrots. Some horses enjoy molasses and freshly pulled grass. Soaked sugar beet pulp improves the palatability of feeds, is non-heating, aids digestion and can reduce the risk of impaction, especially if fed slightly 'sloppy'. Feeding well-soaked, sloppy sugar beet can be a useful way of getting fluid into a sick horse.

If the horse does not eat his food, remove it from the stable. Never leave uneaten food in the stable as it soon turns rancid and attracts flies and vermin. Offer very small quantities of food – horses can often be tempted by hand feeding.

If the horse is eating well and is reasonably mobile he can be kept occupied by being fed using a feed ball, a device which he has to move around to release small quantities of food. A vitamin and mineral supplement may be needed as the horse will be eating below his normal recommended daily amount. This may be provided in the form of a stable lick if the horse is off his normal feed.

Water

Use water buckets for the sick horse so that you can monitor the amount drunk. Switch off the automatic water supply in the box but make sure the horse has seen and will use the water bucket(s). If the horse refuses to use the buckets but will use the automatic drinker then obviously you will have to stick with the drinker.

Ensure that there is a constant supply of clean, fresh 'chilled' water (water which has had a drop of hot water added to take the chill off!) A drink of icy cold water could make a sick horse feel uncomfortable, possibly leading to abdominal pain.

Change the water frequently, especially if the horse has a nasal discharge that will taint it.

Add a small amount of glucose to the drinking water to give the horse an instant source of energy and nourishment. Alternatively, electrolytes can be added to the feed or water if needed. If using electrolytes in the water, always have one bucket of plain water available to the horse so he can choose. Horses have to get used to the taste of electrolytes and not every horse will drink water with them added.

ITQ 9.27

Give three considerations to bear in mind when feeding the old horse:

1.

2.

3.

ITQ 9.28

Why is it important to alter the diet of a horse on box rest and how will you alter it?

ITQ 9.29

What considerations must be made when considering suitable bedding and forage for the horse on box rest?

ITQ 9.30

How might you tempt a sick horse who is off his feed to eat?

ITQ 9.31

What considerations are required in terms of watering the sick horse?

10 Fittening

REQUIRED SKILLS/KNOWLEDGE	Learnt, revised, practised?	Confirmed
Know how to fitten a turned away horse for light work, up to one and a half hours a day.		
• Describe a fittening regime for bringing up a horse from grass into regular work.	☐	☐
• Be aware of the health and welfare considerations when bringing up a horse from grass.	☐	☐
• Discuss feeding in relation to the fittening programme.	☐	☐
• Be aware of possible causes of concussion and strain in the ridden horse.	☐	☐
Caring for a horse after work.		
• Methods of cooling a horse off after work.	☐	☐
• Understand the importance of the care of the horse after work.	☐	☐
Know what's involved in 'roughing off' a horse.		
• Describe a suitable plan for roughing off a horse.	☐	☐

AIMS OF FITTENING

The general aim of fittening a horse is to enable him to take part in a given discipline with minimum fatigue and risk of injury.

A fitter horse should be able to work for longer before tiring, and compete without distress. The requirements for each discipline will vary, for example an Advanced dressage horse must be supremely supple and very fit but, because of the different stresses placed on the various systems of the horse and the difference in skills required, he would not necessarily be fit to compete in say, a point-to-point.

The fitness level for any particular discipline is achieved through regular exercise over a period of time. It should be noted however, that all horses, whether competing or not, need daily exercise. In the wild, horses spend their days roaming, exercising freely, resting as and when they desire. Similarly, a grass-kept horse will exercise himself in the field – although this will not be sufficient to achieve and maintain fitness for competition and/or hunting.

Reasons for daily exercise

Daily exercise is needed for the following reasons:

- Exercise promotes the circulation of body fluids within the circulatory and lymphatic systems, which helps them to function efficiently. Improved circulation promotes effective digestion and the removal of waste products (some waste products are excreted via the skin when the horse sweats).

- The respiratory system is developed, which improves the supply of oxygen to the muscles.

- The muscles respond to the stimulation of schooling and exercise, becoming supple and well developed.

- Correctly performed fittening positively alters bone density and thus strength.

- The horse will become mentally relaxed – horses who are under-exercised tend to be 'uptight' and difficult to handle. (Note that this can also apply to horses who are over-fit for purpose.)

Fitness for purpose

Before carrying out any assessment of fitness you need to know 'fit for what?' As mentioned in the introductory text, requirements vary between the disciplines. A horse could be perfectly fit enough to go unaffiliated showjumping but not fit enough to go hunting or eventing.

The following list of work types is set out in an approximate ascending scale of fitness.

Lowest level of fitness	Light hacking and schooling (regular work)
	Non-jumping showing classes
	Riding Club dressage competition
	Showing classes involving jumping (such as Working Hunter)
	Riding Club showjumping competition
	Showjumping up to Foxhunter level
	Hunter trials
	Riding Club one-day events

Showjumping up to Grade A

32km (20mile) long distance rides

British Eventing (BE) one-day events – Novice

Advanced dressage competition

Hunting three times a fortnight

BE one-day events – Intermediate to Advanced

BE two-day events – Novice, Intermediate

Highest level of fitness BE/FEI three-day events – Novice, Intermediate, Advanced

Flat racing

Point-to-pointing and National Hunt racing

FACTORS THAT INFLUENCE A FITTENING PROGRAMME

When planning a fittening programme and calculating the time needed to achieve the required level of fitness, you need to know the date of your first main event. All fittening programmes aim to increase performance through a combination of correctly balanced work and feeding to condition the horse correctly and bring the unfit horse to full fitness. In order for a programme to succeed it must be well planned, with adequate time set aside for each phase.

The type of event (discipline and level) you are aiming for has another important influence, beyond mere timescale. Before you can begin to plan your fitness programme you need to assess *how fit* you want the horse to be. There are no real benefits in having a horse over-fit, especially for the less demanding disciplines. If over-fit, horses tend to take longer to settle down at a competition, can be difficult to handle and need more work to keep them calm.

When fittening horses, an important factor to consider is that of *individuality*. Every horse is different and the fitness programme must suit each individual horse. Experienced trainers have their own individual methods of working horses towards an event.

When designing the programme, the following factors must be taken into account:

Time of year. If a horse has been out on lush grass and is overweight, he is likely to take longer to get fit than if he had rested over the winter, rugged up, partially stabled and receiving short feeds.

Age. It is more difficult and potentially damaging to achieve full fitness of a very young horse, since youngsters are physically immature. Older horses may have problems associated with soundness.

Type and temperament. The keen, lighter, Thoroughbred type will be easier to get fit than a lazy, heavier sort.

Soundness. Any problem associated with soundness will result in much more time being needed, particularly with the early slow work.

Level of training. Other factors being equal, a horse who has already been fully fit once before will be easier to get fit again.

Type of competition. As mentioned, the type of competition will affect how fit the horse needs to be. It will take longer to get a horse fit for a three-day event than to get one ready for a Riding Club one-day event.

Assessing fitness in an unfamiliar horse

If you are trying to assess the fitness of a horse unfamiliar to you (whether a horse from the sales, a new livery or a potential purchase) it is important to make note of the following:

- Muscle tone – a horse who is reported to be in full exercise should show a good degree of correct muscle tone; if the tone is incorrect or lacking it may indicate the horse is not in work or is working incorrectly.

- Shoeing status – a horse in full work will normally be shod all round; if the horse is unshod you need to ascertain why (some horses do work unshod).

- Evidence of clipping and trimming – a horse in full work in winter will require clipping – look out for this when assessing the horse.

- General demeanour, weight, coat and skin condition of the horse – a fit horse will usually be relaxed and regular grooming will promote a healthy and supple coat and skin.

ITQ 10.1

Arrange these disciplines in an ascending order of fitness levels:

a. Riding Club One-day Event

b. Working Hunter Show Classes

c. Point-to-pointing

d. BE Novice One-day Event

e. Riding Club Dressage

ITQ 10.2

List four ways in which daily exercise alters the systems of a horse:

1.

2.

3.

4.

Pre-fitting checks

Before starting to get a horse fit, the following checks should be made.

Feet. The horse should in most normal cases be shod, with stud holes if necessary. Whilst it is possible to work some horses unshod, the majority of horses eventually become footsore and loss of grip is a problem riding unshod horses on hard ground.

Vaccinations. These must be given as protection against tetanus and equine influenza. Many competitive societies demand proof of vaccination against the latter before allowing the horse to be registered. Check closing/ballot dates for the first events and make sure you allow enough time to get the horse vaccinated and registered.

Worming. A worm burden will prevent the horse from utilising his food to maximum benefit, and may have other serious repercussions. All horses should be wormed regularly in accordance with the drug manufacturer's instructions and veterinary advice, if necessary.

Teeth. These must be rasped annually. The molars develop sharp edges as a result of wear. These sharp edges can affect a horse's ability to chew his food and may also lead to bit evasions.

A BASIC FITTENING PROGRAMME

Bringing the horse up from grass

Most competition and riding horses have a break, spending either some or all of the time at grass. Hunters have their break in the summer months and event horses tend to have their long rest in the winter. The duration of a horse's holiday depends upon the intensity and pressure of his competitive/hunting career. A horse used for riding activities and gentle hacking will only need a short break from time to time, if he needs a rest at all.

A horse who has hunted three times a fortnight for the whole season will benefit from a complete break of approximately 3 months at grass in the summer.

Assuming that the horse has been out at grass for some time, we'll discuss how to bring him up in preparation for a fitness programme.

This programme of bringing the horse gradually from a grass-kept state to being stabled allows for a period of adjustment. It needn't take very long and the amount of time taken will depend very much on individual circumstances. As an approximate guide, 7–10 days should be adequate but the longer he has been on holiday, the longer the period of adjustment required. This period allows for the horse to adapt both mentally and physically to the changes in regime.

Reintroducing stabling

It is possible to keep horses in work and turned out permanently. However, for various reasons, many owners choose or have to keep the horse stabled at least some of the time. If the horse is to be stabled, bring him in for a few hours daily to help him get used to being confined again. Always ensure there is ample fresh air by keeping the top door open. Use dust-free bedding and soaked hay or haylage to prevent coughing. Gradually increase the time he is stabled until he is only being turned out during the day. All working horses should be turned out daily where possible.

Introducing exercise

Start with 20 minutes at walk to accustom the horse to being handled, gently stimulate heart and breathing rates and tone up the muscles. Check for signs of rubbing caused by the bit, saddle, girth or boots. If the horse has not been in work he will be in soft condition and more prone to rubbing.

As exercise is introduced you may notice the horse coughing from time to time. The most likely cause of this is the stable environment, i.e. dust and spores from bedding and hay, which is why is it better to keep horses out as much as possible. Some horses cough as their workload increases as they start to use a greater part of the lung tissue, including some tissue that has not been used for some time. If a dust-free management regime is followed and the cough persists or is accompanied by any signs of ill-health it should be investigated, as coughing is a sign of inflammation and/or infection within the airways.

Introducing short feed

While the horse is stabled he should have soaked hay or haylage to provide roughage and prevent boredom. As work is introduced, he'll need to be fed concentrates. The amount will depend upon the size and type of horse and his condition. Remember to introduce all changes gradually to allow the digestive system a period of adjustment. Keep the amount fed in relation to the amount of work being done.

Starting grooming

If working a grass-kept horse, he can have minimal attention in terms of grooming. His feet must be picked out daily and, when he's to be exercised, the saddle and bridle areas must be brushed clean to prevent chafing. As he spends more time stabled, the grooming can be increased. He may also need clipping and trimming. If it's cold, he'll need to be rugged up.

Continue to watch out for saddle sores and/or girth galls. As mentioned the horse may be more prone to rub injuries as his skin is initially unused to the saddle or girth. With care and good management it should be possible to avoid these injuries.

> **ITQ 10.3** ?
>
> What preparatory checks will you make before initiating a fittening programme?

Weeks 1 and 2

The unfit horse will start off in 'soft' condition, i.e. his muscles will lack tone, his lungs will be incapable of working to full capacity, his heart will not be at its most efficient and he may be overweight.

All the early work should be done at walk, usually along the road. If there are suitable tracks to ride around, so much the better, as roads are not the safest of places. Unfortunately however, there is often no alternative.

Walk exercise increases the blood supply throughout the body, improving the supply of oxygen to the muscles. The gradual increase in circulatory function ensures that the muscles are conditioned and toned in preparation for the harder work to follow over the next few weeks.

All the systems affected by fittening and training work, i.e. circulatory, respiratory and muscular systems, are developed gradually without being overstressed. This preparation reduces the risk of injury, especially if carried out on a flat, level surface (rough, uneven ground should be avoided).

The initial 20 minutes a day should be gradually increased until, by the end of the second week, the horse is being walked for at least 1½ hours a day. As the walking exercise progresses, so body fat is used up and the muscles begin to tone up and develop – note that fat is *not* converted into muscle.

The horse should be asked to walk actively and in a balanced manner to gain maximum benefit from the exercise and reduce the risk of injury.

Some horses, after a long holiday, feel extremely exuberant, making it unsafe to mount up and attempt to walk around the lanes. In such cases, it is better to lunge quietly on a good surface and let the horse use up some energy without the rider on board. Change the rein regularly to reduce the risk of muscle or tendon strain. Once the horse has settled (and this may take several days) mounted walk work can safely begin. Alternatively, if a horse-walker is available, start the horse off with 5 minutes a day on each rein, building up to a total of 20–30 minutes in a good strong walk.

Weeks 3 and 4

Begin suppling work at walk in the school and introduce short spells of slow trotting. Approximately 20 minutes schooling before or after 1 hour's exercise, three times a week, should be sufficient.

The horse may be lunged (in walk and trot only) two or three times a week, avoiding very small circles, which place strain on the limbs. Lunge sessions must be kept short – 10 minutes initially, building up to approximately 20.

Introduce steady trotting on good going only and, if possible, slightly uphill. Once the horse is able to trot up a long slope without getting out of breath he may begin slow canter work.

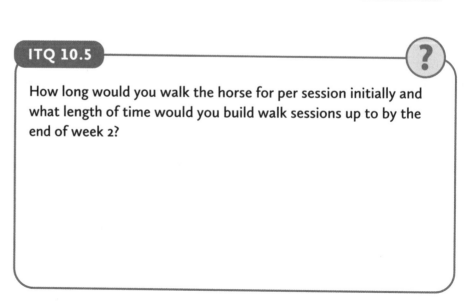

ITQ 10.4   **?**

Why is the early walk work so important?

ITQ 10.5   **?**

How long would you walk the horse for per session initially and what length of time would you build walk sessions up to by the end of week 2?

Weeks 5 and 6

Short spells of canter can now be introduced while schooling or hacking – avoid cantering on tight circles initially, and on very hard or deep ground. Keep to good going only to reduce the risk of concussion or strain. Keep the pace steady and start off cantering for very short periods (1 or 2 minutes). Check the horse's respiratory rate after each canter – if he is not blowing, the next canter can be a bit stronger and maintained for slightly longer.

The horse may be keen to go faster than required but you must remember that his limbs, heart and wind are not yet ready; he must therefore be well restrained. If he is very strong, it may be necessary to make temporary changes to tack, e.g. use a pelham bit for extra control.

Don't canter on the lunge as the horse's muscles and tendons are not yet prepared for the extra strain this would exert.

It may be useful to enter a dressage competition to help gauge your schooling progress and give you an idea of what to work on at home. Gymnastic jumping can also begin – gridwork is an excellent means of suppling the horse.

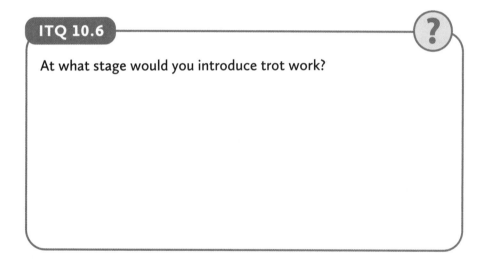

ITQ 10.6

At what stage would you introduce trot work?

Weeks 7 and 8

Four schooling sessions per week should be sufficient. This work can be made interesting by interspersing it with lungeing, gridwork and hacking.

Build up the canter work when out hacking – make it stronger than a school working canter and continue to check the horse's breathing after each canter to determine whether he is gaining fitness and ready to do more. The horse should now be ready to take part in a showjumping competition.

ITQ 10.7 ?

At what stage would you introduce canter work and how will you do this?

Avoiding potential injuries

It is very important, especially in the earlier stages, to be prudent in respect of choosing appropriate ground on which to work. Excessive trotting, cantering and jumping on hard ground can cause concussion, which can lead to injuries such as sore shins, splints and inflamed joints, tendons (tendonitis) and ligaments (e.g. suspensory desmitis.) Working in deep or uneven going can increase the risk of strain injuries, and other injuries such as those caused by brushing and overreaching.

Care of the horse after exercise

After any fitness work or schooling session it is important that the horse is 'warmed down'. Walking for approximately 10 minutes, either in hand or ridden, should allow the horse's breathing to return to normal and the heart rate to lower. The girth can be loosened one or two holes. He will start to cool down during this time too. He should be walked until his breathing is back to his base rate, i.e. he has stopped blowing and breathing heavily.

Always pick the feet out on return from work. Check the condition of the shoes, and for injury. Feel the horse's tendons so any heat or swelling can be detected.

In hot weather

Your main aim is to cool the horse down. Stand the horse in the shade if possible and untack. Wash down with cold water. This can be done with sponges or using a hose. Keep scraping the water off the horse's coat as this promotes effective cooling. Cold water can be applied all over the horse. Make sure you wash off all sweat marks and

SAFETY TIP

▶ It is essential to ensure that you thoroughly scrape water off the horse as if it is left on the coat in hot weather the water will retain the heat and the horse will stay hotter for longer.

remember to wash around the head area (carefully), between the fore and hind legs and under the girth and belly area.

Once the horse is fully scraped down he can be turned out, where he will probably have a good roll. If not being turned out he can be left in the stable without a sheet (as it is a hot day). Once dry, he can be strapped.

ITQ 10.8

What type of injuries can excessive trotting, cantering and jumping lead to?

In cold weather

The horse is likely to be cool but if he is sweaty he can be washed off using warm water to remove all sweat marks. Don't make the horse excessively wet as this would increase the risk of chilling. Scrape all water off very quickly and if the horse has a thick coat, rub him down briskly with a towel. Next, put on a cooler-style rug. These draw moisture away from the horse's coat and so help him to dry more quickly and reduce the risk of chilling.

If you have washed the legs, rub them briskly with a towel and apply stable bandages to help them dry and keep the horse warm. Pay particular attention to the heels – they may crack if left wet. Dry them and apply petroleum jelly.

Once dry, strap the horse and put on a dry rug. If the horse is dry on return from work brush the sweat marks off – don't make him wet.

ITQ 10.9 ?

How will you care for the horse after work:

a. In hot weather?

b. In cold weather?

ROUGHING OFF

If a horse is to be given a break at grass after a competitive season this is frequently termed 'roughing off'. Horses in normal light work don't really need to have a holiday as such; it is generally competition horses and hunters who may be given a break at the end of the season.

Depending on the time of year, roughing off normally involves preparing the horse for prolonged periods of turnout at grass. Workload, concentrate feeds and grooming are reduced then stopped, forage rations and the amount of time spent out at grass increased. Ideally, changes should be made over approximately a two-week period to give the horse time to adjust, but this is just a guide and the time taken to rough off will vary according to individual circumstances.

Some people then choose to leave the horses out 24 hours a day, which is ideal for the horse. This should not, however, mean that the horse is simply abandoned in the field; periodic checks should be made to ensure the horse's welfare. Depending on the individual horse, shoes may be removed or left on.

11 Principles of Stabling and Grassland Care for Horses

REQUIRED SKILLS/KNOWLEDGE	Learnt, revised, practised?	Confirmed
Requirements for stable design and construction.		
• Be conversant with stable design and dimensions for horses and ponies.	☐	☐
• Describe materials for stable construction.	☐	☐
• Understand the need for good ventilation and how this may be provided.	☐	☐
• Appreciate the importance of good drainage and how this may be provided.	☐	☐
• Be able to describe various stable fixtures and fittings.	☐	☐
Behaviour and welfare of stabled horses.		
• Appreciate the effect that stabling has on the horse's natural lifestyle.	☐	☐
• Describe how a new horse might be accommodated.	☐	☐
• Recognise nervous/undesirable behaviour in stabled horses.	☐	☐
• Know how to handle nervous/undesirable behaviour in stabled horses.	☐	☐
Grassland care and pasture maintenance.		
• Know what essentials and features make for ideal horse pasture.	☐	☐
• Know how to go about maintaining good-quality grazing.	☐	☐
• Be familiar with plants that are poisonous to horses.	☐	☐
Behaviour and welfare of horses at grass.		
• Understand the causes of unsettled behaviour in horses at grass.	☐	☐
• Explain why some horses can be difficult to catch.	☐	☐

STABLE CONSTRUCTION

Stables must be:

- Solidly built.

- Draught-free.

- Well ventilated.

- Light and airy.

- Waterproof.

- Facing away from prevailing winds.

- Built on solid foundations or, if sectional, built on a concrete base.

- Free of protrusions, (nails, etc.), which could injure a horse.

- Smartly built and well maintained.

Dimensions

The following are minimum stable size requirements:

Pony under 13hh	3m x 3m (10ft x 10ft)
Pony under 14.2hh	3m x 3.65m (10ft x 12ft)
Horse up to 16hh	3.65m x 3.65m (12ft x 12ft)
Horse over 16hh	3.65m x 4.25m (12ft x 14ft)

Walls should be at least 3.65m (12ft) high. If sloping, the lowest point must be at least 3m (10ft) high.

Walls

Bricks make good solid walls but can be expensive.

Breeze blocks are relatively inexpensive and make wall construction very quick. The main problem with them, however, is that a horse leaning and rubbing on the wall can weaken it. The builders must take steps to strengthen the walls by using metal rods which are set in the concrete floor and go up through the breeze blocks.

Wood can be a less expensive option, depending on its quality, but must be tough enough to withstand a kick. Walls should be lined with wooden kicking boards up to a minimum height of 1.2m (4ft), for extra strength and security.

The roof

The roof should slope to allow rainwater to run off to the guttering. Ensure that adequate guttering and downpipes are used. Ideally the downpipes should lead to a drain as opposed to a water butt, which may overflow. Guttering must be kept clear of leaves and debris if it is to work effectively.

The roof should be durable, noiseless, non-flammable and maintain an even temperature in all weathers. (Insulation in the roof will help maintain an even temperature.)

Roofs must be very secure to withstand gale-force winds. Ideally there should be an overhang of at least 1m (3ft 3in) to give extra protection against the elements.

Suitable roofing materials include **tiles** and **slates** which, although they may break, come loose and leak, are excellent with regular maintenance. Stable suppliers offer a range of roofing sheets, made to look like tiles and slates. These are convenient to use and look smart.

Roofing felt is a popular means of waterproofing a wooden, pitched roof.

Corrugated plastic maintains an even temperature all year and is fairly quiet. Clear plastic must not be used as it becomes too hot in summer.

Corrugated iron gets too hot in the summer, is cold in the winter and is also very noisy in the rain. It rusts and looks untidy – it is therefore not suitable for use.

Thatch is also unsuitable because of the fire risk and maintenance needs.

Flooring

All flooring should be:

- Non-slippery.

- Impervious to moisture.

- Hard-wearing and not strike cold.

The floor should have a downward slope of 1 in 60 towards the rear of the stable, leading to an external drain. (Externally, the gutter leading to the drain should have a 1 in 40 slope.) There should be an open drain, protected with a grid, outside the stable. Poor drainage in a stable means that urine will sit on the floor rather than drain away, making the stable smell and the bedding a lot wetter, which can lead to problems with the horse's hooves, e.g. thrush. Poor drainage will lead to additional costs in bedding materials and make mucking out more difficult. Also, when you wash the stable floor, it is difficult to get rid of the water.

The most common flooring material used is **concrete**, which is roughened to prevent the horse from slipping. A herringbone pattern set in the concrete aids drainage.

Cobblestones and **stable bricks** are sometimes used. They do, however, wear smooth and become slippery or uneven. **Compressed chalk** can be slippery when wet, but otherwise fulfils all criteria.

Rubber matting is now more widely used as flooring and is designed to be used with minimal or no bedding materials.

ITQ 11.1

Give the minimum stable dimensions for the following horses and ponies:

12.2hh pony

14.1hh pony

15.3hh horse

16.2hh horse

ITQ 11.2

a. What is the main disadvantage of using breeze blocks to construct stable walls?

b. What can be done to prevent this problem?

Doors

Stable doors must be at least 1.2m (4ft) wide and a minimum of 2.1m (7ft) high. The door should be in two halves, opening outwards. Keeping the top door open at all times allows the horse to look out and have plenty of fresh air.

The bottom door must have a top bolt, preferably of a design that a horse cannot undo, and a kick bolt at the bottom.

The top of the bottom door should be protected with a metal strip to prevent the horse from chewing the wood. Horses who spend a lot of time stabled often rub their teeth on the bottom door, wearing off the paint and ruining the door itself. Stable doors can be purchased with metal panels covering the top half of the bottom door to protect against this problem.

A stable door should always open outwards so that you can still get in should the horse become cast in the stable.

Fixtures and fittings

The general rule is, the fewer fixtures there are in a stable, the less likely the horse is to injure himself.

Tying rings

There should be a tying ring at the horse's eye level and another just above his eye level for tying up the haynet. The rings should be very securely fitted into the wall and must have a **weak link** (a loop of baler twine) for tying the horse to. Should the horse pull back, the weak link will break. The ring must not come out of the wall or, worse still, bring some of the wall down with it. The haynet is tied directly to the ring – that does *not* require a weak link.

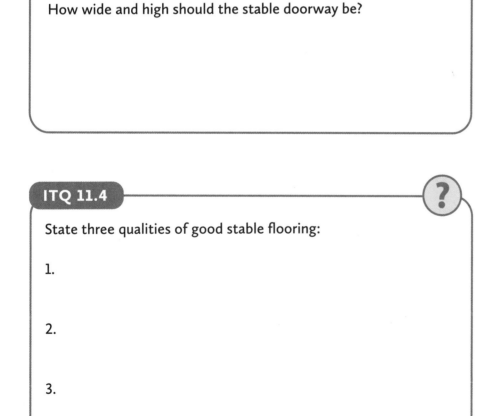

ITQ 11.3 ?

How wide and high should the stable doorway be?

ITQ 11.4 ?

State three qualities of good stable flooring:

1.

2.

3.

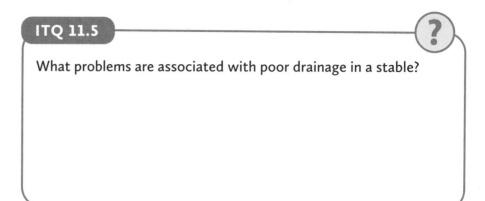

ITQ 11.5

What problems are associated with poor drainage in a stable?

Mangers and feed bowls

There are many different types of manger available and although chest-height mangers are popular, it is worth considering that nature intended the horse to eat from ground level. Therefore a bowl on the ground is acceptable.

Feed bowls should be hard-wearing, difficult to knock over, easy to clean and free of sharp edges which could injure the horse. Heavy-duty rubber or plastic bowls fulfil these criteria and can be removed from the stable once the horse has eaten. The main disadvantage to leaving bowls on the ground in the stable once the horse has finished is that he may tread on and flatten the bowl. It may also end up in the middle of his bed, full of dung.

If the horse is prone to kicking his feed bowl over and putting his foot in his food, a fitted wall manger should be used. It should be fitted in one of the corners, on the same wall as the door at chest height. If the manger is fitted in a corner on the far side of the stable and you need to enter the stable, you will have to walk behind the hindquarters of a horse who has just been fed, which could be dangerous. (Some horses become protective of their feed and kick out).

Metal-framed feed bowl holders should never be left empty in the stable as there is a risk that a rolling horse could get a leg caught.

Another useful type of manger is that which hooks over the stable door but bear in mind that an inquisitive horse, whilst eating, may keep looking out at things going on in the yard and spill more than he eats.

Water provision

Horses should have a constant supply of clean, fresh water. It can be provided in **heavy duty rubber buckets** or by using **automatic drinkers**. Cheap plastic buckets are not suitable as they tend to split and can cause eye injuries.

All water buckets and bowls must be kept clean and free of hay, straw and dung. Buckets and bowls must be scrubbed and rinsed daily. To prevent buckets from being kicked over, stand them in two old car tyres. Alternatively you can attach a clip to the wall and hold the buckets in place by hooking the handles through the clips.

Automatic waterers are widely used as they save labour. The main disadvantages are:

● You cannot monitor the amount that a horse is drinking.

- The pipes can freeze up in the winter.

- The bowls can become clogged with food and hay.

- If the bowl becomes unlevel, for example as a result of a horse rubbing against it, the bowl overflows and the bedding can get soaked.

- The bowls are quite small and take time to refill – this can discourage a thirsty horse from drinking his fill.

Lighting

Ideally, stables should be naturally light and airy to provide a pleasant environment for the horse. Electric lighting will be needed in all stables, and outside lights should be fitted around the yard.

All electric light fittings and wires must be well maintained to minimise the fire risk. They must be encased in approved casings to protect them from vermin and damp, as well as to stop the horse chewing the wires.

Bulbs must be protected by a metal grille and be kept clean and free of cobwebs and dust to reduce the fire risk. Strip lights must also be kept clean and should be high enough to prevent a horse from touching them.

A window provides natural light (see also Ventilation, below).

Ventilation

The object of ventilation is to change the air in the stable frequently, thus keeping it pure and clean. If a stable is not well ventilated the air becomes stale and warm. As the horse breathes out he exhales **carbon dioxide. Ammonia** vapours rise in the warm air from urine in the bedding. This air needs to escape and be replaced with clean, fresh air.

Stale air and a dusty atmosphere will affect the respiratory system and interfere with the horse's fitness. If the stable is dusty, he will be prone to coughing. The horse is kept warm with rugs and blankets if needed, never by shutting the top door or limiting the amount of fresh air in a stable.

In the summer, a poorly ventilated stable will be hot and stuffy. This can lead to the horse becoming overheated and distressed. In hot climates additional ventilation can be provided through the use of electric fans.

In addition to leaving the top door permanently open, ventilation can be provided by a window. The window should be on the same side of the stable as the door to prevent a cross draught. The **'Sheringham' window** opens inwards, thus directing the air upwards and not directly onto the horse's back. All glass should be protected by a mesh or grille.

Ventilation may also be provided by slatted **louvre boards** set at an angle in the ridge at the top of the wall. The angle stops rain and snow from entering through the gaps. **Ventilation cowls** and **tubes** can be fitted in the roof. They are designed to draw warm, stale air upwards and allow it to escape.

Draughts must be considered as distinct from useful ventilation – if a horse is left standing in a draughty, ill-ventilated stable he will be in danger of catching a chill.

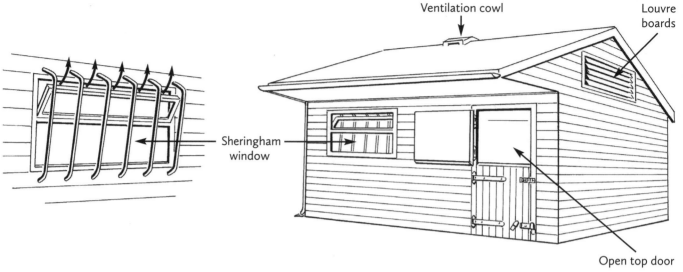

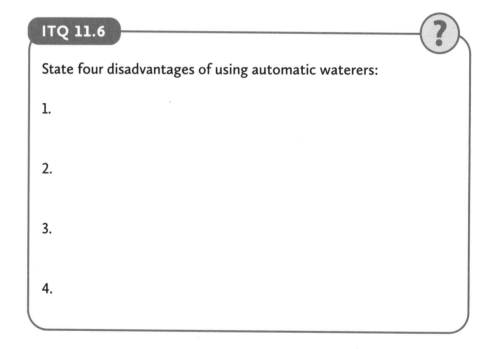

11.1 Means of providing ventilation

ITQ 11.6 ?

State four disadvantages of using automatic waterers:

1.

2.

3.

4.

ITQ 11.7 ?

What affects the quality of air in a stable?

ITQ 11.8

What are the effects of poor stable ventilation on the horse?

IN-TEXT ACTIVITY

Using magazines and equestrian suppliers' catalogues as sources of information, select three different types of stable made by different manufacturers.

Compare the costs and styles of each.

EXAM TIP

In the exam you may be asked to comment on the construction and design of the stables at the examination centre. To help you prepare, make observations about every stable you see at home or in other yards, noting good and bad points. Think about points you would keep, and those you would change.

BARN STABLING

The conventional yard design involves stables built around a square yard. Another method of stabling is the **American Barn System.** This involves loose boxes, tack rooms, feed stores etc. being fitted into a large barn so everything is under one roof. The barn can be either purpose-built, or an existing building modified.

When planning a barn conversion, particular attention must be paid to the ventilation. As the horses share the same air space, the barn must be very well ventilated. It should be light and airy to provide a pleasant environment for the horses and staff.

There must be adequate tap points and fire-fighting equipment in the barn. The internal stable doors may be on rollers to avoid having doors opening into the central alleyway.

The following table compares the pros and cons of barn stabling and conventional stabling.

Conventional yard	Barn stabling
The horses can see the activities of the yard. The horses may feel more isolated in a conventional stable where the walls are high and solid and their view of the other horses may be restricted.	The horses can look up the central alleyway if they can reach out over the top door. They can generally see each other through the bars, although it is not normally as interesting for the horses as they are looking at the same alleyway all day. Some barn designs allow for a stable door opening onto the outside wall. The horses can then look outside.
Each horse has his own air space within his stable. Dust from one stable should not invade the airspace of another. It is easier to isolate airborne viruses.	Horses share the same air space. Dust may travel from one stable to another which can be a problem with horses suffering from a dust allergy. Airborne viruses will also spread more easily.
Air space may be restricted, especially in smaller stables. This can aggravate the respiratory system of a horse suffering from a dust allergy.	Each horse has plenty of air space which, provided it is not dusty, is better for horses suffering from a dust allergy.
Staff have to work outside in all weathers. Pleasant in summer months, not so in winter.	Staff are protected from the elements – pleasant in winter but not so in summer.
Everything is spread around the yard so staff have to walk further, e.g. to the tack room, feed room, etc.	Everything is under one roof, reducing the amount of walking.
It is more expensive to construct individual stables.	Barn stabling can provide an economical means of stabling, especially if using an existing barn.
Fire and smoke will spread slowly through individual brick-built stables. Escape from external stables should be straightforward.	Fire and smoke will spread more quickly through wooden boxes sharing the same air space. The central alleyway must be wide enough to facilitate escape. Externally opening doors in each box will aid safety. There should be main doors at each end of the barn through which horses can escape.

Table 11.1 Comparisons between conventional and barn stabling

NERVOUS BEHAVIOUR IN HORSES

When horses are new to an environment, or very young, they may be nervous and easily upset. Nervous and young horses should be handled regularly by experienced people in a quiet, confident manner to gain their trust and respect.

A horse new to a yard should be stabled away from, but in sight of, the other horses for the first 10 days to prevent the spread of any infectious condition that the horse may be suffering from. He must also be turned out in a separate paddock although, again, this should be within sight of other horses. Once this isolation period is over he can be introduced to the main yard. Generally horses settle down quite quickly as they become accustomed to the new routine and surroundings. However, the time it takes for a new or young horse to settle into a yard will depend on the horse's temperament; each horse must be treated as an individual.

Stereotypical behaviour ('stable vices')

When caring for horses you must take into account their instinctive behaviour. Horses are naturally gregarious nomadic, grazing and browsing herbivores. By confining a horse to a stable we take away his opportunities to express these natural behaviours, which can be stressful to the horse.

Unlike horses in the wild who deal with physical stress with instinctive reactions, the domesticated horse has no way in which to deal with the mental stress inflicted upon him. As a result he may well develop stereotypical or abnormal behaviour patterns, formerly referred to as 'stable vices'.

The majority of abnormal behaviours are the direct result of boredom and social frustration caused by long periods of isolation and confinement in the loose box. The individual behaviours, and specific strategies to alleviate them, are discussed below. However, bearing in mind that prevention is better than cure, the following practices are useful in helping to counteract boredom and reduce mental stress in the stabled horse:

- Turn the horse out daily with others for long periods. If this is not possible, lead out and graze in hand.

- Divide the daily exercise into two lots. This is normally only possible if the yard has a large number of staff, or you are only dealing with one horse.

- Keep the work varied – a variety of hacking, schooling and competing will all make life more interesting for the horse.

- In a large yard a horse-walker can provide a means of exercising horses and getting them out of their stables. Whilst this cannot be a substitute proper work and turning out, it is better than nothing.

- Divide up the feeds to adhere to the 'little and often' rule of feeding. Eating helps alleviate boredom.

- Ensure a constant supply of good quality hay or haylage. Use a haynet with small holes so it takes longer for the horse to eat his ration.

- Provide a salt or mineral lick.

- Stable the horse in a position from where he can see other horses and all the yard activities.

- Stable mirrors have been proven to reduce separation anxiety and reduce the horse's desire to box-walk and weave.

- Provide some sort of toy that the horse can play with. For example, a horse ball – a ball specially designed for horses to play with. Also on the market is the Passifier – a rotating device which is attached to the door. It has a flavoured wheel in the centre that will encourage the horse to 'play'.

While these strategies should significantly reduce the chance of stereotypical behaviour developing, the possibility remains that some such behaviour may still arise in a particularly neurotic individual and, of course, it is always possible that a newcomer to the yard may have some such behaviour already ingrained. We should therefore look at the individual stereotypies to see what threats they may pose to a horse's well-being, and what steps can be taken to minimise their impact.

Crib-biting and wind-sucking

Crib-biters take hold of any projecting object such as the top of the stable door, ledge, or paddock railings and gulp in air. A crib-biter's teeth wear down more quickly than normal, and therefore the tables may give the appearance of an older mouth. A wind-sucker will arch his neck and gulp in air, usually without taking hold of anything.

These are very serious behavioural problems constituting an unsoundness, and must be declared if the horse is being sold. The swallowing of air may cause colic and loss of condition.

These are habits which cannot usually be broken, but they can, to some degree, be controlled.

Control

- The most important course of action is to alleviate boredom and reduce confinement stress as described above.

- Painting exposed woodwork with creosote, or an anti-chew paste such as Cribox may discourage a crib-biter from taking hold. The main disadvantage is that everything and everybody tends to get covered in the sticky paste, and some horses seem to develop a liking for the taste!

- An **anti-wind-sucking strap** fitted around the throat prevents the horse gulping in air. This must not be fitted too loose or to tightly and care must be taken when the horse is turned out in it, in case he gets caught up.

- Fitting a **muzzle** may help. Some are designed to allow the horse to eat and drink, but not actually catch hold of anything with his teeth.

- A **metal grille** on the top half of the stable door will allow the horse to see out but not bite the top of the door.

- Kicking-boards should end above head height to reduce the chance of crib-biting on ledges.

- The top of the lower stable door should be protected by a wide metal strip.

- Protect paddock rails with electric fencing wire along the top or on the inside of the fence line so the horse cannot reach to crib on them.

Weaving

A horse who weaves will sway or rock, transferring his bodyweight from one forefoot to the other as he swings his head and neck from side to side. This is a serious condition and again constitutes an unsoundness which must be declared if the horse is being sold. Although the problem is normally caused by boredom or nervousness, it is also a habit which may be copied by other horses.

Horses who weave put extra stress and strain on their forelimb joints – it is therefore important that the stable is well bedded down. Weavers are also prone to losing condition because the continuous swaying uses up energy.

Control

- Try to alleviate boredom where possible.

- Make sure the horse is well exercised and turned out as much as possible.

- An anti-weaving grille may help, and some horses only weave at feed times. However, a confirmed, neurotic weaver will stand behind the grille and weave.

- Some people hang plastic bottles of water either side of the doorway to discourage the practice, but it is more of a question of finding out why the horse weaves and trying to remove the cause.

ITQ 11.9   **?**

List some of the ways in which boredom can be reduced:

1.

2.

3.

4.

5.

Box-walking

Because of boredom or nervous tension the horse paces round and round the box, digging up the bedding and working himself into a sweat. Some horses will also do a similar thing out in the field when they pace up and down the fence line.

Control

● Try to turn the horse out as much as possible.

● Nervous horses may benefit from the presence of a quiet companion, or a different stable in a quieter part of the yard.

Tearing clothing

The horse chews or tears rugs and bandages either because they are irritating his skin, or because he is bored. Some horses chew tack and rugs that have been left within their reach, e.g. hung over or near a stable door. This can prove a very annoying and expensive habit.

Control

● Alleviate boredom.

● Never leave clothing unattended within the horse's reach.

● Check for skin complaints which may cause irritation.

● Dab bitter aloes on the clothing.

● Use a bib fastened to the underneath of a leather headcollar.

● Use a muzzle.

Eating droppings

This may be caused either by boredom or a craving for minerals.

Control

● Alleviate boredom – in particular ensure that the horse is turned out regularly.

● Keep the stable very clean.

● Provide a mineral lick.

● Add a mineral supplement to the feed.

Biting and snapping

This may vary from the harmless pulling of faces at the handler to the more dangerous habit of lunging from the back of the box with teeth bared and making every effort to bite. It is often caused, originally, by mismanagement, particularly in the early stages when youngsters nip playfully and are not reprimanded. The feeding of titbits, particularly over the stable door can also encourage horses to bite.

Some horses are very sensitive and thin-skinned, or even just ticklish, and dislike being groomed or rugged-up roughly. Such horses may attempt to nip in response to insensitive handling.

Control

- Treat the horse fairly and firmly, reprimanding him quickly if he actually bites you. A quick slap on the shoulder and a verbal reprimand is normally enough punishment. Beware of making the horse head-shy through slapping his muzzle. Also, bear in mind that the horse may pull back violently when reprimanded.

- Grooming and rugging-up must always be carried out carefully. When tightening girths and rollers take care not to pinch the skin.

- Do not feed titbits.

- A confirmed biter must be tied up when being groomed or rugged-up, and should either be muzzled, have a grille on the door or a notice on the stable warning people of the danger.

Kicking at walls

Horses will kick at the stable walls for a number of reasons:

- Irritability – the horse may want his feed, or to be turned out with the other horses.

- Rats and mice – many horses become upset if rats and mice run about in their bedding.

- Parasites and skin irritation – a horse with lice or other skin irritants may kick at the wall or water bucket as a means of scratching his leg.

- Boredom – the horse may simply like the noise.

Control

- Alleviate boredom.

- Pad or line the walls with rubber matting to deaden the sound.

- Put poison down for vermin, but well out of reach of the horses, dogs and other livestock so they cannot eat it.

ITQ 11.10   **?**

Give two reasons why horses may develop stereotypical behaviour:

1.

2.

ITQ 11.11

What can be done to control crib-biting?

ITQ 11.12

Give two negative effects on the horse of weaving:

1.

2.

ITQ 11.13

a. What can cause a horse to bite?

b. What can be done to prevent biting?

ITQ 11.14

a. What is the safest way to reprimand a horse for biting?

b. Why should the horse never be slapped on the head or face?

Kicking the handler or other horses

This is a very dangerous vice because of the damage a shod foot can do. Kickers must be dealt with firmly and effectively.

Causes of kicking can be the same as for biting; some horses kick out when being groomed or rugged-up because they are sensitive or very ticklish. Some kick because they have been badly treated and are using it as a form of defence because they are nervous about what they are going to be asked to do. Some horses kick because they are bad-tempered and aggressive. Horses are more prone to kick at feeding time as they instinctively need to protect their feed. In-season mares may be more prone to kicking than usual.

Control

- Try to identify why the horse is kicking out.

- Tie the horse up when grooming, tacking-up or rugging-up.

- Be considerate when grooming and use a soft brush reasonably firmly so you do not tickle the horse.

- Stay as close as possible to his body at all times to minimise the chance of a shod foot striking you.

- When grooming around the quarters and hind legs, have an assistant hold up a foreleg, and grasp the tail yourself, holding it to one side.

- Be positive in the way you speak to and handle the horse. Do not put yourself in a position where the horse can make contact with you with any of his four legs.

- When exercising a horse who is known to kick, tie a red ribbon in the top of his tail as a warning to others.

GRASSLAND PLANNING

Paddock size and siting

As an approximate guide, **one acre per horse** is the *minimum* land requirement. The ideal size would be between 0.5 and 1.5 hectares (approx. 1¼ –3¾ acres) per horse. 1 hectare is 2.471 acres; 1 acre is 0.405 hectares (ha.).

There are several factors which affect the exact amount of land needed:

- The quality of the grass. If the grass is very good and well looked after it is possible to manage on less land.

- Whether the horses are to live out permanently or to be stabled for some of the time. If the horses are to be partially stabled it is possible to manage on slightly less land.

- Whether there are any ponds or boggy patches in the field. These will need to be fenced off for safety, which will reduce the amount of land available to your horses.

- Whether you going to ride on the fields as well. Riding on fields cuts up the ground and kills the grass – this will reduce the amount of grass available for your horses to eat.

- The number of horses kept.

It is ideal to have more than the practical minimum of space per horse – the field(s) may then be divided up so that parts can be rested to allow the grass to recover and grow.

The siting of fields is usually beyond the influence of the horse owner but ideally should be:

- Near to the house or yard to provide security.

- Well away from main roads.

- As flat as possible. Fields on the side of hills put an extra strain on the horses' legs.

Soil

Soil types

There are many different types of soil – each is a complex mixture of mineral particles, air, water, decaying plant and animal debris and other organic matter. Soils are a composition of coarse and fine sands, silt, clay and humus (organic matter). The name given to the soil depends on the predominant particle.

The three main types of soil are **sand, loam** and **clay**. (The nature of the subsoil must also be taken into consideration when discussing soil types, particularly on the aspect of drainage.)

Sandy soils drain easily, thus calcium, which neutralises acidity, is washed through the sand and lost. Being light soils, they dry out earlier in the year. A major disadvantage of sandy soils is the high incidence of sand colic, which occurs when horses ingest sand as they graze. This leads to an impacted colic, which can be fatal.

Loam soils range from sandy loams through medium to clay loams and are the commonest soil types.

Clay soils are classed as 'heavy' soils, with a tendency to be alkaline. They readily become waterlogged and are unsuitable for many arable uses as the machinery cannot get onto the land. Clay soils are well suited to permanent pasture. As these soils hold water they are rich in nutrients but poorly supplied with oxygen.

Improving soil fertility

The quality and feed value of grasses grown on a paddock is dependent upon the right balance of nutrients being present in the soil. These nutrients include:

- Water (H_2O)

- Nitrogen (N)

- Phosphorus (P)

- Potassium (K)

- Calcium (Ca) – also controls soil acidity

Plant roots also need oxygen – for this reason it is important that soils do not become waterlogged.

Once the soil has been tested, deficiencies can be corrected through the application of fertilisers. This, in the northern hemisphere, is carried out either in the spring between March and April or between August and September, prior to the autumn flush of grass growth.

ITQ 11.15

In terms of grazing, what is the minimum land requirement per horse?

ITQ 11.16

What are the three main soil types?

1.

2.

3.

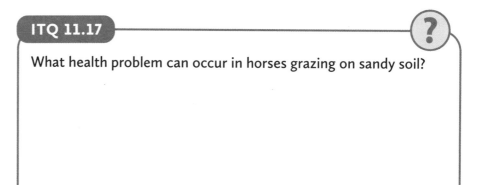

ITQ 11.17　　　　　　　　　　　　　　　　　**?**

What health problem can occur in horses grazing on sandy soil?

ITQ 11.18　　　　　　　　　　　　　　　　　**?**

Name four main nutrients needed in the soil:

1.

2.

3.

4.

Drainage

Drainage is an important aspect of grassland management. Good drainage reduces 'poaching' (churning up of ground). Well drained soil allows oxygen to mix within the soil particles, which helps root growth and the breakdown of organic matter, thus releasing nutrients into the soil. Grass will grow stronger and earlier in well-drained soil, which warms up more quickly.

The method of drainage employed in any field will depend upon:

●　The natural drainage, e.g. whether there are any ditches in or around the field.

●　The level of the ground water table. If the water table is naturally very low the ground will drain better than if the table is high.

●　The type and nature of the subsoil, e.g. clay soil often has a dense, slowly permeable subsoil which leads to waterlogging.

●　The type of topsoil. As already discussed, the soils vary in their drainage capacity.

●　The nature of the land, i.e. whether flat or sloping. Sloping land will drain downwards so the higher levels will be naturally well drained whilst the lower levels will become very wet.

Ditches

These must be checked regularly for blockages. The ditches on your neighbours' land must also be clear if they are to allow the free run of water so, if this is not the case, it may be necessary to approach them politely on this subject.

If putting in new ditches, ensure that the soil is not dumped along the edges – spread it away from the edges to prevent it being washed down into the ditch. Keep the ditch as straight as possible – the water flow slows on corners and silting occurs, which leads to blockages.

Ditches must always be safely fenced off to prevent animals from becoming trapped. Particular care must be taken that foals and small ponies cannot roll under the fence and down into the ditch.

Keep all pipes leading to and from ditches in a good state of repair.

Underground drainage

When considering drainage of paddocks, the advice of a drainage specialist should be sought. In the UK, a consultant from the British Institute of Agricultural Consultants may be able to help. Alternatively, ask a local farmer who may be willing to offer advice as to which method of drainage is most suitable for the land in your area.

The use of underground pipes is always expensive, but the investment is very worthwhile as the quality of the land is greatly improved.

Mole drains are unlined channels which are created in the soil by a conical 'mole' which is approximately 8cm (3½in) in diameter. A mole plough is used behind a tractor. Mole drains are used in the heavier clay soils and are effective for 5–15 years. The presence of sand or drought conditions shortens the life of the channels.

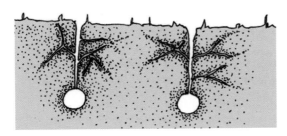

11.2 Mole drains

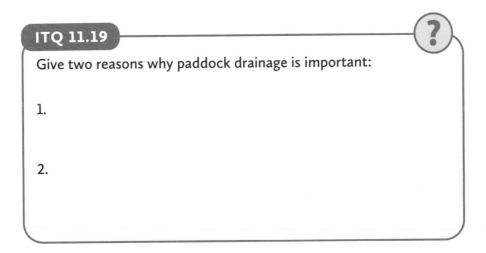

ITQ 11.19   ?

Give two reasons why paddock drainage is important:

1.

2.

Grasses

Having discussed the need to ensure that the soil in the paddock contains the right balance of nutrients and is well drained, we move on to look at the types of grasses that are desirable for grazing horses.

The main characteristics needed by grass for horse pasture are:

- **Palatability.** Grasses which are too stalky and coarse are not palatable enough for horses, although they may provide a good tough turf, helping to stop the cutting up of soil.

- **Digestibility.** There must be a balance between too much fibre, which is difficult to digest, and not enough, an example of the latter being lush spring grass. A certain amount of fibre helps digestion and satisfies the appetite.

Grass mixtures

When deciding which grasses to use, take into account the **heading dates,** i.e. the time at which the grass comes into flower and is at its most nutritional stage. Try to choose a mixture of early and late heading grasses to provide a good level of nutritional value throughout the spring and summer.

Two **perennial ryegrass** varieties should make up 50 per cent of the mixture; 25 per cent of the mixture should consist of two types of **creeping red fescue,** which is very productive, giving a good turf. Types vary in quality but the better ones are of good nutritional value. The other 25 per cent of the mixture could consist of:

- **Crested dog's tail** – 5–10 per cent.

- **Meadow grass** –10–20 per cent – suitable for wet land.

- **Wild white clover** – 1–2 per cent – grows on any type of soil and enhances soil fertility as a result of the formation of nitrogen in the root nodules. Care must be taken that the clover does not take over the paddock.

Other types of grasses used in meadows include:

- **Timothy** – a persistent grass, useful in hay. Produces abundant amounts of seed and enjoys heavy loams and clay soils.

- **Cocksfoot** – hard-wearing, suited to dry areas.

Field boundaries

Field boundaries such as fences, walls or hedges are necessary to keep horses in confined areas. Fences are needed for the following reasons:

- There is a legal responsibility to prevent horses from straying.

- Boundaries prevent horses from coming to harm or causing harm. Boundaries keep horses safe by keeping them away from roads, poisonous plants and any other

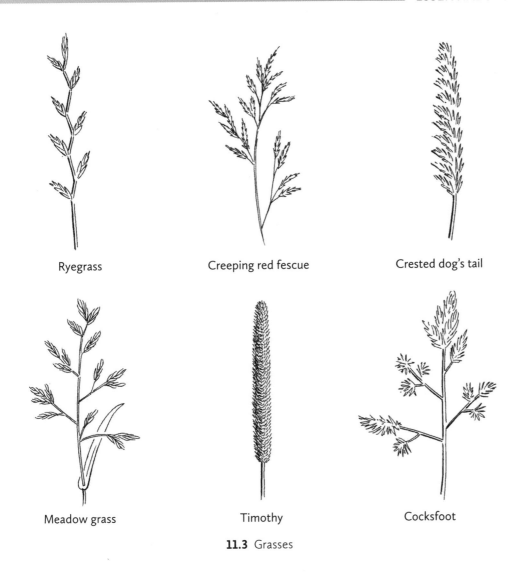

Ryegrass   Creeping red fescue   Crested dog's tail

Meadow grass   Timothy   Cocksfoot

11.3 Grasses

dangerous area and also stop them getting into neighbouring fields and damaging crops.

● Boundaries prevent other stock coming onto your land and eating valuable grass.

Boundaries should be checked regularly to block any escape route before horses use it.

When considering the type of fence boundary to install the following should be considered:

● Availability of capital and ongoing maintenance costs.

● Safety of the horses.

● Appearance.

Walls

Walls should be high enough so that a horse does not feel the urge to jump them. Stones walls last a long time, and need little maintenance. However, they should be checked regularly to ensure they are intact along their whole length. Stone walls are used as fencing in certain areas of the British Isles, i.e. areas with a good local supply of stone. There are many areas where it would be too expensive and impractical to use stone walls.

Hedges

The main advantages of hedges as boundaries are that they are self-renewing and provide excellent wind-breaks. Studies have shown that hedges can slow wind speeds for up to 100m (110 yards), providing excellent protection to large areas of the paddock. A thick hedge is especially beneficial if there is no other shelter in the field. Horses are able to tuck in close to the hedge and shelter from the wind and rain. It has been proved that hedges are better wind-breaks than solid barriers such as walls or panel fencing. This is because when wind hits solid barriers it forms circular draughts on either side of the barrier.

Hedges should be non-toxic to horses (who will eat them if grazing is sparse) and, of the trees and shrubs that fulfil this criterion, **hawthorn** provides a dense growth with its tough, thorny branches, while **blackthorn, hazel, elm** and **beech** are also suitable.

In order to prevent unwanted escapes, hedges need to be examined regularly for gaps. If a hedge has a lot of gaps along its length, a fence, either temporary or permanent, should be put up to make the boundary stock-proof. The hedge itself can then be made stock-proof by employing a contractor to 'lay' the hedge. This will make the hedge thicker at the base. It will take some years for the hedge to grow to a reasonable size.

Hedges should also be routinely trimmed to prevent them from become 'lanky', which contributes to the development of gaps.

When checking hedges for gaps, any poisonous plants should be removed or fenced out of reach. As with walls, hedges should be high enough to prevent horses from jumping them.

The ideal fencing for horses is post and rail (see below) with a hedge behind. This is secure and has the benefits of the shelter provided by the hedge.

Fences

There are many kinds of fencing now available. Fences should be high enough to prevent horses from jumping them. The lowest strand or rail of the fence should be high enough from the ground to prevent a horse getting a leg stuck through the fence. This is usually thought to be about the horse's knee height, although in studs it should be approximately 0.3m (1ft) from the ground to prevent foals rolling under the fence. If there are a number of horses in the field, especially in the case of youngstock, or if there is a problem with bullying, the corners of the field should be fenced across. This provides a rounded corner to the field and will prevent injury if a horse becomes cornered by other horses. Rounded corners are also easier to get into with machinery, e.g. tractor and cutter, paddock cleaner, etc.

Post and rail fencing

Depending on your budget, this can be two, three or four rails. This type of fencing looks smart but is very expensive to erect and maintain. Hardwoods are less likely to be chewed than softwoods, but hardwoods are twice as expensive as softwoods. Post and rail fences will need to be creosoted every year to give protection from the weather, and to deter horses from chewing the rails. If horses constantly chew rails, electric fencing can be attached to the top rail. This will quickly break the horses of the habit and prevent the fence from being demolished.

When building a post and rail fence, the rails should be nailed on the inside of the paddock to prevent horses who lean or rub on the fence from pushing the rails out. If there are horses on both sides of the fence, one strand of electric fence wire on the middle rail will prevent horses pushing the rails out.

The top surface of the top rail should lie flush with the top of the post to prevent injury. The top surface of the post should be slanted slightly to allow the rain to run off. When installing such fences, at least 46cm (18in) of post should be in the ground. However, posts sited at a change in fence direction and/or at intervals of 50m (55 yards) should be sunk in the ground to a depth of 76cm (30in).

The top rail should ideally be at least 1.4m (approx. 4½ft) high to deter the horses from jumping out. Fencing in a stallion paddock should be at least 1.75m (5ft 9in) high. The whole paddock should be close boarded to help regulate the stallion's behaviour, especially when other horses are led past his field.

Plastic fencing

Wire strand fencing is becoming increasingly popular, as it cannot be chewed; it needs very little maintenance and is cheaper than post and rail fencing. The wire is usually encased in a plastic tube. High-tensile strands of wire known as droppers keep the tension correct and contractors usually install such fencing, as they have the equipment needed to set the wire at the correct tension. The wire strands should be spaced at 30cm (1ft) intervals. Some people prefer not to use wire, in case a horse gets a foot caught through the bottom strands, which will then not break under pressure. However, if the lower strands are positioned correctly this should not occur. A further innovation of this type of fencing is two strands of wire encased in a plastic sleeve to give a plastic rail. This lessens the risk of injury from the wire.

There is now also a specialised V-mesh wire fencing which is supported by posts and a top rail. The mesh is very rigid and the holes are too small for a horse to get a foot caught. This fencing is expensive compared to other types but is frequently used on studs.

Electric fencing

This type of fencing is mostly used for temporary purposes. When using it in this way, electrical tape is much preferable to wire. Horses have difficulty seeing wire and may run through it without realising. However, if using electric fencing to prevent fence chewing, then electric wire should be used.

When erecting electric fencing for the first time, any branches or long grass touching the tape should be cut away to prevent the current being earthed.

If possible, although it is more expensive, electricity should be supplied through a mains fencing unit kept in a tack room. This is a more reliable system than battery-powered fences and less likely to be damaged by the horses.

Unsuitable fencing materials

Barbed wire *should never, under any circumstances, be used as fencing for horses.* Barbed wire can cause serious, sometimes fatal, injuries. If you 'inherit' a field fenced with barbed wire it must be a priority to replace it with safe fencing.

Sheep and/or pig netting should never be used for horse pasture. A horse can easily become entangled in the fence. Netting will also stretch under pressure, rather than break, and will then sag, becoming more dangerous.

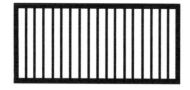

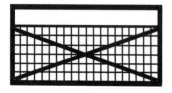

11.4 Safe gate designs

Gateways

Gateways should be in the middle of the fence line rather than situated in the corner of the field. This will prevent injuries occurring if a fight breaks out as horses wait at the gate. When siting the gateway, take into account the distance you have to walk to turn the horses out so, if possible, avoid siting the gate too far away.

The gateway should be sited in a well-drained area if possible, and it is advisable to have some kind of hard standing to prevent poaching in the winter months. The gateposts should be sunk 90cm (3ft) into the ground and the area around the gatepost should be packed with stone or concrete to prevent movement.

The gate should be hung properly so that you do not have to struggle when putting a horse out or bringing in. It can be dangerous to struggle with a gate while trying to separate one horse from others in the field.

The gate itself can be made of either wood or metal. Metal gates are lighter than wood and are usually adjustable, which makes hanging easier. Metal gates are also cheaper and cannot be chewed.

Ideally the gate should have vertical bars to prevent a horse from getting a leg trapped. Alternatively the lower half of the gate should consist of a metal grid which prevents injury.

Security

If the field is situated away from the stables, or if the horses are left overnight, there should be a chain and padlock fitted to both ends of the gate. This will prevent thieves lifting the gate off its hinges. Alternatively, a more effective method is to fix the top hinge upside down.

Even if the horses are only put out while people are around, there should be an effective means of securing the gate, such as a rope, chain or horse-proof catch to prevent horses opening the gate.

ITQ 11.20

What type of fencing should never be used on horse pasture?

ITQ 11.21

How deep should the following posts be put into the ground?

1. Standard fence posts:

2. Fence posts at a change of direction:

3. Gate posts:

Shelters

Shelter in the field is especially necessary for horses at grass all year. Most horses do not mind either wind or rain, but when the two are combined they like to shelter away from the elements. To provide maximum protection from the weather, the shelter should face away from northerly and prevailing winds. Shelter is also necessary in the summer to protect from the sun and the flies.

Providing shelter will keep horses in better condition. Horses are likely to lose weight if exposed to cold wind and rain for long periods of time. In the summer, flies can cause horses distress, preventing them from settling. Horses will wander around the field in an attempt to find an environment with fewer flies, which again will cause them to lose weight.

Hedges

As previously mentioned, hedges provide excellent shelter in the winter, and many horses prefer to shelter against a hedge rather than under cover. Hedges provide excellent shelter because they are not totally solid. Wind hitting a solid structure will produce eddies on either side of the structure, whereas the permeable nature of the hedges reduces wind speed, and so provides shelter.

In order to provide an efficient wind-break, the bottom half of the hedge should be at least 1m (3ft 3in) wide. In order to increase the width, the hedge should be laid. A laid hedge will take time to grow to an adequate height to serve as a barrier to both the wind and the horse. In the meantime, extra fencing, either temporary or permanent, will have to be erected to confine the horses, while artificial shelters will also have to be installed. If the horses are prone to eating the hedge it may be worthwhile installing a permanent inner fence to prevent damage.

If the hedges are not on the northerly edge of the field, or there are no hedges in the field, man-made wind-breaks can be erected.

Man-made wind-breaks

These can be constructed by attaching plastic mesh to a wooden frame. As the plastic forms a permeable barrier, it acts like a hedge and reduces wind speed. The wind-break can be single-, double- or triple-planed. The single- and double-planed wind-breaks will need supporting struts to prevent them from blowing over in the wind, but the three-sided wind-break will stand up on its own. Whichever type is used, it should be sunk solidly into the ground to prevent it from moving in bad weather.

Field shelters

These are especially valuable in shading horses from the sun. If there are a large number of horses in the field, it may be better to provide more than one shelter. This will avoid the dominant horse preventing others entering the shelter. Alternatively an octagonal shelter could be constructed. This has an opening on one side only and gives better protection from the elements. If a horse is being bullied he will be able to escape more easily by running around the edge of the shelter.

Whatever type of shelter is provided it should have a large enough entrance to allow horses to enter and leave safely. For a single horse, the shelter should be the size of a stable. For each subsequent horse, the floor area of the shelter should increase by 50 per cent.

Shelters should face away from the prevailing weather conditions. They should be sited on free-draining land to prevent poaching and should be at such a distance from the gate that checking the horse is not a struggle, but not so close that it causes more poaching in an already overused area. If the shelter cannot be sited on free-draining land, a hardcore base will have to be laid before the shelter is erected. Concrete will become slippery in wet and icy weather. If siting the shelter close to a hedge, there should be sufficient space between the shelter and the hedge so that horses can get around the shelter without injuring themselves. If this is not possible, the gap between the shelter and the hedge should be fenced off.

If the shelter is being used by horses who are only fed by the grazing (i.e. they do not receive any hay or hard feed), it should be possible to build a shelter without planning permission. However, check with the local planning authority to determine whether planning permission is required.

ITQ 11.22   **?**

Give two reasons why should horses be provided with shelter:

1.

2.

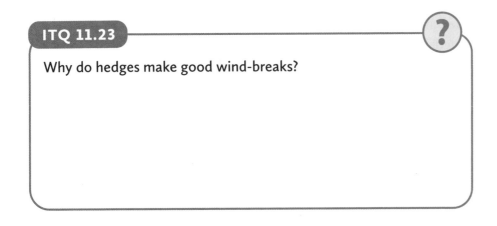

ITQ 11.23 ?

Why do hedges make good wind-breaks?

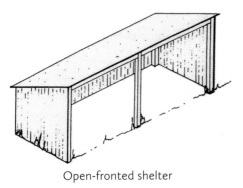

Open-fronted shelter

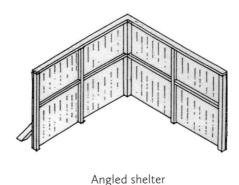

Angled shelter

11.5 Forms of shelter

Water

Water must be provided in the field. If there is not a suitable river supply or water cannot be piped to a trough, a large tub will have to be refilled daily, or twice a day in hot weather. Ponds should be fenced off, as they are likely to contain stagnant water. If there is any worry that the water may be contaminated, it should be analysed. If this is not possible, mains water should be used.

Rivers and streams

If safe to use, a river or stream provides an excellent source of fresh drinking water. It also avoids water having to be piped or carried to fields. However, in some situations, it can be hazardous for horses to drink from rivers or streams. When considering using them as a water source, the following points should be considered:

- There should be easy access, or the horse may injure himself trying to reach the water. The ideal access is a gentle slope down to the river. (Note that banks may give way; this is not only – or even mainly – because to the weight of the horse, but also because of water erosion of the bank.)

- The water should be free flowing.

- The riverbed should not be sandy or muddy. Sand in the river can be ingested by the horse while he drinks. If a considerable amount of sand or mud is ingested, the horse may suffer from sand colic. A gravel bed is much more suitable.

● There is a risk of pollutants in the water from agricultural chemicals or other materials leached into the river upstream. Although some signs of river pollution, such as foam in the water or increased plant life, are visible, others may not be.

● Any boggy areas need to be fenced off as there is a risk that a horse may become trapped in them.

Water troughs

Water troughs provide a labour-saving means of watering horses in the field. Although they have to be checked at the same time as checking the horses, using troughs stops the need to carry several buckets of water to the field every day. The troughs should be large enough for the number of horses in the field. Most troughs are 50cm (20in) in depth and vary between 1 and 2m (3ft 3–6ft 6in) long. They are usually made of stone, metal or plastic. The trough should have a plug at the bottom to allow it to be drained and cleaned.

There are two main types of trough; those that are self-filling and contain a ballcock to control the flow; or those with a tap. Both types do the job well, but any pipes should be insulated to prevent them from freezing in the winter. All pipes should be laid at least 60cm (2ft) deep in the ground. This prevents them being fractured by heavy machinery or broken during soil cultivations and helps prevent the pipes freezing.

The water trough should be sited on free-draining land. If this is not possible hardcore should be laid; this should be well compacted and sand laid on top of it. This will prevent poaching. The trough should also be sited away from trees and shrubs to prevent leaves filling the trough. If possible, the trough should be incorporated into a clear fence line.

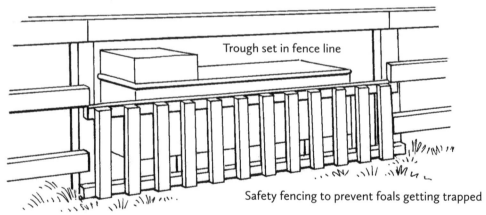

Trough set in fence line

Safety fencing to prevent foals getting trapped

11.6 The water trough

It should lie flush with the fence to prevent injury; the middle rail of the fence may be removed to allow better access to the trough. If the field is used for foals, the trough must be safely enclosed.

If it is not possible for the trough to be incorporated into the fence line, it should be sited a couple of metres away from the fence in order to minimise the risk of injury if several horses are all milling around the trough together.

Water troughs will need cleaning on a regular basis throughout the summer to remove the algae that will accumulate in the trough. If possible the trough should be left to air for a couple of hours before refilling. In the winter, ice will have to be broken on the trough at least twice a day. A large rubber ball can be floated in the trough to prevent thin surfaces of ice from accumulating.

ITQ 11.24

List three factors that should be taken into account when siting a shelter:

1.

2.

3.

ITQ 11.25

Give three considerations that should be taken into account before using a river as a water supply.

1.

2.

3.

ITQ 11.26

If the land is not free-draining, what measures should be taken to reduce poaching around a water trough?

ITQ 11.27 ⟨?⟩

Give three reasons why water pipes should be laid 60cm (2ft) underground:

1.

2.

3.

MANAGING GRASSLAND

Natural behaviour of horses

If you intend to manage grassland used for grazing horses, it is necessary to be aware of aspects of natural equine behaviour that may have an impact on the land. Points to consider include the following:

Grazing. Horses have a natural desire to graze and roam. While still wild, herds of horses would roam freely, only grazing the most succulent areas; they would leave the remainder, and continue on to new pasture. When confined, horses will graze palatable grass, and leave the less desirable until there is nothing else left. This will form the pasture into well-trimmed 'lawns' and ungrazed 'roughs'. Horses will also eat hedges, strip trees and chew on fences, which does not enhance their appeal to farmers. Hedges and trees should be fenced off, while wooden fences should be protected by electric fencing wire to prevent damage.

Dunging patterns. In the wild, horses will move on from their droppings – they do not eat in the area where they dung. This leaves patches of longer grass, which will have to be topped in order to restore growth. The droppings will also have to be removed or broken up in order to reduce the worm burden of the field.

Fence walking/poaching. Horses cause localised damage to the field by continually walking along the fence line, for example when waiting to be brought in, or for a companion to return to the field, and thus poaching it. This damages the grass and covers it in mud, making it unpalatable. In drier conditions, the grass will be worn away by heavy use. This will leave bare patches allowing weeds to invade. Shod horses will cause more damage than unshod horses. This needs to be repaired by harrowing, re-seeding and rolling.

Rolling and galloping. Horses roll for various reasons, one of which appears to be pleasure, and they will gallop if excited or disturbed by something. Both activities will damage the field. Horses usually roll in the same spot; this removes grass from a small area of land, and also compacts the soil. Galloping will tear up divots, which also damages the land.

Dealing with horse-sick paddocks

Fields which have accommodated horses for a long period without any management will show certain characteristics. There will be areas of closely cropped 'lawns' and longer 'roughs', which probably hide a large amount of droppings. Horse-sick fields have a large weed burden, and the ground will be uneven and poached at wetter times of the year.

So long as there are no major drainage problems or weed infestations horse-sick paddocks can be repaired. First, the patches of long grass should be removed. If the grass is very long and has fallen onto itself, it will have to be cut with a scythe, as the mower is not able to pick up extremely long grass, while sheep will ignore these areas. Areas of long grass where the grass is still supporting itself can either be topped with a tractor-drawn mower, or grazed by sheep. Sheep will help to reduce the worm burden in the field. The close cropping by the sheep will also increase grass 'tillering' (the growth of side shoots).

After this, the dung should be removed or harrowed. If the field is going to be rested for a period of time, harrowing is a more suitable operation, as it will also pull out a lot of dead grass in the same cultivation. If the droppings are picked up, the ground should then be harrowed.

If the grassland has not been overgrazed, it could be rested and fertilised if the weather is suitable. However if there are bald patches, the field will have to be re-seeded. Depending on the damage to the field, patches may be repaired, or the entire field may have to be re-seeded.

Avoidance

Horse-sick paddocks can be avoided by the use of good management techniques.

- The sward should not be grazed shorter than 7.5cm (3in) in length. As the grass nears this length, the pasture should be rested to allow grass regeneration.

- Droppings should also be removed regularly to prevent the grass from becoming 'sour'.

- While the field is being rested, it should be harrowed and rolled. The harrowing disperses droppings and pulls out any dead grass, while the rolling encourages grass growth.

- Any areas of long grass should be topped.

- A good weed control policy should be followed to allow for the maximum grass growth in the sward.

- If the field can only be rested for a limited period, a nitrogenous fertiliser should be applied to encourage rapid grass growth.

Dealing with weeds

Paddocks must be kept as free of weeds as possible – weeds have a tendency to take over the fields, using up valuable ground space and soil nutrients. Most weeds are unpalatable, indeed some are poisonous.

The Injurious Weed Order is a protective order made under the Corn Production Act of 1921 and the Weeds Act of 1959. Landowners are legally obliged to eradicate specific weeds from their land. Failure to do so may lead to a fine.

The following weeds need to be dealt with to prevent paddock deterioration and possible harm to horses.

Dock. Serious infestations must be sprayed in April or May and again in August or September.

Creeping thistles and spear thistles. These must be sprayed in the early budding stage, before flowering in June.

Ragwort. Horses will not usually eat ragwort as it grows; it is more palatable in its wilted state and is deadly poisonous. It is particularly dangerous when eaten in hay.

Ideally, ragwort should be uprooted, removed from the field and burned. This will have to be repeated every year, taking great care never to drop leaves on the ground. If a spray is to be used it must be applied while the flower is still in the 'rosette' stage as opposed to waiting for the flowering stem to appear. Never cut or mow ragwort as this promotes more vigorous growth.

Ragwort poisoning causes degeneration of the liver even if eaten in very small quantities and 1–5 kg (2¼ –11 lb) can be fatal.

Nettles are harmless if eaten; indeed some horses relish them if they are cut and allowed to wilt for a few hours. Nettles grow rapidly between April and September and should be sprayed during this time to eradicate them. Nettles soon spread and take over paddocks, so care must be taken to spray or cut them before they go to seed.

Chickweed is a smothering, fast-growing weed; it is unpalatable and is best sprayed when in the seedling stage.

Buttercups are poisonous if eaten fresh, but are totally harmless when eaten in hay. In order to eradicate them, fertilise the soil to encourage strong grasses to smother the buttercups, then apply weed-killer. Large quantities would have to be eaten to affect the horse's health.

Toxic plants, trees and shrubs

Many plants contain **alkaloids** – organic basic compounds that are toxic to horses in varying degrees.

Poisonous plants should be eradicated from all pasture. All poisonous plants, including trees, should be fenced off or dug up from the field to protect the horses.

These methods are faster than spraying, whereby the plant has to die before removal. While there is sufficient grazing, horses will usually avoid poisonous plants that are still alive, but this should not be relied upon. However some toxic plants become palatable when conserved in hay or when they have been removed from the soil but left to rot in the field.

In some cases the toxins can gradually build up in the horse, so that the poisoning takes place over many months without the owners seeing any outward signs. Horses vary in their response to toxins. Age, condition, state of health and management will all affect how a horse responds. For example, if a horse has a fast metabolism, toxins may be ejected from the body quickly, limiting the amount of damage. If there is any suspicion of poisoning a vet should be called immediately.

Poisonous plants

Ragwort (*Senecio jacobaea*)

Ragwort consumption is the most common cause of poisoning in horses in the British Isles. Ragwort is a yellow flowered plant with lobed leaves. It grows to about 0.75m (2ft 6in or so) in height. It flowers from July through to September. Because of its bitter taste, horses usually ignore ragwort as it grows. However, if grazing is particularly sparse, they may be tempted to eat it. The plant becomes more palatable once it has started to die. Ragwort is especially harmful once it has been dried in a hay crop. To reduce the risk of ragwort in conserved crops, you should only buy hay from a reliable source, and have the assurance that there is no ragwort in the hay.

11.7 Ragwort

The alkaloid in ragwort causes permanent liver damage, termed **seneciosis.** The poison accumulates and stops the liver from repairing itself. It is difficult to identify liver damage until the liver is past repair, although in some cases the horse may look depressed and lose condition. A blood test or liver biopsy may identify liver damage. However, if a horse is looking well and performing normally you may not realise that he needs testing. Once the liver is severely damaged conditions such as photosensitisation, jaundice, seizures and dementia can occur. There is no cure for ragwort poisoning.

Measures can be taken to limit the amount of ragwort that grows in the summer. The land should not be overgrazed in winter, spring or early summer. It should also not be heavily poached in the winter. Ragwort thrives in poor soil; a regular fertilising routine should be followed in order to limit its growth. If ragwort can be identified in its developing 'rosette' stage, it can be sprayed or grazed by sheep without any detrimental effect to them. This will reduce the amount of mature plants developing.

Once the plant has reached maturity, pull it from the ground, removing all or as much of the root as possible. *Cutting* ragwort will only produce more vigorous growth and increase the risk of ingestion as the cut plants die on the field.

Once pulled, the dying plant should never be left in the field – it should be removed from the field and burnt. You should also ask your neighbours, and the local authority, to remove ragwort from neighbouring pasture and from hedgerows and verges.

Laburnum (*Laburnum anagyroides*), broom (*Cytisus scoparius*) and lupins (*Lupinus spp.*)

These all come from the same family of legumes and contain alkaloids which are fatal in small quantities. Laburnum is considered to be the second most toxic plant in the

Laburnum

Lupin

11.8 Laburnum and lupin

British Isles. While all parts of the laburnum are toxic, the seeds are the most poisonous, although different strains vary in toxicity. Although usually found in gardens, laburnum should be fenced off to prevent horses reaching the trees. Laburnum poisoning results in convulsions and coma prior to death. Horses who have eaten highly toxic lupins die from respiratory failure. Lupins can also cause **lupinosis**, a fungal disease causing liver damage.

Bracken (*Pteridium aquilinum*)

Bracken is usually found on commons, hillsides and marginal land. As with many toxic plants, horses will only eat bracken if grazing is scarce. Horses will have to eat a large amount of bracken before symptoms of poisoning are seen. Bracken contains the toxin **thiaminase** that attacks vitamin B1 (thiamine). This results in the horse losing weight, becoming weak and uncoordinated. Internal haemorrhaging could also occur. By giving a B1 supplement, the horse should recover from bracken poisoning. The horse should be removed from the pasture.

A good fertilising policy coupled with the addition of lime will reduce the amount of bracken in the pasture. Cutting the bracken biannually for two or three years will also limit the amount of bracken in the pasture.

Buttercups (*Ranunculus spp.*)

Buttercups contain an irritant called **protoanemonin** and are poisonous if digested in large quantities. However, once dried the protoanemonin is destroyed, so there is no danger from poisoning by buttercups in hay. Buttercups will encroach onto poorly fertilised pasture; a good fertilisation policy coupled with chemical spraying before flowering will reduce the incidence of buttercups. Most horses find buttercups unpalatable and so poisoning is rare.

11.9 Bracken

Hemlock (*Conium maculatum*)

Hemlock contains alkaloids and all parts of the plant are poisonous. The seeds especially contain high levels of alkaloid. Hemlock is similar in appearance to other members of the parsley family, although it can be identified by smooth, purple blotched stems and an unpleasant smell. As little as 2.5kg (5½ lb) of hemlock can be fatal. Symptoms include an inactive, coma-like state and paralysis, followed by death.

The sappy stems of the **water dropwort** (*Oenanthe crocata*) and **cowbane** (*Cicuta virosa*), members of the same family, are especially dangerous in dry weather conditions. As little as 0.5kg (approx. 1lb) of dropwort or cowbane can kill.

11.10 Hemlock

> **ITQ 11.28**   (?)
>
> Which plant causes the most cases of poisoning in horses in the British Isles?

Poisonous trees and shrubs

Yew (*Taxus baccata*)

Yew is the most toxic plant in the British Isles. This extremely dangerous tree can be identified by its red berries and distinctively shaped leaves. Every part of the tree is poisonous, from the bark to the leaves, and even dried leaves can kill. Little more than one mouthful can cause a cardiac arrest within minutes. Any yew tree close to horse pasture should be fenced off, so that horses are unable to reach it, or any leaves or berries that may have blown from the tree. If spotted, symptoms of yew poisoning include trembling, breathing difficulties and collapse. There is no antidote to yew poisoning.

11.11 Yew

Oak (*Quercus spp.*)

Oak leaves are poisonous, although by far the greater danger is from acorns. Acorns contain a large amount of tannic acid, which causes dullness and lack of appetite. Horses can also get colic from eating acorns. Oak trees in horse pasture should be fenced off in the autumn, when horses can pick up fallen acorns. Although pigs can be used to eat the fallen acorns, they will also plough up the land. On a limited area, it may be better to pick up the acorns manually.

11.12 Oak

Rhododendron (*Rhododendron spp.*)

Although usually only seen in gardens, rhododendrons should be fenced off or removed from horse pasture. Small quantities are extremely toxic. Rhododendron poisoning causes the respiratory system to fail.

Deadly nightshade (*Atropa belladonna*)

Usually found in hedges, this plant has brown and purple berries. Deadly nightshade is not normally fatal to horses, although it causes narcosis, dilation of the pupils and convulsions. The degree of poisoning depends on the condition of the horse.

11.13 Rhododendron

Laurel (*Prunus laurocerasus*), privet (*Ligustrum spp.*) and box (*Buxus sempervirens*)

These are usually found in suburban areas. Small quantities of laurel and box can kill, although animals in poor condition are more susceptible to laurel poisoning. Signs of laurel poisoning include laboured breathing and convulsions. Privet poisoning is uncommon unless the horse has ingested large quantities.

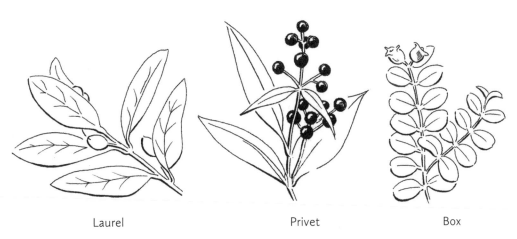

Laurel   Privet   Box

11.15 Laurel, privet and box

11.14 Deadly nightshade

ITQ 11.29 ?

What is seneciosis?

ITQ 11.30 ?

a. Why should ragwort never be cut?

b. How can ragwort be controlled?

c. What precautions must be taken if ragwort is sprayed with herbicide?

ITQ 11.31 ?

Name a plant that loses toxicity when made into hay.

An annual guide to pasture management

Winter

Poaching should be limited for the following reasons:

● The field can be used for a longer period as there will be more grass available, and the field will not damage so easily.

● In the spring, the field may only have to be rested rather than completely re-seeded.

- The horses can be turned out onto dry areas rather than wet, boggy fields, which could lead to mud fever, and poor foot conditions.

Poaching can be reduced by choosing:

- Free-draining fields.

- Land on a sheltered hillside (a positive aspect of hilly fields), rather than land in a valley, or close to a river.

- Permanent pasture, which has a denser sward than most leys.

- A low stocking rate, which will reduce the amount of wear and tear on the field.

- Well-travelled areas such as gateways, water troughs, and field shelters should be reinforced with hardcore to prevent these areas becoming swamps.

- Trees and fences should be cordoned off to prevent horses damaging them.

- A mineral supplement can also be fed to lessen the horses' desire to chew wood.

In some cases, if the stocking rate cannot be kept low, or the fields will not drain well, it may be better to sacrifice a small area of grazing, which can be re-seeded in the spring.

Hedges can be trimmed any time from the autumn through to the spring.

Spring

With the onset of spring, the weather becomes warmer and monthly rainfall lessens. These factors combine to heat the land. When the land is warm enough, the grass will begin to grow. If the paddock has been rested over winter or only lightly grazed, so that it is not poached, it can be prepared for grazing in the following way.

First, the field should be harrowed. Chain harrows can be attached to a tractor or ATV. The hooked metal spikes of the chain harrows are used to pull out dead grass, and to scatter any droppings that have been left on the field. This will break up the surface of the soil and, coupled with the removal of dead grass, will allow more air to the soil and roots. This will encourage grass growth.

Harrowing should be carried out throughout the spring and summer. If droppings are not being picked up and removed, the field should be harrowed in hot, dry conditions to break up the droppings and allow the sun to desiccate the droppings and worm larvae. However, paddocks must not be over-harrowed, as this will pull growing grass from the soil and reduce the amount of grass in the paddock, which may lead to weeds developing.

Fertiliser should be applied to the land in mid-March or April, depending on spring weather conditions. Fertiliser should be applied when there are light showers forecast, or when there are heavy morning dews in order for the granules to be absorbed. Although horses can be returned to the pasture once the fertiliser has been absorbed, in order to get optimum use of the fertiliser the field should be rested for approximately four weeks before it is grazed.

All grazing areas should not be fertilised at the same time. Owing to the spring flush of growth, there is usually more grass than horses can graze at this time of year. If grazing areas are fertilised as weekly intervals, after one paddock is grazed, the next will be ready for grazing.

Rolling can take place either before or after fertilising. Rolling levels the ground, pushes any stones into the soil, and crushes the grass; this will encourage it to tiller by forming secondary growing points.

If rolling takes place after fertiliser has been added, the fertiliser will be pushed into the soil, which will aid absorption.

Summer

During the summer, the field should be kept clear of droppings, as already discussed. Long areas of grass should be topped, to prevent the areas from going to seed, and to encourage growth. Weed control should also be undertaken.

Maintenance can also be carried out during the summer months. Fences can be painted and any necessary field drainage can be installed.

Autumn

Ditches should be checked for blockages, and cleared ready for the winter. Gateways susceptible to poaching should be reinforced with hardcore. If the paddock is being rested for the winter, once the horses have been removed from the pasture, farmyard manure can be spread if required.

12 Lungeing

REQUIRED SKILLS/KNOWLEDGE	Learnt, revised, practised?	Confirmed
Lungeing a horse.		
• The requirements of areas suitable for lungeing.	☐	☐
• Protective clothing for the lunger.	☐	☐
• Be able to choose and fit suitable lunge tack.	☐	☐
• Carry out appropriate lungeing exercise, as instructed.	☐	☐
• Remove lungeing tack correctly and safely.	☐	☐
Work safely.		
• Maintain health and safety while lungeing, bearing in mind current codes of practice relating to this area of work.	☐	☐
Understand the principles and practice of lungeing.		
• Understand why lungeing can be substituted for ridden exercise.	☐	☐
• Be conversant with different types of equipment and protective clothing.	☐	☐
• Be aware of how conditions such as weather, surface and other horses can affect the lungeing process.	☐	☐
• The lungeing process and how to recognise and deal with problems.	☐	☐

REASONS FOR LUNGEING

Carried out correctly, lungeing has the following benefits:

- It helps to exercise an excitable horse and use up excess energy before the rider mounts.

- It is a good way to begin the early training of a young horse, getting him used to wearing tack and obeying verbal commands.

- It is a useful method of exercising, particularly in bad weather when you may be unable to ride out on the fields or on the roads. It is also useful if you are short of time, as lunge sessions should never exceed 30 minutes.

- It allows the horse to move without the rider, encouraging him to use his back freely.

- It promotes:
  - free forward movement
  - calmness
  - rhythm
  - suppleness
  - balance
  - even muscle development (if carried out equally on both reins)

- It can be very useful to maintain fitness if the horse cannot be ridden, for example if he is suffering from tack sores.

LUNGEING PRELIMINARIES

You must learn to lunge under instruction and then practise lungeing a variety of quiet horses, preferably with a knowledgeable person looking on.

> **Clothing/equipment notes:**
>
> Wear gloves and fastened crash helmet.

The lungeing area

As with ridden schooling, lungeing should be carried out on a surface that is:

- Flat, level and consistent.

- Non-slip.

- Not too hard or deep.

- Enclosed. If you don't have an enclosed area, try to cordon off a corner in a field using safe hurdles or bales.

An all-weather arena is ideal.

LUNGEING EQUIPMENT

Lunge cavesson

The lunge cavesson normally has three straps – a throatlash, middle cheekstrap and a noseband. When lungeing in your Stage 2 exam, a snaffle bridle with the noseband removed is worn under the lungeing cavesson. The noseband of the lungeing cavesson should lie the width of two fingers beneath the projecting cheekbone. The noseband and middle strap should be fastened fairly tight to prevent the cavesson from being twisted round and pulled across the face. If this happens the cheekpiece of the cavesson can press against the horse's outside eye. The reins should be twisted up out of the way and secured through the throatlash.

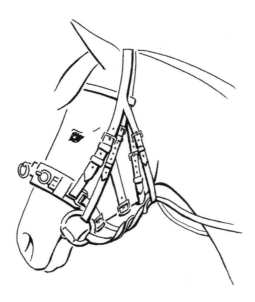

12.1 A correctly fitted lunge cavesson

> **EXAM TIP**
>
> It is important to ensure that the straps of the cavesson do not interfere with the action of the bit when fitted over a bridle. It is best to fit the noseband and middle straps under the cheekpieces of the bridle to ensure a snug fit and prevent rubbing and interference. Depending on the fit of the cavesson it may also be sensible to fasten the throatlash strap under the bridle throatlash. The aim is to ensure a secure and comfortable fit for the horse.

Brushing boots

The horse should be fitted with brushing boots all round to protect his legs. The physical effort required from the horse on the lunge and the fact that his inside hind should take extra weight, increases the likelihood of him knocking one of his legs against its pair (brushing).

Saddle

When lungeing in your Stage 2 exam the horse will be wearing a saddle. The stirrups should be secured by passing the leathers back up through the irons. The 'spare' end of the stirrup leather is passed through this and then through the surcingle loop (see Figure 12.2). This stops the stirrup irons from banging around on the horse's sides.

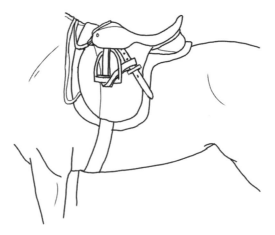

12.2 Method for securing the stirrup Irons

Side-reins

Side-reins are used for the following reasons:

- To teach the horse to accept a contact. The side-reins have the same role as the rein contact given by the hands.

- To encourage the horse to work in a rounded outline (as opposed to sticking his nose out). Working in a rounded outline helps the horse work his muscles correctly on the lunge.

- To help control a lively/naughty horse.

- If lungeing on grass it stops the horse from grabbing mouthfuls as he goes round.

Fitting and adjustment

In the lungeing section of the Stage 2 exam the side-reins should already have been adjusted for the horse. However, it is essential that you know how they should fit and be adjusted.

They should be attached at the girth – undo the second girth buckle and pull the girth strap out of the buckle guard. Pass the side-rein under the first girth strap and thread the second girth strap through the side-rein before putting it back through the buckle guard and re-fastening.

To adjust the side-reins to the correct length: with the horse standing with his neck straight, with his head in a normal position, adjust the length so you can hold the side-rein taut, with the clip touching the bit ring.

With the side-reins adjusted correctly, pass each one over the top of the withers and clip it onto the opposite 'D' ring of the saddle. Don't attach them to the bit

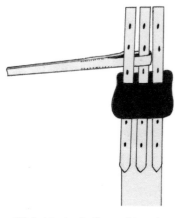

12.3 Method of attaching the side-reins

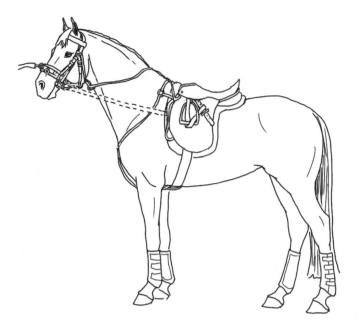

12.4 Horse tacked up for lungeing

immediately as it can be dangerous to have the horse standing around in side-reins.

The side-reins should be of equal length, not too long and – more importantly – not too short. If the side-reins are set too short they will force the horse's head into a false position, putting constant pressure on the horse's mouth, which is likely to be resented. This could prevent the horse from going forwards properly and may cause him to run back or even rear. The horse will also move with his head tucked into his chest – this is known as **overbending.**

If the side-reins are too loose they will swing in a big loop as the horse trots and the horse may lower his head and put a foot over them. They should also be set at the same height at the girth on both sides. You must stand in front of the horse to judge whether the side-reins are level or not.

Lunge line

The lunge line should be at least 10m (33 feet) long and attach by a buckle or rotating clip to the middle ring of the cavesson. It is usually made of 2.5cm (1in) wide webbing and has a loop at the opposite end to the buckle or clip, through which you can put your hand to stabilise the end. Make sure the lunge line doesn't get knotted or worn.

ITQ 12.1 ?

Give two points to consider regarding fitting the lunge cavesson:

1.

2.

ITQ 12.2   ?

Give three reasons for using side-reins:

1.

2.

3.

ITQ 12.3   ?

How will you adjust the side-reins?

ITQ 12.4   ?

What problems might occur if the side-reins are fitted too tightly?

ITQ 12.5   ?

What problems might occur if the side-reins are fitted too loose?

EXAM TIP

In an exam, if you are presented with a horse tacked up ready for lungeing make sure that you check the fitting and adjustment of all tack and equipment yourself before beginning the lungeing session. It is your responsibility as handler to ensure that the horse is comfortable and the exercise is safe – so don't rely on someone else's tacking up!

THE LUNGEING PROCESS

Leading the lunge horse

Before leading the horse into the lungeing area, check the girth and fitting of the equipment.

Once in the area, standing on the horse's nearside (left), the lunge line is held in the right hand approximately 30–40cm (1ft–1ft 4in) from the cavesson, with the bulk of the line in equal length loops in your left hand. The line is attached to the middle ring on the cavesson. Hold the lunge whip, with the thong, under your left upper arm. It should be pointing back and downwards to prevent it trailing and frightening the horse.

Staying level with the horse's shoulder, lead the horse into the centre of your lungeing area and make him stand still, using in succession the verbal commands 'Walk on', 'Whoa' and 'Stand'.

12.5 Leading the lunge horse

Methods of holding the lunge line

At this point we need to discuss the two methods of holding the lunge line. Both are correct, so it is your personal preference as to which method you use.

Line in one hand

The rein is held in even loops in one hand only. When the horse is on the right rein, the line is held in your right hand and vice versa. The line is played out through the one hand.

Advantage of this method

● The whip hand has only the whip in it. Some find this easier to manage.

Disadvantages of this method

● It is more difficult to feed the line out evenly and straight, i.e. without any twists.

● Should the horse pull away, you have only the strength of one arm to hold him.

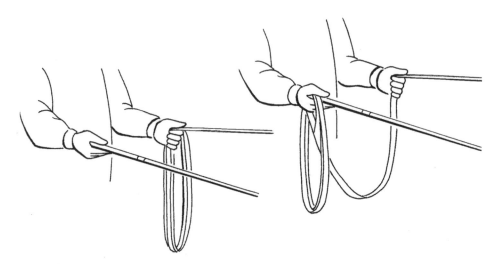

12.6 Methods of holding the lunge line

Line in two hands

On the right rein, the bulk of the line is held in even loops in the left hand (with the whip), whilst the right hand holds the rein, feeding it out as needed.

Advantages of this method

● It is easier to feed the line out evenly, and to straighten any twists.

● Should the horse pull away, you have the strength of two arms to hold him.

Disadvantages of this method

● Some students find holding the whip and rein in one hand too bulky.

● If the line is handled incorrectly, a low loop can form between the two hands, which can hang dangerously around your feet.

Methods of looping the lunge line

Around the hand

The lunge line must be free of twists. With the line unattached, prior to tacking up, hold the buckle end in the left hand and, keeping the line free of twists, loop the rein evenly around the hand. Form even loops of approximately 45cm (18in) and put your fingers through the sewn end loop for greater security. Never loop the line tightly around your hand as this could cause injury should the horse pull away suddenly or violently.

Across the hand

Holding the loop end in the palm of your left hand, pass the flat lunge line backwards and forwards across your palm, forming even loops of approximately 25cm (10in) on either side of the palm. Once this is done, put your fingers through the sewn end loop as above. Many students find it easier to keep the line from becoming twisted using this method. The main disadvantage is that of bulk – the line feels bulkier in the palm until it is played out.

When holding the horse

Sorting out the lunge line when it is attached to the cavesson and horse causes the novice handler many problems and is one of the most common causes of failing the lungeing section of an exam. Always sort the line out carefully before you lead the horse into the arena. If it starts out straight and tidy, it is easier to keep it that way.

If you need to adjust the line and 're-loop' it, be sure never to drop the line in front of the horse. Holding the 'tangled' loops in your right hand, straighten out some twists at the swivel on the cavesson and re-loop in your left hand. It is essential to practise handling the line until you are fully competent and can prevent it from getting into a twist in the first place.

If it is very tangled you can drop the bulk of the rein *behind* you whilst holding the line near the horse's head. Then untangle and sort out the line.

If it becomes repeatedly tangled in an exam you will probably fail for poor handling of the equipment. The occasional twist, promptly rectified, will not go against you.

Starting off

Walk around the front of the horse for a final check of equipment, including the girth. From the offside (right) of the horse, with the lunge line in your right hand and the whip in your left, you are ready to start lungeing the horse on the right rein. Release the whip thong.

It is the pitch, tone and inflection of the voice that are important when commanding a horse on the lunge. You must speak positively and, if in an exam, quite loudly so both the horse and examiner can hear you clearly. This is particularly important if there are two candidates being examined in the same school. Whilst you must not drown out the other candidate, you must be heard clearly.

Most horses respond to the word 'And' as a preparatory command – use it as a way of getting the horse's attention. Encourage the horse to walk on by giving the command 'And – walk on!' and by pointing the end of the lunge whip at the horse's hock level. The pitch of the command rises towards the 'On' part of the command,

EXAM TIP

At home, clip the lunge line to something such as a gate and practise playing the line out and re-gathering it.

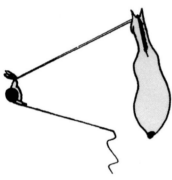

12.7 The lunger's position

ITQ 12.6

How will you hold the whip when leading the lunge horse?

which indicates to the horse that an upward transition from halt to walk is required.

As the horse walks forward, the rein is played out until the horse is on the desired length of rein. You must not step backwards – the horse must move away from you.

Standing in the middle of the circle, a cone shape is formed by the whip, horse and lunge line, with you forming the point of the cone. Your body should be level with the horse's girth, inclined towards the horse's shoulder. Never get in front of the shoulder, as this would have the effect of discouraging the horse from going forwards. He may also turn in to face you.

If the horse is active, you can stay in the same spot, pivoting on your right heel as the horse goes around. Although you stand level with the girth area of the horse, you send the horse forwards from the voice and whip, not by pulling him along by the lunge line.

If the horse is lazy, try to send him forwards without walking around yourself. In exam conditions you should stand as still as possible. Flick the whip at the horse's hocks and use your voice very positively to encourage him to go forwards.

If the horse is lazy it is acceptable to flick him with the thong on the hind leg below the hock. Sometimes adjusting your position so that you are standing in line with the horse's flanks can help to drive him forward a little more; when he is moving forward more actively you can resume your position level with the girth.

When holding the lunge line in two hands, it is held and used like the rein when riding. There should always be a contact – the line should be taut and free from twists. At no time should the line become very loose or touch the ground.

When ready, the horse can be asked to trot. Give the command 'And – trot on!', again using a raised note towards the end to indicate an upward transition and also an indication with the whip by raising it to hock level.

The circle used should be approximately 15m in diameter. It is very hard work for the horse to move on a smaller circle for any length of time and, if doing so, there is more chance that the horse will lose momentum.

Downward transitions

Downward transitions such as trot to walk, or walk to halt, are asked for with a slight downward intonation to the voice and an elongation of the command, which should have a calming effect – 'And – wa-a-a-lk' or 'And – woah-oh'. Once the horse has halted, give the command 'And stand'. Be quick to reward obedience with a kind word.

For downward transitions, in addition to using the voice, the hand holding the lunge line closes briefly to give a slight half-halt feel on the line to encourage the horse to balance and to go forward into his downward transition.

If the horse is unwilling to slow down and is ignoring your voice aids you can move slightly to the side so you align yourself with the horse's shoulder. This has a 'blocking' effect and can be enough to slow a horse. If this doesn't work, still using your voice, you should start to shorten the lunge line and walk slowly towards the horse, gathering the line and maintaining an even contact as you do so. Most horses will start to take more notice as you move closer to them.

Changing the rein

The horse must be lunged equally on both reins before fitting the side-reins, if you choose to use the side-reins. Once the horse has been halted, the rein can be changed. The horse should halt on the perimeter of the circle – he should not be allowed to turn in and face you.

Assuming the horse has been on the right rein, you can pick up the whip thong (but you do not need to do so). If you choose to pick up the thong you must do so without leaning down. If you bend over and take your eye off the horse whilst organising the whip you are putting yourself in a vulnerable position. There is the possibility of getting kicked, especially if lungeing a young horse.

Organising the whip
To organise the whip:

- Holding the whip in your left hand, point the tip of the whip upwards *slightly* to raise the thong.

- Slide your left hand towards the tip and take hold of the thong, holding it against the whip.

- Slide your left hand back down the whip towards the handle, still holding the thong against the whip.

- Put the whip and thong under your left arm so that the handle is near your armpit and the main length of the whip points downwards behind you. This conceals the whip from the horse and avoids upsetting him.

The lunge whip is a cumbersome item which requires practice to handle with ease.

Starting on the new rein
While the horse remains still, walk towards the horse's shoulder and collect up the lunge line in neat, even-sized loops in your right hand. At no time must the line touch the ground.

Having reached the horse, give him a pat and pass the lunge whip behind your body, changing it into your right hand, still keeping it pointing downwards, and tuck it under your right armpit. Move in front of the horse to his nearside.

EXAM TIP

In an exam you are permitted to trail the thong when changing the rein but not when leading the horse.

Lead the horse forwards two or three steps and push him away from you to turn him around. He should now be standing on the perimeter of the circle, on the left rein with you standing on his nearside.

Organise the lunge line according to the method you prefer: if rein in one hand, the line should be in your left hand; if rein in two hands, the bulk of the line is in your right hand, fed out through your left hand.

Now warm up the horse on the left rein in walk and trot.

ITQ 12.7

When lungeing, how should the lunger be positioned in relation to the horse?

ITQ 12.8

Give four points to note regarding the contact on the lunge line:

1.

2.

3.

4.

ITQ 12.9

What effect will it have if you move in front of the horse's shoulder whilst lungeing?

ITQ 12.10

Which verbal command and voice intonation would you use to:

a. Make an upward transition (i.e. from halt to walk or walk to trot)?

b. Make a downward transition (i.e. from trot to walk or walk to halt)?

Fitting the side-reins

Once the horse has warmed up in trot on both reins, he can be halted and the side-reins unclipped from the 'D's on the saddle. In the Stage 2 exam the side-reins will have already been adjusted to be the correct length for the horse. You must, however, be aware of gauging the correct length.

It is up to you whether to attach the side-reins or not. If the horse is not going forwards at all willingly and you are having to work hard to keep him moving, there is probably nothing to be gained from attaching the side-reins, indeed they may inhibit his forward movement even more. Other than this scenario, the side-reins should be attached.

Check the length and height of the side-reins at the girth before attaching them to the bit rings below the reins. The horse is then lunged on both reins in the side-reins. When changing the rein, the horse must be led forwards, never turned on the spot as he may resent the pressure exerted by the side-reins. You do not need to unclip the side-reins when changing the rein.

Once the horse has been turned to work on the other rein, the side-reins can be adjusted if needed, i.e. if they appear too tight or too loose when the horse is working.

Notes on working the horse

General principles

1 The horse should work on a true circle without falling in or pulling out. If the horse falls in, point the whip to the girth area and use the command 'Out' to encourage him to stay out. If the horse pulls out you need to maintain a firm contact and try to keep him on the circle, using the technique in the Exam Tip overleaf.

2 When walking, the horse should **overtrack**. This means the hind feet step beyond the prints left by the forefeet. In working trot (the form of trot required in the Stage 2 exam), he should **track up.** This means the hind feet should step into the prints left by the forefeet.

SAFETY TIP

▶ Beware of using side-reins that are too short. This can cause the horse to pull backwards or rear. In contrast, side-reins that are too long will be a trip hazard for the horse, who may get a foreleg entangled should he put his head down low.

EXAM TIP

If the horse falls in on the circle you must correct this. Try to ensure that the horse is moving with impulsion and is bending in the correct direction as this will mean he is less likely to fall in. For the horse who pulls out, repetitive squeezes (of similar strength to the rein aid in a half-halt) on the lunge line can help to keep the horse's head facing the desired way and focus his attention. The use of transitions can also help to focus his mind on the job in hand!

③ Make the work interesting with regular transitions and changes of rein. In the Stage 2 exam you are not likely to be asked to canter the horse on the lunge; it is up to you to decide. If the horse is not working actively in the trot, a short canter may wake him up and improve the subsequent trot work.

Ideally the horse should be worked forward with an even rhythm, which will help him to stay balanced on the lunge.

Quality of movement
Controlled forward impulsion

The horse should go forwards willingly when asked to do so. If the voice aid is ignored it must be reinforced quickly with a flick with the lunge whip. However, impulsion mustn't be confused with speed – a horse working with impulsion doesn't necessarily need to be travelling quickly. If the horse is working well, a slower rhythm can often be established. Impulsion must be controlled – ideally the horse should be calm and settled in his lunge work. If the horse is calm he will be relaxed and therefore more likely to be obedient and responsive.

Rhythm

In terms of gait, rhythm can be described as the regularly recurring sequence of footfall. The interval between footfalls remains the same. The aim should be to develop an even rhythm in all gaits. Rhythm follows on naturally after free forward movement has been achieved. Good rhythm is easiest to achieve in trot because of its pronounced two-time beat.

By maintaining rhythm, the horse is encouraged to become more balanced as the hocks must be used to maintain an even rhythm on a circle. Some horses are naturally more balanced than others and will find it easier to maintain a good rhythm.

Balance

If the horse is working with controlled impulsion, an even rhythm and is supple and straight, this is evidence that he is well balanced. If the horse is balanced, he will be able to carry his own weight (and that of the rider) equally over all four limbs.

Cantering

As the horse is constantly working on a relatively small circle, lungeing places increased strain on the joints, muscles and associated tissues, so should not be 'overdone', particularly with young horses. Cantering on the lunge is particularly strenuous, even for mature horses, and should only be carried out for a very short period.

However, practise cantering horses on the lunge so that you are prepared to do so, should you decide to canter the horse in the exam, or should the horse canter, unasked. (In the latter case, you should bring him quietly back to trot.)

Ending the session

When you have finished lungeing, bring the horse forwards to halt. The horse remains on the lunge circle and you must walk up to him, gathering up the line as previously described.

ITQ 12.11 ?

How would you correct the horse who is:

a. Falling in?

b. Pulling out?

EXAM TIP

Remember to control the lunge whip at all times, it is easy to be so relieved after the lunging session of your exam that you forget to control the lunge whip as you undo the side-reins and lead the horse out of the arena.

Unclip the side-reins and fasten them to their opposite 'D' ring. The horse must never be allowed to stand around with the side-reins attached to the bit. Some horses get upset and may react badly – either by pulling back or rearing.

Loosen the girth one or two holes and praise the horse to reward him. End by standing on his nearside in position ready to lead.

NOTES ON LUNGEING IN THE STAGE 2 EXAM

When assessed in the Stage 2 exam, candidates are required to lunge an experienced horse in a 20 x 20m area. Often there will be two candidates in a 40 x 20m arena – the school will be divided up by poles on the ground.

Efficiency is very important as you do not have long to lunge – 45 minutes is allowed for the lunge section of the exam; some of this is spent discussing lungeing. Once the horses are brought into the arena you need to work efficiently.

1 Check tack and equipment. Alter as necessary, check the adjustment of the side-reins without fastening them and organise the lunge line. Check the condition of the tack and tighten the girth.

2 Warm up briefly without side-reins. Walk one circuit, trot two, then walk, halt and change the rein. If, at this point the horse has been very lively, it would be sensible to attach the side-reins to increase your control. If the horse has been quiet, walk half a circuit, trot for one, then walk and halt. Then attach the side-reins.

3 Walk the horse for half a circuit before sending him into working trot. Make sure he is working actively forwards into the contact.

4 You do not *need* to canter in the Stage 2 exam but you *may* canter the horse if you feel it would be useful.

EXAM TIP

During the lungeing section of the exam, the examiner will be looking for:

A calm, effective approach.

Good control of the horse with appropriate commands given.

Correct use of equipment, including lunge line, whip and side-reins.

A workmanlike approach which exercises the horse safely.

⑤ Change the rein regularly to keep the horse interested and improve his suppleness.

⑥ Try to get the horse working calmly forward in an even rhythm.

⑦ If the horse does not go forward you must use your voice, body language and the whip to encourage him to be active. It is acceptable to flick a lazy horse below the hocks with the whip – however, avoid cracking the whip or waving it about to no effect.

The most important point about preparing for the lungeing element is to practise regularly. Whilst one minor mistake will not result in failure, the following are the most common reasons for failure:

- Consistent mishandling of the equipment, e.g. lunge line twisted, line touching the ground.
- Circle consistently too small.
- Horse not working forwards properly.
- Dangerous positioning of the lunger in relation to the horse.
- Lunger walking about excessively.

ITQ 12.12

How would you warm up the horse before attaching the side-reins?

EXAM TIP

Try to lunge a wide variety of horses and ponies with different stride lengths and ways of going to prepare you for any horse you may be given in an exam. The correct way of going for a small, short-striding, nippy pony will feel very different from a long-ranging hunter stride, so be aware of the correct speed, impulsion and rhythm for each individual horse.

13 Riding on the Flat

REQUIRED SKILLS/KNOWLEDGE	Learnt, revised, practised?	Confirmed
Ride with a secure, independent and balanced position in walk, trot and canter, with and without stirrups.		
• Walk, trot and canter with and without stirrups with a secure, independent, supple and balanced position showing an ability to ride forward from leg to hand.	☐	☐
• Ride using the correct diagonals in trot.	☐	☐
Apply natural and artificial aids when riding horses in an enclosed area.		
• Using coordinated aids, carry out transitions and school movements, maintaining the horse's rhythm and balance.	☐	☐
• Maintain a suitable rein contact at all times.	☐	☐
• Use natural and artificial aids as necessary.	☐	☐
• Ride with the reins in one hand.	☐	☐
• Prepare for and ensure a correct canter lead.	☐	☐
Ride horses in harmony and in conjunction with others using the area.		
• Build up a rapport with the horse when riding.	☐	☐
• Abide by the rules of the school when riding with others in closed and open order.	☐	☐
Know the principles of the horse's way of going.		
• Understand the horse's behaviour and responses whilst being ridden.	☐	☐
• Describe the way of going of the ridden horse.	☐	☐
• Understand the aids used on the ridden horse.	☐	☐

THE CORRECT RIDING POSITION

Reasons for adopting the correct position

The correct position is needed for the following reasons.

1. To balance the rider over the horse's centre of balance, so there is no feeling of a need to grip in order to remain in the saddle at walk, trot and canter.

2. To harmonise the rider with the movement of the horse to avoid unintentional interference with the horse's action, i.e. the rider should 'go with' the horse.

3. To establish a light communication acceptable to the horse, through the seat, legs and reins, enabling the rider to apply the aids correctly.

The correct position in the saddle is similar to the position that we take when standing. The body is held vertically, with the legs underneath and supporting the body. This natural and balanced position is also correct when riding a horse on the flat, with the minor alteration of a slight bend in the knee.

If an imaginary plumb-line were dropped from the rider's ear, the correct alignment of the body would be: ear in line with shoulder – in line with elbow – in line with hip – in line with heel.

There should be an imaginary straight line drawn from the rider's elbow, down the forearm to the hand and down the rein to the horse's mouth.

The joints of the ankles, knees and hips act as shock absorbers – the capacity to absorb shock is at its highest when the joint is slightly flexed. Setting or forced fixing of the position causes tension in the body, which will prevent the rider from going with the horse.

The head

You should look up and ahead in the direction of movement in order to maintain balance. Looking down, collapsing the chest and rounding the shoulders affect balance and make your position less effective.

To help maintain correct head position, imagine:

- A full-length mirror in front of you – look your reflection in the eye.

- A piece of string attached to the top of your crash cap, pulling you upwards.

Loss of balance is nearly always caused through tipping forwards, which results in the rider's weight being lifted off the seat bones and onto the front arch or fork only. To correct this, exaggerate looking up; this will raise and correct the body angle. The head and shoulders are the heaviest parts of the rider's body; any tilting of the head, either forwards or to one side, will cause loss of balance. Therefore your head should not tip

13.1 Correct riding position

forwards, backwards or to the side. The chin should be raised so that the jawline is perpendicular to the ground. To help prevent your chin jutting forwards, think of bringing the back of your neck back towards your collar.

Riders often feel compelled to look down at the horse's neck – as mentioned, dropping the whole head alters weight distribution and affects your balance. As long as the head stays up, you can look down if necessary by moving your eyes only.

There should be no tension through the jaw, neck or shoulders, as this will transmit to other parts of the body and also to the horse.

The shoulders

The shoulders should be held square and level, with a slight feeling of drawing the shoulder-blades together, whilst avoiding tension. It is easy to become tight and stiff when trying to do this so it is often better to get the same result by thinking of raising and opening the chest.

Tightness in the shoulders affects the back and arms, which will impede the horse's free forward movement.

If you are naturally round-shouldered you will need to work on improving your posture, otherwise this rounding will cause tipping forwards in the saddle, which will spoil your position and weight the horse's forehand. A round-shouldered rider often also has a rounded back, which then cannot be used effectively in absorption of movement or as an aid.

The back

When riding, your back should be 'straight' yet supple. The spine naturally curves inwards at the small of the back. This doesn't mean that the back should be hollowed or rounded; it should maintain its normal slight 'S' shape. When sitting in the correct position you will be able to follow the horse's movement, using the muscles in your back in a 'concertina' effect to absorb the horse's movement. An incorrect position limits the use of the back.

When the spine is following its natural arch or curve, the rider's pelvis shows a slight forward rotation.

The seat

The seat provides the support for the body when the rider sits in the saddle. The rider effectively sits on a bony tripod or 'three-point seat', made more comfortable by the fleshy tissue-covering in that area (and hopefully a comfortable saddle!).

Sit in the deepest part of the saddle, which is nearer the front than the back. Sitting on the back of the saddle will cause you to be 'left behind' as you will not be over the horse's centre of movement.

Aim for a feeling of closeness between the seat, thighs and inside legs with the saddle and horse's sides. To help achieve this open your hips as wide as possible to enable your legs to drop down naturally.

Try to ensure that you sit evenly in the saddle with weight distributed equally on each seat bone.

The aim is to develop an independent seat – a seat that can be maintained independently of the reins or any other false safety net. Gripping causes tension and compromises the seat.

The legs

As mentioned above, the legs should descend naturally from open hips. The hips play an essential role in the absorption of the horse's movement. Imagine your hips are twice as wide as normal so your legs can drop down around the horse's sides without undue stretching.

The leg should be directly under you, as if you were standing with slightly bent knees. This will ensure the alignment of the ear-shoulder-hip-heel. When not in use, the legs should stay lightly in contact with the horse's sides, not gripping but soft and relaxed.

Differences in rider conformation will affect the ability to take up the ideal position. For example, the short-legged rider with broad thighs will find it less easy to keep the legs close to the horse, but with practice a perfectly good position should be achievable.

With regard to function, the leg can be divided into two parts:

1. **The thigh** is an integral part of the seat, acting to hold the seat in position.

2. **The lower leg** applies the aids. It serves no purpose in gripping and will actually act to force the rider out of the saddle if used in this way.

Riders often grip up when first learning to maintain their balance and use their legs. To correct this tendency to grip, think of the knees descending as low as possible, as if kneeling.

The position of the lower legs can affect your overall balance. If they move too far forward this will cause the upper body to become behind the movement; too far back and the upper body will tip forwards.

The feet form the lowest point of the riding position with the stirrups holding some of the weight of your legs. Generally, most of your weight is supported on the seat, with just sufficient weight bearing down on the stirrups to keep them in place on the balls of the feet. This weight through the legs travels down into the heels as the lowest point. The deep heel position should not be forced as this will cause tension in the body. Instead, gravity should be allowed its influence. The fact that the heel is lower than the toe tightens the calf muscle at the back of the lower leg which, in turn, helps you give clearer leg aids, because to the tone of the calf muscle.

The arms and hands

The arms should hang naturally down by your sides, with the elbows brushing against the outside of the pelvis.

The bend in the elbow permits a straight line to be drawn along the forearm, wrist, hand and rein to the bit in the horse's mouth. This is the rider's direct line of communication, which should not be broken by faults in the position of the arm, wrist or hand. The hand should be positioned 'thumb on top' to allow flexibility of the elbow and ensure that the bones of the forearm (the radius and ulna) are parallel, with the radius above the ulna. Turning the hand over, as if to play the piano, results in twisting of the bones of the forearm and restriction of the use of the elbow.

The reins are held in a gentle fist, the fingers closed lightly around the reins. The reins enter the hand between the little and ring fingers, come over the palm and up between the thumb and index finger, where the excess is allowed to drape down over the horse's neck. The tightness of the fist will vary, but imagine that you are holding a small bird in each hand. You don't want them to fly away, yet you mustn't crush them.

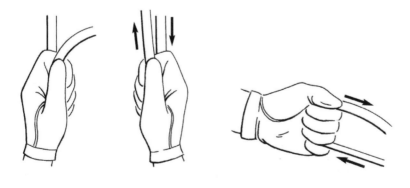

13.2 Holding the reins correctly

The fist can open slightly to allow the horse forward, or can close in a resisting action to prevent or check forward motion.

The hands must never come back towards your body, or pull, as this is a negative attitude and will result in the horse pulling against you. Human beings rely on their manual dexterity in almost every other walk of life, but must be retrained when learning to ride to give the seat, legs and back priority and not rely on the hands.

The hands assist the seat and legs to unite the horse and have two main functions:

1. **Passive resistance** – when slowing or stopping, the hands cease to allow and reflect the blocking of further forward movement employed by the seat and back.

2. **Allowing** – the seat, legs and back ask the horse to move forward, and the hands permit the horse to obey by allowing – opening the fist slightly.

At all other times the hands maintain a steady, even, yet elastic (i.e. not rigid) contact.

BASIC INDICATORS OF CORRECT RIDING

When riding any horse, whether at home or in the Stage 2 exam, as a minimum you should aim to have:

- Obedience.

- Controlled forward impulsion.

- An even rhythm in all gaits.

Combined with effective use of the arena and accurately ridden school movements, whilst maintaining a correct position, this will help you to demonstrate a good level of competence.

You should ideally also show awareness of:

- Straightness.

- Balance.

- Acceptance of the bit.

- Suppleness.

The level to which these qualities are present in the horses you ride in the Stage 2 exam will vary. However, while standards of schooling and responsiveness may vary, you should not be asked to ride horses who are downright disobedient.

The following are notes on some key issues.

ITQ 13.1

Why is it necessary to adopt the correct riding position?

ITQ 13.2

Which two imaginary straight lines can be drawn when the rider is sitting correctly?

ITQ 13.3

What are the two main functions of the hands?

Controlled forward impulsion

The horse should go forwards willingly when asked, i.e. be responsive to the leg aids and show free forward movement. If a leg aid is ignored it must be reinforced quickly with a tap with the schooling whip. The hands must then soften accordingly.

Impulsion mustn't be confused with speed – a horse working with impulsion doesn't necessarily need to be travelling quickly. If the horse is working well, a slower rhythm can often be established. Impulsion must be controlled – ideally the horse should be calm and settled in his work. If the horse is calm he will be relaxed and therefore more likely to be obedient and responsive.

Rhythm

In terms of gait, rhythm can be described as the regularly recurring sequence of footfall. The interval between footfalls remains the same. The aim should be to develop an even rhythm in all gaits. Rhythm follows on naturally after free forward movement has been achieved. Good rhythm is easiest to achieve in trot because of its pronounced two-time beat.

By maintaining rhythm the horse is encouraged to become more balanced as the hocks must be used to maintain an even rhythm on circles. Some horses are naturally more balanced than others and will find it easier to maintain a good rhythm.

Suppleness

For the horse to be able to move freely he needs to be supple. Suppleness can be demonstrated as the horse working in a relaxed manner, free of tension: he should bend evenly on either rein and change bend smoothly when asked. The supple horse's back appears to 'swing' – the tail is relaxed (as opposed to clamped or swishing), hanging naturally.

Straightness

The horse is said to be straight when his hind legs follow the tracks of the forelegs. The horse should be on two tracks whether on a straight line or on a circle. (That is, his offside hooves fall on one track, the nearside hooves fall on the other.) When on a circle the horse's body uniformly follows the curve of the circle. Excessive neck bend to the inside should be avoided as this leads to the horse 'falling out' through his outside shoulder. When the horse falls out, his outside foreleg moves on a third track with the result that the horse is then not straight. Excessive neck bend to the outside will cause the horse to fall in on his inside shoulder.

The horse will find it easier to be straight when he is supple – any uneven muscular development and stiffness will cause the horse to be crooked.

Balance

Once the horse is working with controlled impulsion, an even rhythm and is supple and straight, this is evidence that he is balanced. Good balance is necessary if the horse is to carry his own weight, and that of the rider, distributed equally over all four limbs.

EXAM TIP

When riding unknown horses in an exam, try to think about each aspect of their way of going. Compare how they feel to horses of varying standards that you have ridden previously and try to produce a description of them in terms of how they feel when ridden on straight lines and how they feel when ridden around corners or on a circle: are they balanced and supple or do they find bending and changing bend difficult and/or unbalancing? Consider whether they feel forward-going and responsive to the leg aids or whether you are having to push them along constantly and tap them with the whip. In this way you will be prepared to answer any questions and make comment on each horse as and when required.

THE AIDS

The aids provide the means of communication between rider and horse and can be regarded as a language which the rider teaches and the horse learns. The aids are applied through varying pressures with the seat, legs and hands. The horse learns to yield or respond to this vocabulary of pressures. The reward for correct yielding or response is a cessation of the aid.

A trained horse will respond to refined aids which enable him to be light and responsive to ride.

The aids control and mediate:

- The rhythm.

- The energy, impulsion or desire to go forwards.

- The gait – which includes halt and the transitions between and within gaits.

- The bend.

- Turning.

The aids can be divided into natural and artificial:

The natural aids	**The artificial aids**
Seat	Whip
Legs	Spurs
Back	Martingale
Hands	Various gadgets
Voice	

In the early stages of learning to ride you will use natural aids and should only ride with artificial aids once balance and coordination are established and you understand the need for and use of such aids.

The natural aids

Seat influences

The seat can help initiate, maintain and control impulsion. It is also helps establish the horse's correct outline by assisting the engagement and drawing under of the hind legs with the subsequent rounding of the horse's back.

It also plays an essential role in determining direction of movement through the use of weight. When the rider is in the correct central position, the upright position of the pelvis enables the legs freedom to operate. Through turning of the pelvis (*not* tipping) the horse is encouraged to turn. This is described in more detail under Turns and Circles later this chapter.

Leg influences

The legs produce impulsion by activating the horse's hindquarters. If the hindquarters are inactive, the horse will seem to pull himself along from the shoulders, instead of the desired pushing forward from the hindquarters. To produce more activity in walk, the legs are used alternately, in time with the lateral steps of the gait; in trot and canter they are used together – although in canter the outside leg will be a little further back. The legs are also used to produce bend in the horse's body and indicate changes of direction.

The legs should give changing pressure against the horse's sides, as constant pressure will be resented and later ignored. The leg aid acts by a closing in or nudging action, not a kick. The legs should not be moved further back on the horse's body if there is no initial response, as this puts you into the wrong position, which will confuse the horse and affect your balance. The inside of the leg, from under the knee to the instep of the foot, is used to give the aid. The back of the heel is not used, as this turns the knee and toe out, forcing the rider out of the saddle.

Back influences

The back can be used to encourage the horse forwards or to slow him. It can quietly follow the movement of the horse through its concertina action, enabling the horse to move freely under the rider. It can be used more strongly, to drive the horse forward for extension or to encourage a horse who is thinking about refusing a jump (both uses requiring that the rider's seat is fully in the saddle).

Hand influences

The hands channel the impulsion produced by the legs and seat. They help regulate speed – the outside hand being chiefly responsible for this when riding in an arena. The hands also work as a pair to indicate direction – the inside hand asking for the bend, the outside hand supporting with the rein against the neck. Used in this way the reins are referred to as the **direct** and **indirect rein** respectively. It is useful to consider the hands as an extension of the seat.

Voice influences

The voice is a very useful aid – it can be used to calm, reward and correct and is important in the initial training of the young horse. It is the *tone* of voice used, rather than the actual words, which the horse will listen to – although some riding school horses seem to recognise words used by the instructor, which can leave the rider as an unwilling passenger. For example the instructor may say, 'Prepare to walk' and before the rider can respond the horse is walking.

The voice should not be used as punishment; shouting at a horse is likely to upset him rather than correct him. A raised voice tends to indicate fear in the rider or handler.

The artificial aids

The whip

A whip is only carried to back-up or reinforce the leg aid. It should not be used to punish the horse.

There are two types of whip used for general equitation:

Schooling whip – usually about 100cm (39in) long, used only for flatwork.

Jumping whip – approximately 76cm (30in) long used when showjumping or cross-country jumping.

When working in the school, the whip is carried in the inside hand to support your inside leg and help discourage the horse from 'falling in'. Each time the rein is changed the whip should be changed.

When needed, the whip is used once immediately behind the rider's leg. The whip should not be used further back than this as it will not be reinforcing the leg aid and will probably cause the horse to buck or kick out.

To use a schooling whip, keep hold of the rein, bring the whip hand away from the horse's neck and flick the wrist to apply the whip just behind your leg.

To use a short whip, the reins should be taken into the outside hand and the free hand used to apply a light tap with the whip. This prevents the horse from getting jabbed in the mouth. Allow the horse to go forwards once the whip has been used.

When not in use, the whip should rest across your thigh, being held by the inside hand when riding in an arena. Only a short length of whip handle should protrude at the top of the hand to avoid injury should the horse throw his head up suddenly.

To change the schooling whip from one hand to the other

1 Point the end of the whip upwards as you take both reins into the whip hand (the hand holding the whip).

2 Bring your free hand across the top of the horse's neck and take hold of the handle of the whip.

3 Take the whip over the top of the horse's neck, handle downwards.

EXAM TIP

Try to use the voice in a similar manner to how it is used when lungeing. A slow, low-pitched and relaxed voice will calm the horse and steady him down whilst a higher-pitched faster voice will encourage him forward.

SAFETY TIP

▶ Note that when praising the horse he will much prefer a gentle stroke on the neck and a verbal 'Good boy' to a big slap on the neck or rub around the head, which may startle him.

④ Retake the reins in both hands and position the whip so it rests across your thigh.

To change the short whip from one hand to the other

① Put both reins in the whip hand.

② Take hold of the top of the whip with the spare hand and pull the whip through over the horse's withers.

③ Retake the reins in both hands and position the whip so it rests across your thigh.

Spurs

Only experienced riders with a secure leg position should wear spurs. They should be regarded as a refinement of the leg aid and should never be worn pointing up into the horse's sides. You will not wear spurs in your Stage 1 or 2 exams.

The running martingale

A running martingale can usefully be worn by the novice rider's horse. Its main function is to prevent the horse carrying his head too high by exerting pressure on the bit when the horse raises his head beyond the point of control.

Gadgets

Balancing reins, draw reins, Market Harboroughs and other such gadgets have no place in the tack worn by a horse ridden by beginners or novices. It is a point of contention with some trainers as to whether they have a place at all and it is beyond the scope of this book to debate the subject; suffice to say that in the hands of an inexperienced rider, such gadgets can do irreparable harm to the horse, both physically and to his mental attitude to work.

SAFETY TIP

▶ Remember that a martingale is never used to force the horse's head down so must be fitted correctly. Make sure you check a martingale on any horse you ride to ensure it is well fitted and has all the required rubber stoppers.

'On the aids'

While we are discussing the aiding system it is relevant to look at the term 'on the aids'.

A horse is said to be 'on the aids' when he appears alert, responsive, yet calm and trusting – ready and able to carry out the rider's requests with ease and enthusiasm. In other words, he is finely attuned to all of the rider's aids; in no way alarmed by them but ready and willing to obey they signals they send.

Not every horse presented in the Stage 2 exam will be completely 'on the aids'; you must practise riding a range of horses, including slightly staid, even 'lazy' horses, so you are effective on these types.

Rein contact – acceptance of the bit

In the early stages of learning to ride you should aim to maintain a light and even rein contact, allowing the horse to position his head naturally.

As training progresses, you can ask the horse to accept a light and 'elastic' contact on both reins without resisting your hands. Gradually the horse is encouraged to lower

ITQ 13.4 ?

List the artificial and natural aids available to the rider.

his head, slightly rounding the neck. This should happen naturally without being forced.

The horse should gradually yield softly to the hand when asked and accept the rider's aids without resistance. As training of both horse and rider progresses the horse is asked to work consistently 'on the bit'. The horse is said to be 'on the bit' when:

- He moves freely forward with controlled impulsion.

- He is straight, accepting and taking the same contact on each rein.

- He accepts the bit without resistance.

- He is submissive to the rider's aids.

- His neck is slightly raised and arched, with the poll being the highest point of the neck.

- His whole outline gives the appearance of being generally convex (rounded upwards) rather than 'hollow'. The degree of 'roundness' will be dependent on his level of training and the movement being performed.

- His head remains steady, with the front line of the face slightly in front of the vertical.

- He is free from stiffness, in particular through the neck and back.

At Stage 2 level you are not expected to work the horse 'on the bit' but you should demonstrate a non-restricting, yet controlling, rein contact.

It is worth noting that the expression 'on the bit' is used because it is mainly through astute use of the rein contact, carefully metering and directing the horse's forward impulse, that the desired head-carriage and overall body posture are achieved. However, this situation cannot be attained before the horse is substantially 'on the aids' – i.e. he first must be willing to move forward in response to the seat and leg aids, and he must not be resistant to the bit. In other words, while the first four bullet points above are indications that the horse is 'on the bit', they must be substantially in evidence *before* this can be achieved.

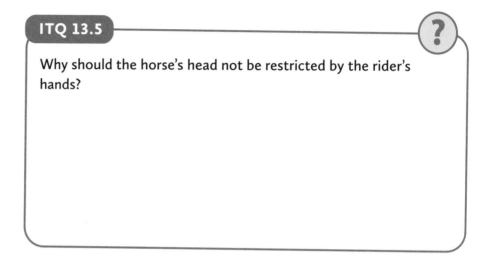

ITQ 13.5

Why should the horse's head not be restricted by the rider's hands?

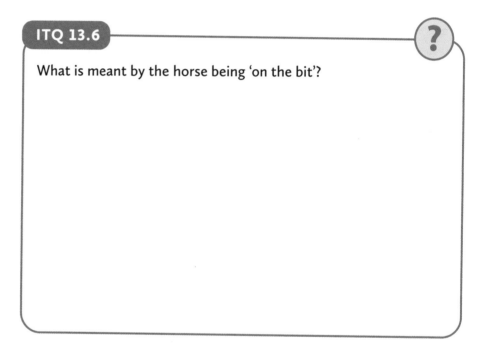

ITQ 13.6

What is meant by the horse being 'on the bit'?

TRANSITIONS

Preparation

To increase the chances of making a smooth and clear transition you must first ensure that the horse is moving actively forwards in an even rhythm.

Before making any transition you should give the horse a preparatory signal. As you progress in your training this is often referred to as a 'half-halt'; it helps balance and prepare the horse for another instruction. Very simply, before you want to make your actual transition you need to get your horse's attention and make sure he is prepared for, and therefore 'listening' to the upcoming aids. To do this you should make sure you have sufficient impulsion by using your legs and seat and, as you do so, apply slight pressure to the reins (which is almost immediately released). This acts as if to say: 'Listen to me – I'm about to ask you to do something else…' Then follow on with the aids to make your transition.

You must prepare the horse slightly in advance of the arena marker at which you wish to make your transition. If you have been instructed to make a transition in between two markers, you should aim to do so in the middle of the two. Do not leave it too late to prepare or you are likely to miss the arena marker.

> **EXAM TIPS**
>
> Remember that when carrying out a half-halt the leg and seat aids are always applied before the hand aids. The whole half-halt should last around a second.
>
> A good way to think of making downward transitions is that you are trying to slow the entire horse, not just his head, thus you must use your seat and legs as well as rein aids to have the desired effect on the entire horse.

Upward transitions

A good upward transition is active, smooth and positive. The horse must be attentive and listening, ready to move immediately in response to your leg aids. Good preparation increases the chance of making a clean transition.

To make an upward transition from halt to walk, keep a light and even contact on the reins, maintain an upright position and squeeze with both legs simultaneously. The rein contact must allow the horse to move forwards. As he moves forwards the leg aids can cease unless he is reluctant to move actively forwards, in which case the leg aid can be repeated.

To move from walk to trot make sure you have a good quality (calmly active) walk and apply a preparatory aid. Most horses naturally hold their heads a little higher in trot than walk, so shorten the reins slightly in preparation.

Use both legs to ask the horse to move off into trot and, as he does so, ensure your hands allow him to move forwards. Remain sitting for the first three or four strides – start to rise as the outside shoulder goes forwards to ensure you are on the correct diagonal. If you find you are incorrect, sit one extra beat straight away to make the correction.

The aids from trot to canter are discussed later in this chapter (Riding at Canter).

Downward transitions

Examples of downward transitions are from canter to trot, from trot to walk and from walk to halt. At this stage (the Stage 2 exam) transitions from canter to walk or trot to halt are made progressively, i.e. through the intervening gait, and are termed **progressive transitions**. **Direct transitions**, which miss out the intervening gait (e.g. canter to walk or trot to halt), are more demanding of horse and rider and require effective use of the half-halt. You will not be required to make such transitions at Stages 1 or 2.

To make a downward transition, apply a preparatory aid, then, keeping your legs close to the horse's sides to maintain impulsion, sit tall yet deeply into the saddle and brace your back slightly while applying light resistance with the reins. As the horse obeys your instructions release (but do not lose) the rein contact. You must practise riding downward transitions using the seat and back, making sure you never rely solely on the reins.

THE ELEMENTS OF SCHOOL FIGURES

School figures are basically made up straight lines, turns and circles (or part-circles). Riding these elements correctly is, therefore, the foundation for riding accurate figures.

Keeping the horse straight

When moving on straight lines, e.g. when riding down the straight sides of the school, across the school on a diagonal, or up a centre or quarter line, the horse's body should be straight, without lateral bend in the spine and, on each side of his body, the hind foot should follow the track made by the forefoot. His head and neck should be straight, i.e. there must be no flexion in the neck and his head should not tilt one way or the other.

Straightness is achieved by maintaining a good level of impulsion and an even rein and leg contact. If the horse deviates from straightness, you should make the necessary correction using leg and/or rein aids. If the horse's quarters swing inwards or outwards, draw your relevant leg back slightly behind the girth and apply it to correct the deviation of the quarters. If the horse's neck flexes inwards or outwards, use the appropriate rein to make a correction. This will usually entail taking a slightly firmer contact with the rein on the opposite side to which the horses is flexing his neck. However, be careful that you do not *cause* the flexion by taking too strong a contact on the side to which the horse flexes.

The most common cause of lack of straightness is loss of impulsion and forward momentum – just as when riding a bicycle, it is easier to stay on a straight line when moving positively forwards; much more difficult when moving slowly.

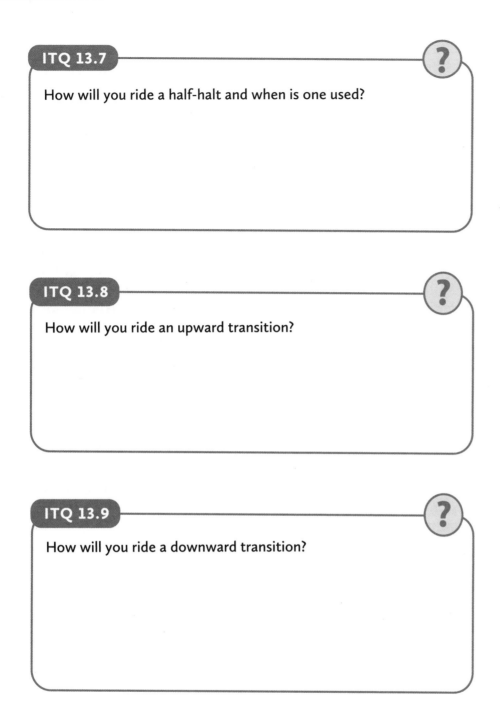

ITQ 13.7 ?

How will you ride a half-halt and when is one used?

ITQ 13.8 ?

How will you ride an upward transition?

ITQ 13.9 ?

How will you ride a downward transition?

Turns and circles

Turns and circles will be dealt with together because their aids are the same, i.e. the aids to ride a circle to the right are the same as to ride a turn to the right, and the principles for correct circling are the same as for correct turning.

The horse changes his direction of motion by turning either to the left or the right – his body following the shape of the turn laterally. For example, when the horse turns to the right, his right side contracts as it follows the inside of the bend and his outside lengthens to take the longer route through the turn.

The horse's body effectively takes on a slight curve from poll to tail when viewed from above. The horse's hind feet follow in the tracks of the forefeet and he looks in the direction in which he is travelling. The same is true when working on a circle.

The aids to turn and circle

In this example, we will assume the intention is to turn or circle right. To do so to the left, the aids are reversed.

As the horse is moving forward in the chosen gait, ask him to flex and look slightly to the right by closing the fist of your right hand so you can just see the horse's right eye. The outside (left) rein limits the bend and speed, and controls the horse's outside shoulder. 'Controlling the outside shoulder' can be a difficult concept to understand when learning.

As the horse turns or moves on a circle he must travel on **two tracks**. This means that his right hooves are on one track, his left hooves on another. In the event that the horse's neck is bent too much to the inside, it can cause the horse's outside shoulder to drift outwards, termed 'falling out' or 'losing the outside shoulder'. The outside foreleg then takes up its own track, i.e. the horse moves on three tracks, which is incorrect in these situations.

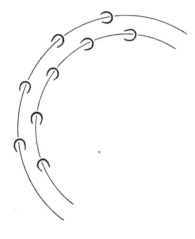

13.3 Working on two tracks

To prevent this, a contact must be maintained on the outside rein; this stops the neck from bending too much to the inside and therefore controls the shoulder. The outside leg behind the girth stops the quarters from swinging out. If the quarters swing out, the outside hind leg takes up a third track and the horse does not genuinely bend through the turn or circle.

The rider's legs are used to bend the horse by maintaining the inside leg (inside the bend of the body – in this case the right leg) on the girth, but pressing a little more weight down onto the right stirrup and seat bone, and drawing the outside leg (left leg) back a little behind the girth to control the swing of the horse's quarters.

The inside leg on the girth therefore helps to produce the bend but also acts to stop the horse from falling in. The whip is carried in the inside hand to reinforce the leg aid.

Forward momentum must always be maintained and ideally there should be no loss of rhythm through the turn. If the rider's legs are not used correctly through a turn or on a circle, and the reins are relied on, the horse will be unbalanced, probably falling out through his outside shoulder, or swinging his quarters out, and the rhythm will be lost.

The smaller the circle or more acute the turn, the greater the degree of bend required from the horse. Therefore, in early lessons the novice rider is taught to ride 20m and 15m circles, and turns must be made simply through oblique angles.

ITQ 13.10   **?**

What are the functions of the following when riding a turn or circle?

a. Inside leg:

b. Outside leg:

c. Inside rein:

d. Outside rein:

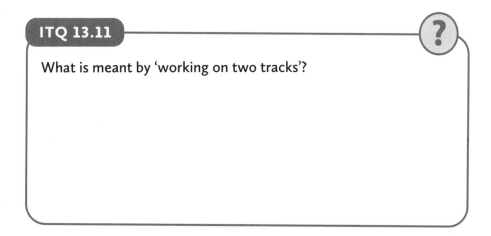

ITQ 13.11

What is meant by 'working on two tracks'?

BALANCE, SECURITY AND HARMONY IN THE GAITS

Riding at walk

The walk is the easiest gait in which to practise and show correct posture. Avoid obviously 'pushing' the horse along with your seat; use the legs alternately to maintain impulsion, ensuring that your hands move gently in harmony with the horse's head movement in order to retain the correct contact.

Riding at trot

Rising trot

As the horse moves into trot, sit for the first three or so strides, before starting to rise.

When riding in the school, you should sit as the outside diagonal comes to the ground. The diagonals are identified as inside or outside according to the foreleg, e.g. on the right rein the outside diagonal is the left foreleg and right hind leg.

To be on the correct diagonal you should rise as the horse's outside shoulder moves forward away from you and sit when the outside shoulder comes back towards you. To begin with you can glance down at the shoulder but you should eventually be able to tell by feel whether you are on the correct diagonal or not.

If incorrect, i.e. rising when the horse's outside shoulder comes back, correct by sitting for one beat and then rising again. When the rein is changed, so is the diagonal to ensure that both sides of the horse's body muscles are worked equally. At each changing of the rein across the diagonal you should sit for an extra beat as you pass over X.

The reason for selecting the outside diagonal is to ensure that your seat is in the saddle when the horse's inside hind leg is on the ground, prior to propelling the horse forward. You can then use your back, seat and legs more efficiently to promote balance and impulsion. When hacking, the diagonals should be changed occasionally to avoid either horse or rider favouring one or the other.

Sitting trot

When sitting to the trot with stirrups allow your back and seat to absorb movement and your legs to stretch down, without gripping, which would cause you to lose your stirrups.

ITQ 13.12

Why is it important to ride on the correct diagonal in trot?

ITQ 13.13

When riding on the left rein, how would you check that you are riding on the correct diagonal, and which diagonal is this?

Riding at canter

The aids to canter

During the transition to canter, the horse should look very slightly to the inside – being the side of the desired leading leg. This is most easily achieved if the canter strike-off is asked for in a corner of the school, when the horse should naturally be bent to the inside.

The corner also helps to balance the horse for the transition to canter, making it more likely that he will strike off on the correct leg. As you become more practised you can progress to cantering on a named leg on a straight line without the assistance of a corner but, for the purposes of your Stage 2 exam, you must ask for the transition in a corner.

Plan which corner you are going to use and prepare several strides in advance. The rein length used for trot should not need altering but you should ensure that the trot is active and the horse attentive.

Take sitting trot approximately 4–6 strides before your planned transition.

Sit with the inside hip slightly in advance of the outside hip and allow the inside (inside of the bend) leg to come deep as it stays at the girth. The outside leg (on the outside of the bend) is drawn back behind the girth.

To make sure the horse is listening, give a preparatory aid just before your planned transition.

Stay upright and look ahead during the transition – do not tip forward over the horse's shoulders. Apply both legs in this position and slightly open the fingers to permit the horse to obey. The contact is maintained as the fingers allow for the rocking motion of the horse's body. As in sitting trot, you must remain sitting deep in the saddle; the legs can be reapplied as necessary to maintain the canter.

You will feel and follow sinking, advancing and lifting movements as the horse canters.

Cantering on the correct lead

At Stage 2 you must be able to identify the correct lead. If the horse is on the correct leg, the inside foreleg should feel as if it is advancing further forwards than the outside foreleg. It is important to practise feeling this. When learning it is acceptable, initially, to look for the canter lead. Do so by glancing down towards the front of the horse's inside shoulder *without* leaning or tipping your head forwards. You should see the horse's inside foreleg stretching out further forwards than the reach of the outside foreleg.

When you know you are on the correct leg, spend time developing a feel for this. You are aiming to be able to tell which leg you are on purely through feel. As your training progresses you will ultimately be able to tell which foreleg the horse is going to lead with simply by feeling which hind leg has taken the first step of the sequence during the transition and, if it is the inside hind, you will be able to correct it before the horse has even taken one complete stride!

If the horse strikes off on the incorrect lead you must make a transition back to trot immediately (this proves to the examiners you knew you were on the incorrect leg), and prepare and ask again on the next corner. If the horse strikes off on the incorrect lead yet again, trot and bring him on to a 20m circle to ask again. Do not panic and rush him off into canter as he will be likely to strike off incorrectly again. Take your time to rebalance him, establish a good rhythm and make sure your canter aids are very clear.

EXAM TIP

Never canter on the incorrect lead in your exam. If the horse is problematical you must keep trying to correct the canter lead.

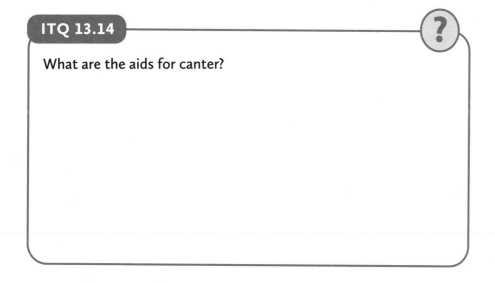

ITQ 13.14 ?

What are the aids for canter?

ITQ 13.15

If the horse strikes off on the incorrect canter lead what will you do?

?

EXAM TIP

If it is proving very difficult to get the horse to strike off correctly there are a number of things you can try:

- Be a little firmer with your outside leg when asking for the canter transition.

- Move your outside leg a little further back to insist upon the correct strike-off.

- Ask for a little more bend of the head to the inside (providing you are applying enough support via the legs and seat).

- Ride a 15m or 20m circle and ask for canter on the circle.

- Ride a different school exercise such as a figure of eight or serpentine to ensure the horse is listening and then ask again for the canter.

The disunited canter

In a correct, united, canter the sequence of footfall is outside hind, inside hind and outside fore together (the outside diagonal) and finally, inside fore. When looking at a horse cantering correctly, the inside foreleg and inside hind leg appear to be coming forwards together, although if looked at in slow motion, you would seen the inside hind is fractionally ahead of the inside fore.

In a disunited canter the horse moves incorrectly – although he is correct in front, the diagonal is split and the inside hind does not move with the outside fore. It appears that the inside foreleg and inside hind are moving away from each other – the hind leg moves backwards as the foreleg moves forward. This is sometimes termed as 'incorrect' or 'wrong behind'.

Alternatively, the opposite may occur when the horse leads with the incorrect foreleg *and* is disunited.

In these cases, the three-beat rhythm will be lost and the horse will be crooked and will probably fall into a hurried trot as it will be difficult to maintain a disunited canter in the confines of the school. You will feel that something is wrong as it is an uncomfortable movement to sit to. The corrections for a disunited canter are the same as for an incorrect lead.

Riding without stirrups

Riding without stirrups demonstrates your balance and proves that you do not rely on the stirrups to remain secure in the saddle.

When instructed to ride without stirrups you must halt your horse in line, a safe distance away from other horses. Take your feet out of your stirrups, remove the leather from the stirrup leather loop and pull the buckle of the right-hand stirrup leather down approximately 10cm (4in). Cross the stirrup leather and iron over onto the left-hand side of the horse's neck/shoulder. Turn the leather so it lies flat and untwisted in front of your thigh.

Repeat with the left leather and iron, crossing this over onto the horse's right shoulder. Keeping the left iron on top means that if you have to dismount (or fall off) and need to remount, the left stirrup is easy to pull down.

When riding without stirrups it is important to maintain a balanced position, allowing the seat to absorb movement and the legs to stretch down, without gripping, whilst keeping the toe lifted slightly. When trotting without stirrups you will maintain sitting trot.

Riding with the reins in one hand

When asked to demonstrate riding with the reins in one hand you should make sure they are short enough to give control, bridge them together and hold both reins in your outside hand. Allow your inside arm to hang down by your side. In this particular instance, the whip should be held under the thumb of the outside hand, i.e. the hand holding the reins, but positioned so that it rests down the horse's inside shoulder or across your thigh.

13.4 Holding the reins in one hand

ITQ 13.16

What is a disunited canter, and how will you correct it?

?

ITQ 13.17

How should you hold the reins and whip when asked to ride with the reins in one hand?

?

RIDING IN AN ARENA

This section has dealt so far with flatwork *technique*. Some of the issues relating to school commands and riding in company are now explained – this will help you in the presentation of your flatwork in the Stage 2 exam.

Names and dimensions

The original *haute école* (high school) manèges of centuries gone by were very much smaller than those used today because the horses were worked mostly in a state of great collection, which required less room (and the horses themselves were generally smaller). Arenas today tend to reflect the dimensions of the dressage competition arena.

There are various names for the place where horses are worked, these include:

● School (this can be indoor or outdoor).

● Arena (tends to indicate either an area marked out for dressage, or a large jumping area.)

• Manège (*not* ménage, which is French for household!).

The standard size of arena is 20 x 40m: an international-size arena measures 20 x 60m and permits riders to perform more advanced dressage tests. It has more marker letters than the smaller arena. In the Stage 2 exam you will use the markers of the standard-sized arena only so we shall not discuss the international size arena further.

An easy way to remember the sequence of marker letters around the 20 x 40m arena is to recite the following:

All **K**ing **E**dward's **H**orses **C**an **M**anage **B**ig **F**ences (Clockwise from A)

A **F**at **B**lack **M**anx **C**at **H**ad **E**leven **K**ittens (anticlockwise from A)

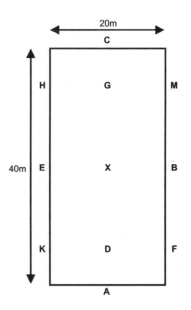

13.5 Standard 40 x 20m arena

Alternatively, you can make up your own memory jogger. In addition, the (usually imaginary) letters D, X and G are located along the centre line. D marks the point midway between F and K, being 6m in from A on the short side of the school. X marks the point at the centre of the school, being halfway between A and C, and halfway between B and E. G marks the point midway between M and H, being 6m in from C on the other short side.

The relative locations of the markers in a 20 x 40m arena are shown in Figure 13.5. There are a couple of useful points to note about the arena:

1 The markers M, F, K and H are called **quarter markers:** they are *not* in the arena corners and should not be referred to or thought of in these terms. If you think of them in these terms, you may well finish up riding 'diagonals' into the corners of the arena, which will make a correct turn through the corner impossible.

2 Although it should not be the case in your exam, some arenas are not of the correct dimensions, and this will affect the relative placing of the marker letters which, in turn, may affect the size and shape of figures ridden using them for reference.

School commands and terminology

Commands

When being taught and during the ridden element of your Stage 2 exam you will (should) receive two types of command:

1 **The preliminary command**

2 **The executive command**

The preliminary command gives you early warning of what will be required within the next few strides. It gives you the opportunity to prepare the movement. Examples of preliminary commands include:

• 'Prepare to go forwards to working trot rising.'

- 'Prepare to halt.'

- 'Prepare to turn right at E.'

So for example, upon hearing the preliminary command: 'Prepare to go forwards to working trot rising', you should ensure that you have suitable rein contact for the trot, check your position to avoid tipping forwards or dropping behind the movement, and give a preparatory aid to balance the horse and encourage his hind legs under his body to produce a clean, impulsive transition into trot when the executive command is given.

The executive command is the command which results in the execution of the movement or exercise. It is the culmination of the preparation that preceded it. Examples of executive commands include:

- 'And…go forwards to working trot, rising.'

- 'And…go forwards to halt.'

- 'And…right turn at E.'

Having had time to prepare the horse, when you hear the executive command, you should be in a position to carry out the exercise successfully. The word 'and' fills the gap between the preliminary command and the executive command and acts as another form of preparation – bear in mind, however, that not every commander in an exam may give their commands in exactly this way.

Time must also be allowed when asking a ride to perform a movement at a specific marker. For example, if the ride is in trot and you are expected to change the rein across the diagonal at H (from the left rein), the preliminary command should be given before the leading file reaches B. The command is likely to be: 'With Fred (or rider number) as leading file, whole ride change the rein across the long diagonal, HXF.'

Terminology
Having had riding lessons at an approved centre you will be familiar with the terminology used. In the exam you may hear very much the same sort of terms used.

- **'Form a ride behind Fred (or number one).'** This means that the other riders in the group lesson should fall in line in single file behind Fred who will be at the front. In an exam you will be wearing your candidate number on each arm so must listen out for your number.

- **'Check your safety distances.'** Ensure that your horse is out of kicking range of the horse in front. The normal safety distance is the length of another horse, or approximately 2m. You should be able to see at least half of the tail of the horse in front when you look between your horse's ears.

- **'Leading file.'** Refers to the rider at the front of the ride.

- **'Rear file.'** Refers to the rider at the rear of the ride.

- **'Whole ride.'** Refers to all of the riders. For example, the commander might say, 'Whole ride prepare to trot', followed by 'Whole ride trot-on' – when all of the riders should send their horses into trot simultaneously.

- **'Work in open order.'** This is where the riders in the group do not follow each other, but ride independently. They can pass each other, work at different gaits and different exercises as determined by the instructor, but need to observe school protocol (see page 284) if they are to do so safely. You may be given a few minutes to warm up in open order.

- **'The track'.** This is the long route all the way around the perimeter of the arena, sometimes called the 'outside track'.

- **'Track left.'** This means turn left at the track. The track is the perimeter of the arena, running along the fence line. 'Track right' means the opposite.

- **'Down the centre line.'** This is the route taken by the horse when ridden off the track at C (or A) and proceeding in a straight line to A (or C).

- **'Down the three-quarter line.'** This is the route taken when the horse turns halfway between A or C and the next long side, i.e. three-quarters of the way along the short side (15m). The three-quarter line is 5m in from the perimeter of the school.

- **'Across the centre.'** This is the route taken from B to E or E to B.

- **'Across the diagonal.'** The long diagonals are FXH or HXF when ridden on the left rein and MXK or KXM when ridden on the right rein. The short diagonals are M to E, B to K, H to B and E to F (and vice versa).

- **'Go large.'** This means, on completing the exercise being ridden, rejoin the outside track.

- **'Change the rein.'** This means change the direction in which you are going around the arena. When going around the arena anticlockwise, the horse is said to be on the left rein. When going clockwise, the horse is described as being on the right rein.

  There are many different ways of changing direction, some examples being:
  1. F X H or K X M across the long diagonal.
  2. C X A or A X C down the centre line.
  3. B X E or E X B across the centre.
  4. H B, K B, M E or F E across the short diagonal.
  5. B 10m half-circle right to X; X 10m half-circle left to E (or vice versa).
  6. Four-loop serpentine from A or C.
  7. 20m half-circle A to X; 20m half-circle X to C.
  8. 10m half-circle from F, for example, inclining diagonally back to the track at M This can also be reversed – ride a diagonal line off the track to the centre line and 10m half-circle back to the track.

- **'Inside'** and **'outside'** (leg, hand, etc.) When the horse is bent through his body

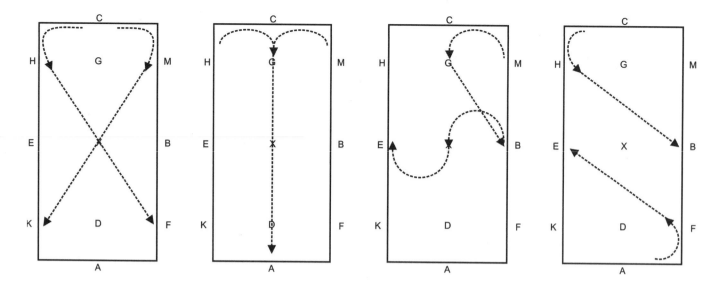

13.6 Some example methods of changing the rein

length, for example when turning, he will contract the side to which he bends. The rider's leg (etc.) on the inside of the horse's body bend is the inside leg. The rider's leg on the outside of the curve is the outside leg.

- **'20m circle.'** This size of circle takes up half of the standard size arena. If the 20m circle starts at A it will touch to track between K and E (about 4m up from K), at X and between B and F (about 4m up from F). To be a true circle it must be round, with no straight sides. Riders often go straight when they hit the track, or ride too much into the corners of the arena. The horse should be bent in the direction of the circle from poll to tail.

- **'15m circle.'** This is 5m smaller than the 20m circle, so requires increased bend from the horse's body. If started at A or C, it will not touch X or the outside track; it will be 2.5m in from the track at the two long sides of the school.

- **'10m circle.'** This is half the width of the arena. A 10m circle at B (or E) will touch the centre line at X and return to B (or E) to complete.

- **'Figure of eight.'** To ride this figure, you need to visualise what the number 8 looks like before trying to ride that shape in the arena. If starting the figure of eight from A on the right rein, you would ride half a 20m circle to the right to bring the horse onto X where the bend would be changed to the left. A complete 20m circle to the left is then ridden to bring the horse back onto X, where the bend is changed to the right once again to complete the other half of the 20m circle to the right. The horse will now be back at A.

- **'Two/three/four-loop serpentine.'** A serpentine is where the rider follows a path which will describe two, three of four loops of equal size within the arena. If asked for a two-loop serpentine from A, the exercise would start as the rider's shoulder passes A. If on the right rein (clockwise) the rider would bring the first loop to touch the track halfway between the short side on which A is situated, and E. The rider would straighten the horse over X before changing the bend to ride the second loop to touch the track halfway between B and the

EXAM TIP

Be very accurate as you ride to the markers. Take into account that you are deemed to be level with the marker when your body passes it.

short side on which C is situated. In this way two equal-sized loops be ridden, joined by a few straight steps over the centre of the school at X. With three- and four-loop serpentines, the same principle applies, that each loop should be of equal size, with a short straight line between each, which allows for the change of rein.

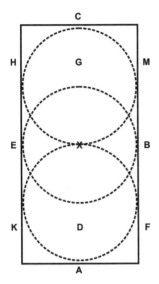

13.7 20m circles

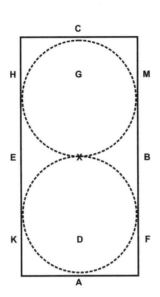

13.8 The figure of eight

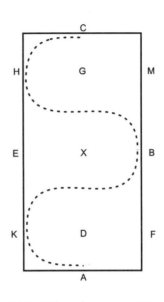

13.9 A three-loop serpentine

ITQ 13.18

What is meant by:

a. The preliminary command?

b. The executive command?

ITQ 13.19

What is meant by the 'safety distance'?

ITQ 13.20 | ?

What is the difference between working 'as a ride' and in 'open order'?

ITQ 13.21 | ?

List five ways of changing the rein in an arena:

1.

2.

3.

4.

5.

School protocol

For safety reasons there is a generally recognised protocol for working in a school.

● Permission should be gained before entering the arena to ensure the entrance is clear.

● The gate/door to the arena should be closed before ridden work commences to ensure an enclosed area to work in.

● Riders altering stirrups and tightening girths at the halt should come in off the track so as not to interfere with those already working.

● The session should commence and finish with the ride lined up off the track. Horses should not be halted too close together, when nipping and kicking are possible.

● A rider executing an exercise which requires passing the ride should be given plenty of room. Horses should never be boxed in or sandwiched between the wall and other horses as squabbles can ensue, which can include kicking.

- When working as a ride, correct safety distances must be maintained at all times unless instructed otherwise. The safety distance is the distance at which the horse behind cannot be kicked by the horse ahead (normally about 2m).

- Having completed an exercise in succession, i.e. one at a time, riders should ensure that they ride their downward transition in plenty of time to avoid running into the back of the rear file.

- When carrying out an exercise in succession – for example, cantering to the rear of the ride – the new leading file should wait to be told to go by the commander to ensure that the previous rider has completed the exercise.

- No rider may dismount or leave the arena without permission from the instructor.

Additional protocol relevant to working in open order

You will recall that 'open order' refers to riders working independently, not as a ride one after the other. This is a greater test of rider control and requires attention to the following points.

- When approaching each other head-on, riders should pass left to left. This means the rider on the left rein will take the outside track and the rider on the right rein will take the inside track.

- Riders working in walk will take the inside track to permit those working in trot or canter to have the outside track.

- Downward transitions and halt transitions are ridden down the long centre line A to C as much as possible to leave the track free.

- A rider wishing to canter whilst other riders are trotting on the outside track should request 'Track please' so that the track can be cleared.

- Since riders will be working independently, there will be those practising transitions, serpentines, circles, figures of eight, leg-yield, etc. The riders must always remain aware of the other horses and riders around them to avoid collisions and interrupting someone else's work. Working in open order requires riders to be intelligent, observant and adaptable.

- Riders performing more advanced movements are given priority in their use of the arena.

- Young horses, or those who have not worked in open order before, should be given plenty of room. Riders should be sensible about cantering past these newcomers, who can get anxious about all the apparently hectic activity going on in a confined space.

- A rider needing to use the whip should do so only when in a space. This should avoid accidents if the horse resents the whip and kicks out.

- Riders need to be aware of the instructor's location at all times. This can pose a

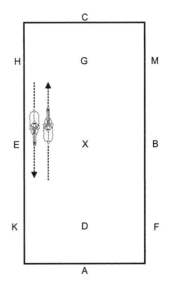

13.10 Passing left to left

EXAM TIP

Make sure that you practise riding in open order many times before your exam as it requires a huge amount of concentration, control and awareness. Be prepared to adapt the movement you are riding at any time to avoid collision.

SAFETY TIPS

▶ If you are riding a horse who is behaving badly in open order it is wise to initially make every effort to interest him in performing school movements to take his mind off being high-spirited! If this does not work, try removing him from the situation to calm him down before re-entering the arena to try again.

If you are in an exam and the horse is reacting very badly you should inform the examiner. Note, however, that horses used in Stage 2 exams are well used to working in open order so you should not encounter a problem.

problem as the instructor needs to move around in order to watch and comment on the work of the riders. It is the rider's job to avoid the instructor, not vice versa.

ITQ 13.22

List three points regarding school protocol and three points regarding working in open order.

Protocol:

1.

2.

3.

Working in open order:

1.

2.

3.

14 Riding Over Fences

REQUIRED SKILLS/KNOWLEDGE	Learnt, revised, practised?	Confirmed
Walk a showjump course.		
• Walk a route suitable for riding a course of showjumps.	☐	☐
Prepare for jumping, including over a grid of fences.		
• Maintain a secure, independent and balanced position at trot and canter, with stirrup leathers at jumping length.	☐	☐
• Ride safely according to the ground and weather conditions to maintain the horse's balance.	☐	☐
• Jump through a grid of fences in harmony with the horse.	☐	☐
Jump horses over a course of fences up to a maximum of 76cm (2ft 6in) high.		
• Ride horses over a course of fences in a secure, independent and balanced jumping position.	☐	☐
• *Use coordinated aids when riding over a course of fences.	☐	☐
• *Ride with a suitable rein contact at all times.	☐	☐
• *Show an effective control of pace.	☐	☐
• *Apply natural and artificial aids as required.	☐	☐
Ride and jump horses in harmony and with an awareness of others.		
• *Build up a rapport with the horse when riding.	☐	☐
• Jump horses with confidence.	☐	☐
• *Ride horses in harmony, to produce a fluently ridden course.	☐	☐
• *Ride safely with others.	☐	☐

* Many principles of riding are equally pertinent on the flat and over fences. For further information on the asterisked points, see Section 13.

THE ACT OF JUMPING

How the horse jumps

The horse's jump can be divided up into five phases:

1 The approach.

2 The take-off.

3 The suspended bascule.

4 The landing.

5 The departure.

14.1 The five phases of the horse's jump

1. The approach
The quality of the approach determines the success of the jump. The horse should be going straight forwards with calm, balanced, rhythmical impulsion – whether jumping out of trot or canter. You should be thinking 'forwards and straight' when riding the approach. The horse may raise his head slightly during the approach, to focus on the fence in front of him.

2. The take-off
The horse will lower his head and stretch his neck before taking off. His neck will shorten as he raises his forehand off the ground, folding his forelegs up. With his hocks underneath him, his quarters bunch as the power of the hind legs sends him up and over the fence.

At the point at which the horse takes off, he can no longer see the fence because it falls into the visual blind spot which is directly in front of him. As an approximate guide, for most standard types of fence, the horse should take off at a distance from the ground line of between 1 and 1½ times the height of the fence. So, for a fence 1.2m (4ft) high, he should take off between 1.2m (4ft) and 1.8m (6ft) feet from the ground line. (As a Stage 2 rider you will not be attempting such heights just yet!)

A horse taking off further away than this is referred to as '**standing off**'; if he takes off closer this is referred to as '**getting in too close (or deep)**'. Many riders place too much emphasis on 'seeing a stride' – i.e. being able to see the exact point at which the horse will take off and judging the horse's stride on the approach. Provided the approach is active, straight and positive, and you are in the correct position, the jump is likely to be comfortable. At Stage 2 level, do not worry about being able to 'see a stride'. As your training progresses you will develop this skill further.

3. The suspended bascule

This phase is sometimes referred to as 'the flight'. During this phase the horse is airborne with no feet on the ground. He will stretch his head and neck down, rounding his back underneath the rider. This rounding is termed the **bascule**.

A horse who 'shows a good shape over a fence' shows a good bascule. The horse's forelegs are folded up underneath him and his hind legs are also held clear of the fence. Ideally, none of the legs should trail. It should appear to the observer that the horse snaps his legs up and out of the way. If the horse does not bascule, but instead flattens his back, his ability to clear the fence will be greatly reduced and the whole experience will be uncomfortable for him.

4. The landing

The horse raises his head to balance himself during the descent as he straightens his forelegs in readiness to meet the ground. The first foreleg to touch the ground will take the brunt of the concussion upon landing – often resulting in the back of the fetlock touching the ground. This is a time of great physical stress on the horse's support structures, i.e. the ligaments and tendons. An awkward jump will produce an awkward landing – subsequently increasing the stress. On landing, the horse should round his back to draw his hind legs underneath his body to facilitate the first stride away from the fence.

5. The departure

This is sometimes referred to as 'the getaway'. If the landing has been a balanced one, with the hind legs being drawn underneath the body, the departure from the fence should be balanced, calm and rhythmical, with no loss of impulsion.

When learning to jump, you will initially only have one fence to negotiate, so should concentrate on riding straight towards, over, and away from the fence. This is a good habit to get into so that when it comes to jumping a course, you are practised at good departures. An active, balanced and calm departure from the previous fence will set the horse up well for the approach to the next fence.

ITQ 14.1   ?

a. Give two words to describe how a horse should approach a jump.

b. How can you work out where, approximately, the horse will take off?

c. What is meant by the term 'bascule'?

The rider's jumping position

You will need to shorten your stirrup leathers by two or three holes from your flatwork length, to enable you to balance over the horse's forward-moving centre of motion and enable you to lift your weight off the saddle. Shortening the stirrup leathers closes the angles of the ankle, knee and hip joints.

If the leathers are too long you will have difficulty maintaining the jumping position, your lower leg position will be insecure and you will probably lose your stirrups. If they are too short, you will be unable to use your legs properly to send the horse forwards and will find it more difficult to balance. Additionally, your muscles will become tired very quickly.

The approach position

When adopting the approach jumping position your seat should move very slightly towards the back of the saddle as you fold forward from the waist, placing your body in front of the vertical plane at an angle of 30–40 degrees – the back should remain straight and the shoulders open (not rounded).

If you do not push the seat to the back of the saddle, but merely fold forwards, the horse's shoulders and neck will be beneath you, causing you to unbalance the horse's forehand and getting 'in front of the movement'. This term describes what happens if the rider simply leans forwards, over the horse's neck, thereby being ahead of the horse's centre of balance. In such cases, there will also be a tendency for the legs to move back, which causes a loss of balance, and further tipping forward.

For maximum security of position, your knees should come into contact with the knee rolls – the built-up area at the front of the saddle flaps, and the heels should be well down.

When in the approach position at walk, trot or canter you must look ahead, taking the forward position. In trot, cease rising – the weight is taken on the thighs and

14.2 The approach position

stirrups and the seat 'hovers' lightly above the saddle. This approach position makes it easier to 'go with' the horse as he takes off.

As you become more proficient and able to go with the movement of the horse, you can adopt a slightly more upright position on the approach. The advantage to this is that you are in a stronger position and more able to influence the horse positively should he be hesitant on the approach or thinking about refusing. In the event that he does refuse, you are also in a stronger, more secure position and less likely to get ejected forward out of the saddle.

The take-off position

Still looking up and ahead, you should start to fold a little more in order to stay in balance with the horse. The dimensions of the fence (width is a factor, as well as height) will determine how high the horse jumps and therefore how much you need to fold – generally, the bigger the jump the more you should fold. As your training progresses you will develop these skills further, taking into different types of fences, e.g. drop fences, etc.

In this forward seat, the weight is lifted slightly off the seat bones and transferred to the thighs, knees and stirrups. This position is maintained through balance – hence the need for the shortened stirrup leathers. Keep one hand either side of the horse's neck, with the elbows bent. As the horse takes off, give your hands up towards the horse's head, allowing the horse to stretch. This is often the point at which the novice rider gets 'left behind', i.e. the horse takes off and the rider does not fold forward and go with him. This normally results in the horse being pulled in the mouth and the rider banging heavily in the saddle. Horses expecting to be pulled in the mouth when jumping soon start to refuse as a way of evading the discomfort. Holding the neckstrap or a good piece of mane helps in the early days of learning to jump. This should be practised over poles before attempting a fence.

The suspended bascule position

While the horse is in the air, continue to look forward, maintain the body fold with the back straight, the leg position secure and hands allowing the horse to stretch.

The seat is close to the saddle but the weight is taken in the stirrups to allow the horse freedom to use his back over the fence. Provided the take-off has gone smoothly, this part of the jump is normally relatively easy for the rider.

The landing position

As the horse begins his descent you must continue to look forward – make a positive effort to look up at this point. Novices tend to look down as they land, which has the effect of inclining the upper body too far forwards. The upper body should be straightened as you start to sit up again. If you sit back too early it can result in banging heavily into the saddle, causing the horse discomfort. The weight should still be in the stirrups as the horse lands over the fence.

The departure position

As the horse moves away from the fence you should sit up properly – i.e. back into the flatwork position. It is at this point that problems occur if the rider has lost balance over the fence. Sitting up and back can make the difference between staying on the horse or falling off!

Always ride straight away from the fence and start looking towards the next one.

ITQ 14.2

a. Why should the stirrup leathers be shortened for riding in jumping position?

b. By about how much will you shorten the stirrup leathers?

ITQ 14.3

List the five phases of the jump and note how horse and rider should present at each phase.

1.

2.

3.

4.

5.

JUMPING IN THE EXAM

Initial procedure

You will be assessed riding two horses in the jumping section of your Stage 2 exam.

On your first horse, you will most likely be asked to trot to a cross-pole which may or may not have a placing pole on the ground. Ensure that you have a good, active trot and look to your fence in good time to ensure you approach it absolutely straight.

This fence will be built up and a second, at one or two non-jumping strides away, will be included. Keep the horse straight and active through the two fences. Always move away from the fences in a straight line – do not let the horse fall in and cut the corner. After this, you may jump two or three other fences and then change horses.

Ground conditions

Take into account the ground conditions. In your Stage 2 exam you are unlikely to be asked to ride on unsafe (e.g. frozen or slippery) ground, but weather conditions can change, for example dry ground can quickly become slippery after rain – so you must be aware of alterations in the going. Note, for example, that minimal grass coverage on hard, dry ground, can produce a very slippery surface. This can be a particular problem when riding downhill, turning corners and jumping. If the ground is soft after heavy rain, the horse's stride will be a little shorter and jumping will require greater effort on his part.

You must judge the ground conditions and ride accordingly.

Walking the course

Prior to jumping a course in your exam (as in a competition) you have the opportunity to inspect the course on foot – referred to as 'walking the course'. If you are mounted prior to being able to walk the course you must dismount and hand your horse to an assistant to hold. Remember to run your stirrups up.

Each fence will be numbered on the take-off side (and in a competition there will be flags or markers indicating the start and finish, which you *must* go through).

Having noted where the first fence is, plan where you will circle to warm up and which rein you will be on as you turn onto the approach line for the first fence. Make a note at this point – is the start moving away from the collecting ring/other horses in the exam setting, or towards them? Horses can be less enthusiastic initially moving away from the others, more forward-going if moving towards them. You must take this into account when you start to ride the course.

If fence two is on a right-hand approach it is sensible, if possible, to warm up on the right rein and approach fence one in canter with the right leg leading. This will help maintain a balanced right-lead canter as you approach fence two.

Start to walk the course through the start flags approaching the first fence absolutely straight. Look towards the second fence and walk the exact line you plan to ride. As you walk from fence to fence make sure you continue to walk the path you plan to ride – don't be tempted to cut corners. Do, however, make sure you walk briskly to save time.

Your approach lines must allow you to approach every fence absolutely straight and at an angle of 90 degrees. You must also plan to move away from each fence in a straight line, noting where the next fence is. Plan to 'use the arena', i.e. ride deep into the corners linking approach lines – do not cut any corners. If you cut corners your approach lines will be wrong and you will be more likely to incur run-outs and refusals. (Experienced competitors who get involved in timed jump-offs practise very short, sharp turns between fences, but these are not your aim at Stage 2.)

Note where you will be changing direction and where you may need to change canter leads.

Whilst there should not be anything really 'tricky' in the exam, note any spooky fillers that the horse may object to – these may need slightly stronger riding.

During the course-walk, after the first four fences or so, look back to the start and visually retrace your steps so you are consolidating the course plan in your mind. Having walked the course, look back at the whole course and make sure you remember it and know exactly where you are going.

Return to your horse and mount up.

Distances between fences

A 'related distance' is one where the course designer has designated the exact number of strides the average-striding horse should take between two fences. At Stage 2 level the course will be relatively straightforward, with no complicated related distances involved. Therefore, at this stage you don't need to worry about measuring distances between any of the fences other than those between doubles. Doubles are a combination of two fences with either one or two non-jumping strides in between, and you need to check these to ensure that you know how many strides to expect between elements. At the sort of height being jumped at Stage 2, a one-stride double will have a distances of about 6.4m (21ft) between elements, and a two-stride double about 10m (33ft).

As you progress with your jumping and start to compete, it will be important to be able to measure distances pretty accurately – both between elements of doubles and trebles, and the related distances mentioned above. To *be totally accurate* when measuring distances a measuring wheel as used by course designers is needed. However, in everyday situations this is impractical – you must learn to 'pace' out distances using your stride length. To do this, you will need to develop a consistent stride – everyone has their own comfortable stride length; those with long legs will have a longer stride than those with shorter legs. Lay a tape measure on the ground and measure the length of your stride. If you can get the feel of a stride either 1m or 3ft long, measured from the back of the heel of one foot to the tip of the toe of the other, this will be most useful when measuring distances. For example, to measure the distance between a double, stand with the back of your leg just touching the landing side of the centre of the first fence and stride straight towards the centre of the second fence, counting the number of strides until your toe reaches the ground pole or ground line of the second fence. Referring to the two-stride double just mentioned, if you take 1m strides, there will be ten strides between the elements; if you take 3ft strides, there will be eleven. Being able to measure distances accurately will help you relate them to the natural stride length of the horse you are riding. For example, the distances between elements of a double (or other combination) may be slightly shorter or longer than those quoted here and horses' stride lengths also vary – a long-legged, scopey horse is very likely to have a longer stride than a smaller short-coupled cob. You will need to take these points into account when riding a course, especially when you reach the stage of jumping bigger, more technically demanding courses.

Jumping the course

As with the flatwork phase, preparation is key. Decide which rein you will approach the first fence on and start to trot a large circle on this rein. Keep your eye on the first fence and, in plenty of time, establish canter, making sure you are on the correct canter lead. This is important – see Section 13 for information on recognising correct and incorrect canter leads.

Make sure the canter is active but not too fast and approach the centre of the first fence positively on a straight line.

Having jumped the first fence you must identify the canter lead immediately to allow time for corrections before the next fence. If the horse has been jumping out of canter, he will normally land in canter, but which lead he lands on can be determined by the rider. If the horse jumped the fence out of a left turn, the chances are that he will continue in left lead canter on landing. If the next fence is to be met from a left-hand curve the horse should be leading with the left foreleg and vice versa for a right-hand curve. If the next fence is to the right you can indicate the change of leading leg in mid-air by looking to the right, feeling the right rein, very slightly weighting the right stirrup and drawing the left leg back. Do not exaggerate the weighting of the stirrup or you risk unbalancing the horse and ruining the jump.

If, upon landing, the lead is incorrect, go forwards to trot before asking for the desired canter lead. Corrections should be made early – preferably before the corner prior to the next fence. To continue on the incorrect lead will unbalance the horse and demonstrates a lack of awareness and feel on your part. Do not try to change the canter lead in the final strides of the approach as it will cause the horse to lose concentration, rhythm and balance.

Throughout the course, aim for an active canter and maintain an even, flowing rhythm at all times. Make the best use of the arena – use the corners, i.e. ride the horse around and into each corner properly, not allowing him to fall in. Do not cut corners.

In between fences sit up and look to the next fence – never look down at the ground. Look and plan ahead the whole time.

When you finish over the last fence make balanced downward transitions to trot and then walk, and return to your place. Pat and praise your horse. Maintain a good position throughout – do not collapse in a heap at the relief of having survived the jumping!

> **EXAM TIPS**
>
> At this level, try not to focus too much on 'seeing the stride' at each fence. It is more important to balance and direct the horse and establish a good rhythm whilst maintaining the correct position; this should ensure that you meet each fence satisfactorily without having to think about getting the correct stride.
>
> However, you should be aware of the non-jumping distance between a double combination in order that you ride in correctly.

ITQ 14.4 （?）

Explain how you can influence the canter lead when landing after a jump.

> **ITQ 14.5** — ⑦
>
> What should you do if the horse lands after a jump and is on the incorrect canter lead?

If things go wrong

The horses used in the Stage 2 exam should be well-schooled and used to having different riders. They are likely to be the horses used in lessons at the examination centre. These horses may, however, have the odd trick up their sleeve; never assume they will just 'do it'. Riding school horses can be quite canny at evading the task – prepare well and be ready.

The main problems encountered when jumping are refusals or run-outs, i.e. the horse approaches the fence but does not jump it, either stopping in front of it or running to the side of it.

The main causes of refusals and run-outs include:

1. Lack of impulsion. The horse needs to be ridden actively forwards from the leg.

2. Loss of rhythm and impulsion owing to the rider being a passenger. You must actively help the horse by keeping him forward, straight and into a contact.

3. The horse may be genuinely lazy – be ready to give a tap with the whip behind the leg on the approach.

4. Confusion between speed and impulsion. You must not 'chase' the horse into the fence – you will have less control if the horse is rushing into the fence at speed and when things go wrong it tends to be more dramatic and more difficult to stay on board.

5. Dropping the contact a few strides from the fence. This can make the horse feel disconcerted and unsure whether you still want to jump. Your legs must maintain the forward momentum whilst the hands channel it. If this contact is abandoned in the last few strides, the horse is effectively left to make his own decision as to whether to jump or not.

6. Ungenuine or 'cheeky' horse. The horse may have become disobedient having learned that some riders are weak and ineffective. Ride this sort of horse very positively so he knows you mean business.

7. Poor approach lines on a bad angle. If you have cut the corner and approached on a bad angle (i.e. not straight, at 90 degrees) you make it much more difficult for the horse.

To correct:

- Make sure you are approaching absolutely straight, channelling the horse between legs and hands. Sit up more on the approach. A forward seat is much less effective in these situations and, if the horse whips round the side of the fence quickly, you are more likely to jump it without the horse. Do not cut corners.

- If the approach is good and the horse refuses for no good reason, i.e. he is being disobedient, he should be reprimanded with a good tap with the whip immediately and be re-presented at the fence. Often a more positive attitude from the rider is enough to convince the horse that he ought to jump the fence. Controlled vocal encouragement can sometimes be used to good effect too, but not at the expense of effective leg and seat aids.

- If the horse has run out, when re-presenting him, your whip should be held in the hand on the side to which the horse ran out. Make sure that the horse is being presented on a straight approach line, and that you are using positive leg aids. Maintain the rein contact on the opposite side to which he previously ran out.

- On a horse prone to running out or refusing, make sure you ride each fence positively.

ITQ 14.6

List six reasons why a horse may refuse to jump.

1.

2.

3.

4.

5.

6.

EXAM TIP

When you are warming-up the horse for jumping in an exam, ensure that you complete plenty of transitions to ascertain the responsiveness of the horse. Get a feel for how he moves and any 'quirks' he may have. Make sure that you walk, trot and canter before proceeding to perform a few turns/circles and pop a practise fence or two. In this way you will have an idea of how the **horse is likely to go** (and be ready to make corrections) and will have experienced his jump so as not to be put off when you begin your round.

ANSWERS TO IN-TEXT QUESTIONS

1.1 The government department that has responsibility for health and safety law is the Department for Work and Pensions.

1.2 The organisations that are responsible for enforcing health and safety legislation are the Health and Safety Executive (HSE) and local authorities.

1.3 The two types of enforcement notices that can be served on businesses are improvement notices and prohibition notices.

1.4 The differences between the two types of enforcement notices are that improvement notices bring the employer's attention to specific issues that need to be rectified in order that the business operates within the law. This notice has a timeframe within which they must be completed. Prohibition notices stop businesses carrying out certain activities when people are at risk of serious injury, and might stop a business from trading altogether until the situation has been fully rectified to the satisfaction of the HSE.

1.5 Four responsibilities of employers under the Health and Safety at Work Act 1974 are:
1. Employers must have employers' liability insurance.
2. A trained first aider and well equipped first aid kit must be accessible at all times.
3. Employers must ensure the safety of their employers by maintaining safe systems at work.
4. A named person must be specified to whom any potential hazards, faults in equipment or accidents must be reported.

1.6 It is unsafe to leave a nylon headcollar on a horse who is loose in the stable because it may get caught on the top bolt of the door as the horse looks out. Nylon headcollars do not break and the horse would panic and be difficult to free.

1.7 Four safety points to observe when tying horses up:
1. Always use a quick-release knot.
2. Always use a weak link, attached to a secure object, as this will break in the event of the horse pulling back and panicking. If there is not a weak link the horse may injure himself.
3. Never leave a tied horse unattended.
4. Never tie horses up close together.

1.8 Two examples of accidents that can happen whilst the horse is turned out in the field:
1. Putting a foot through the fence or gate. This is dangerous if wire fencing is used and is most likely to happen when horses are turned out in adjacent fields as they tend to fight or play over the fence.
2. Kick injuries can occur when horses don't get on together.

1.9 Three safety measures that can be taken to prevent accidents in the field:
1. Never use barbed wire as fencing.
2. Keep all fencing in a good state of repair.
3 Only turn horses out in small, amenable groups.

1.10 When introducing a new grazing member to a group of horses, introduce new members gradually after allowing them to meet in the yard. Watch them closely and be prepared to change the group if there is any sign of bullying. Ensure that there is plenty of space and grazing for all horses in the group to reduce the risk of fighting.

1.11 At the beginning of a lesson for a novice rider you must check that all tack is correctly and securely fitted, with keepers in place. Ensure that all rider equipment is up to standard and that the equipment you will use is in good order.

1.12 In the event of a rider falling off your immediate course of action should include:
1. Halt the rest of the ride.
2. Assess the situation for dangers to yourself – you mustn't end up as another casualty. Move the casualty if necessary – but always avoid moving if possible.
3. Assess for consciousness.
4. Check the airway is clear.
5. Check that the casualty is breathing. If not, call an ambulance and begin CPR.
6. If the casualty is conscious find out if they have any pain and try to make them comfortable.
7. If necessary, send someone to call an ambulance.

1.13 The main danger of moving a casualty unable to get up unaided is that they may have damaged their spine in the fall. Any movement could worsen the damage and cause permanent disability.

1.14 A casualty who is unconscious but breathing should be placed in the recovery position and medical help summoned.

1.15 If the casualty is conscious but appears to be injured:
1. Give reassurance and tell them not to move until their injuries have been assessed.
2. Ask whether there is any pain and, if so, where.
3. Ask whether they can move fingers and toes. If not DO NOT MOVE THE CASUALTY.
4. If necessary, send someone to call an ambulance.
5. Meanwhile, continue to reassure the casualty and check bleeding, which should be stemmed unless pressure to the wound would make matters worse, e.g. pushing foreign matter further into the wound.
6. Immobilise fractures as best you can with the equipment you have with you.
7. The casualty should not be offered anything to drink in case surgery is necessary.

1.16 To stem bleeding:
- Pressure should be applied to a wound to stem bleeding.
- If there is a foreign body in the wound don't try to remove it as it can worsen the damage done to arteries and veins.
- The limb should be raised if there is no underlying fracture.
- Once the bleeding has slowed a clean dressing should be bandaged firmly over the wound.
- The casualty should then be taken to the local Accident and Emergency Department.

1.17 The following information should be entered into the *Accident Book*:
- Date, location and time of the accident.
- A diagram depicting the location of those involved and how the situation progressed.
- Names and addresses of those involved, including witnesses.
- Description of events, i.e. what happened and why.
- Record of injuries sustained and to whom.
- Record of any treatment given and by whom.
- Admission to hospital if necessary.
- Signatures, preferably, of all parties involved including the escort or instructor in charge at the time.

2.1 Quartering is a short groom given before exercise to tidy the horse up.
Strapping is the full groom given after exercise to tone the muscles and thoroughly clean the coat and skin.

2.2 Strapping is carried out after exercise because the pores of the skin are open, allowing oil in the skin to give the coat a shine. The dirt in the coat will loosen off more easily too.

2.3 Whilst picking out the hooves you should check the condition of the shoes.

2.4 When quartering a clipped horse on a cold day the rug should be folded back. First undo the front buckle and the belly straps and fold the front half of the rug back. To groom the hindquarters, fasten the front buckle and fold the rear half of the rug over the front half. This way the horse will not get cold.

2.5 a. A dandy brush and/or plastic curry comb are suitable for use on a horse with a thick and dirty coat.
b. A body brush is most suitable for a thin-skinned horse.
c. A stable stain can be removed by brushing back and forth with a dandy brush or by washing off with a wet sponge.

2.6 a. When brushing a horse's head the first thing you must do is untie the quick-release knot.
b. This must be done so that if the horse pulls back whilst you are brushing his face he will not have the headcollar pulling tight around his neck.
c. The body brush should be used on the head.

3.1 A correctly fitted rug will:
- Not be too tight at the shoulders.
- Extend to the top of the tail.
- Extend to just below the level of the elbows, covering the horse's abdomen .

3.2 The horse should not be left standing with only the belly straps of the rug fastened as there is a risk that the rug will slip backwards and become entangled around the horse's hind legs.

3.3 The horse should not be left standing with only the front buckles fastened as there is a risk that the rug could slip and become entangled around the horse's forelegs.

3.4 The cooler or thermal rug has now largely superseded the anti-sweat sheet.

3.5 Four reasons for using bandages:
1. To provide protection when travelling.
2. To provide support when working.
3. To provide warmth in the stable.
4. To hold a dressing in place.

3.6 Padding is needed beneath bandages to even out the pressure and provide extra protection.

3.7 Two advantages of using bandages as leg protection when travelling:
1. Bandages provide a degree of support to the limbs.
2. If applied correctly they are secure and don't tend to slip down.

3.8 Two advantages of using travelling boots as protection:
1. They are quick to apply.
2. Provided they don't slip down, travel boots provide a good level of protection.

3.9 Two factors that affect the choice of rug worn when travelling:
1. The weather.
2. Whether the horse is clipped or not.

3.10 A tail bandage should not be left on for longer than four hours to prevent loss of circulation in the dock area.

3.11 A poll guard is a leather or sometimes reinforced neoprene pad which is threaded onto the headpiece of the headcollar to protect the poll during travel. Horses who are known to raise their heads or who may be nervy and inclined to rear or jump around should be fitted with one during travel.

4.1 Six points upon which the bit acts:
1. The bars of the mouth.
2. The corners of the lips and mouth.
3. The tongue.
4. The side of the face.

5. The poll.
6. The nose.

4.2 'Nutcracker' action refers to the action of a single-jointed snaffle. As pressure is applied to the reins the two sections of the mouthpiece close together, in the same way that a nutcracker does. This exerts pressure on the tongue.

4.3 The French link and Dr Bristol are double-jointed snaffles. The centre plate of the French link has rounded edges and is allowed in dressage tests. The Dr Bristol has square edges and is not allowed in dressage tests.

4.4 Three qualities of nylon mouthpieces on a bit:
1. Hard-wearing.
2. Flexible so more comfortable in the horse's mouth.
3. Encourage the horse to mouth and accept the bit.

4.5 A narrow mouthpiece is sharper in action than a wider one because the rein pressure is concentrated on a smaller surface area.

4.6 Four points to consider regarding the fitting of a bit:
1. Check the size of the horse's mouth. Look at the thickness of his tongue and the height of the roof of the mouth.
2 The bit should protrude 1cm (approx. ½ an inch) either side of the mouth.
3. The bit should be fitted so the corners of the lips have approximately two wrinkles, but no more.
4. If too low in the mouth, the horse may put his tongue over the bit and the bit may bang on the teeth.

4.7 Four points indicating that a horse is uncomfortable in his mouth:
1. Head raised and mouth open when working.
2. Drawing the tongue back and putting it over the bit.
3. Sudden 'snatching' at the bit.
4. General control problems including rearing and bolting.
Note that the causes of these problems may be poor training or riding and actually have nothing to do with the choice or fitting of the bit. Check the mouth and fitting of the bit but also look to the standard of the rider.

4.8 If the horse is showing signs of discomfort in his mouth you should check his teeth for sharp edges, his mouth for sores and the bit for fitting. As mentioned in 4.7, the standard of the training should also be checked.

4.9 Four causes of discomfort in the horse's mouth:
1. Sharp teeth.
2. Excessively severe bit.
3. Incorrectly fitted bit.
4. Poor riding – heavy, rough hands.

4.10 All saddles need to be re-flocked at least once a year as the flocking packs down and shifts, causing uneven lumps which create pressure points. Uneven pressure will give the horse a sore back.

4.11 A spring tree is made from two flat panels of steel which run from pommel to cantle. The panels are thin enough to give the saddle a 'springy' feel. The rigid tree is constructed of laminated wood and has a more solid tree with less 'spring'.

4.12 You should fit a saddle without a numnah because the numnah will disguise the true fit of the saddle. All saddles should fit the horse without a numnah, although a numnah should be used when riding.

4.13 Four points to observe about a well-fitting saddle:
1. The saddle should sit level on the horse's back – it should not tilt forwards or backwards as this would make it difficult for a rider to maintain position and would exert uneven pressure on the horse's back.
2. The saddle should rest evenly on the lumbar muscles, which cover the top of the ribs. It must not touch the loins. The full surface of the panels must be in contact with the horse's back to distribute the weight over the largest possible area.
3. The saddle must not pinch the shoulders. The knee rolls, panels and saddle flaps should not extend out over the shoulders, as this would restrict the horse's freedom of movement.
4. With the rider mounted there should be sufficient clearance beneath the pommel when the rider is in an upright, flatwork position and a forward, jumping position. You should be able to see daylight through the gullet. At no time should the saddle touch the horse's spine. When viewed from behind, the saddle should not appear crooked or twisted.

4.14 To test for a damaged or broken tree, place the front arch of the saddle on your knee and try to pull the cantle towards it. If it bends easily and does not spring back into position when released, the tree is damaged. Press the front arch inwards. Any grating sounds or excess movement indicates damage.

4.15 a. A running martingale is used to prevent the horse from carrying his head high, beyond the point of control.
b. To tell if a running martingale is fitted correctly:
- When the horse stands with his head in the normal position the martingale straps must be slack.
- It should come into action only when the horse raises his head beyond the point of control.
- Before passing the reins through the martingale rings, take both straps and hold the rings together towards the horse's withers – the rings should not touch the withers as this would make the fit too loose.
- Then pass the reins through the rings and re-buckle; standing beside the horse, hold the reins up in the position they would be in if the rider were holding them on the horse.
- Check the fit – the straps should be slightly loose.
- The neckstrap should be adjusted to admit the width of your hand.

• A rubber stopper must be used on the neckstrap to prevent it slipping along the main strap, which will affect its action. Rein stops are used on each rein to prevent the martingale rings running up too near the bit rings, which could panic a horse.

4.16 A standing martingale should not be used on a drop noseband because sudden pressure when the horse throws his head up could injure the nasal bones.

4.17 The Aintree breastplate consists of a strap passing around the chest held in place by straps attaching to the girth and a strap fitting over the top of the withers. The hunting breastplate consists of a 'V' of leather running from the withers area to a strap which runs between the forelegs to the girth. The 'V' secures to the 'D' rings of the saddle. An Aintree breastplate is used for racing and cross-country whereas a hunting breastplate is most often used for hunting and often showjumping.

4.18 Three reasons for using protective boots:
  1. To protect against brushing.
  2. To protect and support the tendons.
  3. To prevent overreach injuries.

4.19 The straps of a knee boot should be fastened so the buckles are on the outside with the strap pointing forward. The top strap is fastened first, securely to prevent it slipping down. The lower strap is fastened next, quite loosely to allow the joint to flex.

4.20 The tendon boot is often open-fronted and acts to support and protect the tendons, whereas the brushing boot is a closed boot with extra padding around the fetlock area to help with protecting the fetlock from the effects of brushing.

4.21 Three areas which need to be checked for safety when cleaning tack:
  1. All stitching on the bridle.
  2. Girth straps – stitching and leather for signs of stretching and cracking.
  3. Stirrup leather – stitching and leather.

4.22 Two causes of saddle sores:
  1. Ill-fitting saddle – too low on the withers or lumpy stuffing.
  2. Dirty numnah and/or horse.

4.23 If a horse has a sore back, the cause must be removed. Don't continue to work the horse in ill-fitting or dirty equipment. Clean the area using salt water and apply a hydrogel to aid healing. Rest his back until it has healed properly.

5.1 The two sections of the horse's skeleton are:
  1. The axial skeleton – the skull and spine.
  2. The appendicular skeleton – the limbs.

5.2 The two top cervical vertebrae are the atlas and axis.

5.3 Starting at the poll the vertebrae are:
  1. Cervical – 7
  2. Thoracic – 18
  3. Lumbar – 6
  4. Sacral – 5
  5. Coccygeal – 15–20

5.4 a. The scapula attaches to the skeleton by muscles and tendons. There is no shoulder joint.
  b. This form of attachment results in great mobility of the shoulder in both the extent and direction of movement which is a real advantage when galloping and jumping.

5.5 The periople is a waterproof, varnish-like horn which covers the hoof wall, helping to prevent excessive evaporation of moisture from within.

5.6 Five functions of the frog:
  1. To protect sensitive underlying structures.
  2. To assist in weight carrying; if the frog is not bearing weight, more pressure is borne by the walls of the hoof.
  3. To prevent slipping – the rubbery texture and depression formed by the clefts provide grip.
  4. To protect against concussion. As the foot comes down, the heel touches the ground first, therefore taking the bulk of the weight. The jarring effect is lessened by the rubbery compression of a healthy frog.
  5. To promote a healthy blood supply. The insensitive frog becomes compressed which, in turn, causes pressure on the sensitive frog and **digital cushion** – a wedge-shaped fibro-elastic pad which fills the hollow behind the heels and is of a firm but yielding consistency. Frog pressure compresses the digital cushion which, in turn, causes the expansion of the lateral cartilages. This forces the lateral cartilages against the horny wall, which flattens out and empties the blood vessels between the cartilages and wall. Once the pressure is relieved (when the foot is lifted off the ground), the blood vessels refill. This process thus aids the circulation of blood within the foot.

5.7 The horse's digestive tract needs to be relatively long in order to deal with the large quantities of cellulose that the horse eats. The horse's diet should be high in fibre (roughage/bulk/cellulose) which actually takes a lot longer to digest than cereals (short feeds).

5.8 a. The horse's stomach is approximately the size of a rugby ball. It has a capacity of 9–15 litres (2–3.25 gallons).
  b. Food is regulated in and out of the stomach by two sphincter muscles. It is allowed into the stomach by the cardiac sphincter and out of the stomach by the pyloric sphincter.

5.9 Peristalsis is the involuntary contractions of the muscles lining the intestines, which pushes food along.

5.10 The correct order for the organs of the digestive tract is:
  1. Stomach

2. Duodenum
3. Jejunum
4. Ileum
5. Caecum
6. Large colon
7. Small colon

Compare the comments you have made (one of the things you remember about each organ) with the information given within the text.

5.11 a. The foregut is made up of the mouth, pharynx, oesophagus, stomach and small intestine.
b. The hindgut is made up of the caecum, large colon, small colon, rectum and anus.

5.12 a. Fibre aids digestion and ensures that the horse's digestive tract functions properly. It has to be remembered that the horse's digestive tract is designed to break down and ferment large quantities of roughage.
b. Fibre is fermented in the hindgut. This process is activated by a population of bacteria and protozoa.

6.1 The skin of a healthy horse should be supple and loose. Small 'ripples' should appear as you run your hand over the skin. The coat should be glossy and smooth.

6.2 The mucous membranes should appear salmon pink and moist.

6.3 The droppings of a stabled horse should be yellow-brown, fairly firm and break on hitting the ground. Time at grass will make the droppings darker and looser.

6.4 Normal resting rates:
a. Temperature 100.5 °F (38 °C).
b. Pulse 25–42 beats per minute.
c. Respiration 8–16 breaths per minute.

6.5 Two reasons why a horse may not eat his feed:
1. Ill-health.
2. Dislikes feed or additives.

6.6 Five signs of colic:
1. Loss of appetite.
2. Dull attitude.
3. Looking round at flanks repeatedly.
4. Sweating.
5. Rolling.

6.7 The urine of a healthy horse should be more or less clear and free from odour.

6.8 Very loose droppings may be caused by worm infestation, excitement, too much rich grass, sharp teeth preventing the horse from chewing his food properly.

6.9 Four causes of poor condition:

1. Poor diet.
2. Sharp teeth, preventing the horse from chewing properly.
3. Worm infestation.
4. Overwork.

6.10 Laminitis causes the horse to move with a pottery, stilted action.

6.11 Ideally, hooves should feel cool, although on a hot day they may feel warmer than normal. Provided all four hooves feel the same, this is normal.

6.12 If a horse feels lame whilst out hacking dismount and pick out the hooves – look for stones wedged in the foot. Remove any stones and lead the horse up to see if he is still unsound. If he is sound you can remount and ride home. If, however, he still feels lame or there are no signs of stones jammed in the foot, then the horse must be led home. If home is far away it will be necessary to get someone to bring out a trailer or lorry and give him a lift back.
Once home you must try to decide exactly which leg he is lame upon.

6.13 When watching the horse trot up, if he is lame in a foreleg he will lift his head up as the lame leg comes to the ground in an effort to keep his weight off it.

6.14 Lameness in a hind leg will show as uneven rise and fall of the hips as the horse trots away from you. The hip on the affected side will appear to rise higher as the horse tries to keep the weight off that leg. He may also drag the toe of the affected leg.

6.15 a. A horse is said to take 'pottery steps' when his stride is shortened and shuffling.
b. Laminitis will cause the horse to move with shortened, pottery steps.

6.16 It is important to observe the horse from the side so that you can note any shortened strides, irregular footfalls or abnormalities in the way the horse lifts and places each foot.

6.17 a. When examining the hooves to find the seat of lameness you should feel the hoof wall for heat and look for bruising or a puncture wound on the sole.
b. When examining the limbs you should feel for heat and swelling. Look for cuts and/or bruising.

6.18 Four types of open wound (and one cause of each):
1. Incised – sharp object, e.g. glass, knife.
2. Tear – e.g. barbed wire.
3. Puncture – e.g. treading on a nail.
4. Abrasion – e.g. rubbing from an ill-fitting rug.

6.19 It is important that a horse who has sustained a puncture wound is vaccinated against tetanus as the tetanus bacteria thrive in such a wound. Tetanus is often fatal.

6.20 a. As the blood is being pumped by the heart, arterial bleeding occurs in spurts. The blood contains oxygen which gives it a bright red colour.

b. When a horse bleeds from a vein the flow is continual and steady. The blood has given up most of its oxygen (it is deoxygenated) so is a dark red colour.

6.21 Bleeding can be stemmed by:
1. Holding the edges of the wound together and applying pressure with the thumbs.
2. Bandaging a pressure pad in place on the wound.

6.22 Once it has been hosed, the wound can be flushed through with a dilute solution (2 per cent Hibiscrub). It is important to ensure that the solution is dilute because strong antiseptic can damage healthy/surviving tissue surrounding the area, which will increase healing time.

6.23 One advantage of cleaning a wound by cold hosing is that it causes the blood vessels to constrict, which helps to stem bleeding.

6.24 To clean a wound with Gamgee swabs:
1. Wash your hands.
2. Dip the swab in dilute Pevidine or Hibiscrub solution.
3. Start at the centre of the wound and wipe outwards.
4. Repeat, using clean swabs until the wound is clean.

6.25 Keep the top door open to allow fresh air in.

6.26 Adequate ventilation can be ensured via a window on the same side of the door that opens inwards to encourage the air to lift upwards. A ventilation cowl in the roof allows warm, stale air to escape as it is replaced by cool, fresh air.

6.27 Three signs that indicate a horse is cold:
1. Coat dull and staring.
2. Shivering
3. Tucked up, miserable-looking appearance.

6.28 a. If the horse is on box rest after colic surgery a non-edible, low-dust bedding such as paper or shavings should be used to prevent him eating the bedding, which could lead to an impaction.

b. If the horse has a leg injury, the bedding must not be deep as it will drag on the limb when the horse moves around. Use minimal bedding on rubber matting if possible.

6.29 When a horse is on box rest the heating (energy-giving) carbohydrate content of his diet must be reduced. The horse should only be fed non-heating feedstuffs and good-quality meadow hay or haylage. Make sure he is not able to eat straw bedding as this can lead to an impacted colic.

6.30 If the carbohydrates are not reduced the horse may suffer from laminitis and/or rhabdomyolysis (azoturia). He will also gain weight and be very lively once he comes out of the stable for the first time.

6.31 To reduce the risk of explosive behaviour when turning a horse out for the first time after a spell of box rest:
● When a horse is first turned out after box rest, put him in the smallest paddock available on his own. Make sure horses in nearby fields do not 'wind him up' by galloping around. A small turnout 'cage' is ideal as the horse cannot build up any great speed and thereby injure himself. It is also impossible for the horse to jump out of a cage (although only specialist yards tend to have them).
● When the horse is first turned out he will be more likely to stay calm and eat grass if he is a little hungry. Only give a small feed and minimal hay the morning he is due to be turned out.
● As the horse will be unused to grass, increase the amount of time spent out gradually, especially if spring grass is available. This will allow the horse's digestive tract time to adjust and should help reduce the risk of colic.
● Discuss with the vet the benefits of mildly sedating the horse for his first turnout to prevent him from galloping around.

6.32 a. The term quarantine refers to the separation and segregation of infected or potentially infective horses from those presumed to be free of infection and is often used in relation to horses who are to be kept separated before travelling abroad and/or upon arrival at a new yard.

b. Quarantining is necessary to prevent the spread of infectious disease. Yards receiving new horses, especially horses who have come from the sales or whose health status is unknown, should quarantine all new horses for approximately ten days before allowing them to mix, in case they are incubating an infectious disease.

6.33 Four points to consider when keeping a sick horse warm:
1. Use layers of lightweight sheets rather than one heavy rug. This way you can adjust them easily. If the horse is prone to breaking out in a sweat, place an anti-sweat/cooler sheet beneath the top rug to help the air circulate; alternatively a thermal rug can be used.
2. Do not close the stable top door or window.
3. Stable bandages applied over Gamgee help to keep a horse warm.
4. Heat lamps/panels may be used. These are suspended above the horse.

6.34 Call the vet for:
1. Severe or prolonged (more than 20 minutes) colic.
2. Laminitis.
3 Serious wounds.
4. Severe lameness and suspected fractures.
5. Repeated coughing.
6. Abnormal temperature.
Other signs of ill-health which cannot be attributed to anything or appropriately treated.

6.35 Three examples of internal damage caused by worms:
1. The lining of the intestines is damaged, which impairs the absorption of nutrients.
2. Blood flow is impaired, which leads to tissue death within the digestive tract.
3. Arteries become weakened as worm larvae migrate through them.

6.36 Internal parasites can be controlled by:
1. Keeping paddocks clear of droppings through regular muck collection.
2. Topping grass to remove stalks upon which worm larvae become attached and then ingested.
3 Regular use of appropriate anthelmintics.

6.37 A faecal egg count is a laboratory test which counts the worm eggs in a droppings sample to estimate the horse's worm burden. It does not take into account immature or encysted worms or tapeworms so bear this in mind. Egg counts can enable worming to be more targeted at specific species and may reduce the need for anthelmintic use. It is also a very good monitoring method and can assess new horses to the yard to ascertain their worm burden before introducing them to a group of horses.

6.38 Three problems indicating a horse has had problems with his teeth:
1. Quidding – dropping food from his mouth while eating.
2. Reluctance to accept the bit when ridden.
3. Loss of condition.

7.1 Four reasons for clipping:
1. The horse cannot work effectively with a thick winter coat as he will sweat easily.
2. Excessive sweating can lead to a loss of condition.
3. The horse is difficult to dry and can become chilled after sweating up.
4. It is easier to groom a clipped horse.

7.2 a. A circuit-breaker is a plug used when clipping which will automatically cut off the electricity supply if a problem occurs, e.g. the horse stands on the wire.
b. The extension lead should be uncoiled when in use as otherwise heat is generated and the outer cable may melt.

7.3 Three ways of reducing the risk of electric shock when clipping:
1. Use a circuit-breaker plug.
2. Use rubber matting as flooring in the clipping box.
3. Wear rubber-soled boots.

7.4 a. A twitch is a device used to control a fractious horse. It works by applying pressure to an acupuncture point in the horse's upper lip. It is proposed that this pressure causes the release of the body's natural analgesics known as endorphins, which causes the horse to become more

relaxed. However, studies indicate this is not the case and it actually restrains the horse because it is so painful.
b. Sedation would be a more humane method of restraining a horse who is difficult to clip.

7.5 To keep the blades working properly when clipping and to prevent overheating you must regularly clean the blades and apply blade-cleaning fluid during the clipping procedure. Test the temperature of the blades with your hand and if they are getting hot, either leave them to cool or change them.

7.6 To clip around the horse's elbow you must get an assistant to hold the foreleg well forwards. This pulls the skin taut and makes it easier to clip the area. Care must be taken not to nick the folds of skin under the elbow.

7.7 Five areas that can be trimmed with scissors:
1. Headpiece area.
2. External ear hair.
3. The withers.
4. The feathers.
5. The end of the tail.

8.1 Three signs which indicate that a horse needs re-shoeing:
1. The shoe has slipped forwards or inwards.
2. The shoe is loose.
3. The clenches have risen.
There are other signs – you may have selected different ones from those mentioned here. The most important thing to remember is that the horse must be re-shod every five to seven weeks, even if the shoes look okay. The hoof wall grows down and needs to be trimmed back in order to keep the foot balanced.

8.2 Horses need to be shod every five to seven weeks or more frequently if a shoe is loose or missing.

8.3 a. The clenches are knocked up with the buffer and driving hammer.
b. The pincers are used to lever off the shoe.

8.4 a. Fine nailing is the term used to describe clenches that are too low down the hoof wall. The nails will not have a secure hold in the hoof wall.
b. Coarse nailing describes clenches that are too high up the hoof wall.
c. With fine nailing, the shoe may be wrenched off easily. With coarse nailing, there may be pressure on the sensitive laminae. In extreme cases, a nail may penetrate the sensitive laminae.

8.5 When the shoes are taken off and put back on again they are called 'removes'.

8.6 The rasp should not be used excessively on the hoof wall as this removes the periople – this could lead to drying out of the wall.

8.7 Points to look for which indicate that the shoe fits the foot:
1. The shoe must be made to fit the foot and not vice versa. If the toe has been cut back too much it can adversely affect the balance of the foot.
2. The foot must be evenly reduced in size at the toe and heel, inside and outside of the foot.
3. The correct type of shoe and weight of iron must be used according to the size of the horse and the work he is required to do. A small pony would have a lighter iron than a large hunter.
4. No daylight must show between the foot and the shoe.
5. The heels must not be too short or too long.

8.8 The toes will grow long and the feet will be out of balance. If the toe grows too long it will unbalance the foot, which increases the force exerted onto the navicular bone and causes excessive strain to be exerted upon the tendons.

9.1 The three main cereals fed to horses:
1. Oats
2. Barley
3. Maize

9.2 Bran contains high levels of phosphorus.

9.3 Sugar beet cubes should be soaked until they have swollen fully. This normally takes 12 hours for shredded pulp, 24 hours for cubes.

9.4 The advantages of feeding chaff:
It aids digestion.
It provides bulk/roughage in the diet.
It helps to satisfy the horse's appetite without having a heating effect.

9.5 This horse is in medium work so does not require a large proportion of cereals in his diet. It would be preferable to have at least 60 per cent of his diet provided for by forage with the remaining 40 per cent consisting of moderate energy providers, probably in the form of a cool mix/cube. If feeding straights it would be preferable to keep quantities of barley and oats fed to a minimum providing the horse is receiving enough for work. Oils are a safe and effective slow-release energy form that would be suitable for this horse and can make up around 10–30 per cent of the horse's diet according to palatability.
Remember that the feed ration should be closely and constantly monitored so that any lack or over-provision of energy can be amended quickly.

9.6 Any feedstuff with a high-energy content will be fattening for the horse and thus unsuitable for an overweight animal. Barley is especially fattening.
Try to feed a low-energy, high-fibre diet supplemented with oil where energy is required. In order to lose weight the horse must use more energy than he consumes, thus a steady increase in exercise coupled with appropriate reduction in

feed rationing should help this process. Remember to always reduce a ration quantity slowly and ensure you are providing the required essential dietary components; this can be done through feeding a supplement if needed.
Unmolassed chaffs and sugar beet are high in fibre and will keep the horse interested in feed whilst slowing down the rate of eating.
There are specially formulated diet rations on the market aimed at the more portly horses.

9.7 This horse requires large amounts of energy to perform the work asked of him. If fed a compound feed it will be a competition mix or cube and if on a straights ration it is likely to include high proportions of barley and oats with some maize, sugar beet (possibly molassed) and potential inclusion of oil and a feed balancer.
Remember that the diet, even of a horse in hard work, should ideally not contain less than 50 per cent forage. Unfortunately many hard-working horses have diets containing only 30–40 per cent forage and if this is the case it would be preferable to include chaff into the concentrate ration to add more fibre. Forage is vital for a healthy digestive tract and to maintain as natural as possible a diet for the horse. Forage also provides an activity for the horse who is stabled for long periods and ensures that the digestive system is topped up on a natural 'little and often' basis.

9.8 The main differences between meadow and seed hay:
Meadow hay is taken from pasture normally used for grazing and consists of a mixture of grasses.
Seed hay is a specially grown crop consisting mainly of rye grasses.
Meadow hay is generally softer and greener than seed hay.

9.9 Three qualities of good hay:
1. It should smell sweet, not musty.
2. The hay should fall loosely apart.
3. It must be free of poisonous weeds.

9.10 Hay should be soaked in a dustbin or old bath/water trough for up to 20 minutes to ensure that the dust particles are stuck to the hay preventing them from being inhaled (it is quite safe for them to be ingested).

9.11 **Soaking hay:**
Disadvantages
Nutrients are leached from the hay. The resultant soaking water is considered a pollutant and should not be tipped down the drain. Haynets of soaked hay are heavy to handle. It can take quite some time to soak a large number of haynets.

Advantages
Nutrient leaching is useful for laminitic or obese ponies. Soaking is a simple method with little equipment required. Soaking is a quick method for one or two horses.

Steaming hay:

Disadvantages

Requires more equipment than soaking and can be expensive. Takes longer than soaking hay. Requires an electricity source.

Advantages

Nutrients are not leached. There is much less water to deal with. Whole bales can be soaked at a time. Steaming kills spores in the hay.

9.12 Alternative forage for the allergic horse is haylage or vacuum-bagged hay as these are much lower in dust than baled hay.

9.13 Horses should be given two or three smaller feeds a day rather than one large one because their stomach is relatively small (the size of a rugby ball). Also, nature intended the horse to be a 'trickle' feeder – to eat little and often.

9.14 Three reasons why horses need plenty of hay in their diet:
1. Their digestive tract is designed to cope with large quantities of roughage. It therefore helps to keep the system functioning properly.
2. Eating hay helps to keep the horse occupied, mimicking the way he would act in the wild – eating more or less continuously.
3. The process of digesting hay generates heat within the body, so helping to keep the horse warm. This is important for the grass-kept horse in winter.

9.15 Changes should be introduced gradually because a sudden change would affect the horse's ability to digest the new feedstuff, which could lead to colic.

9.16 You should always allow 1½ hours between feeding and exercising. This allows the stomach to empty and for most of the food that has been eaten to be digested. When the horse starts to work, blood is directed towards the muscles to supply oxygen. This means it is taken away from the digestive tract. (A good blood supply is needed for efficient digestion and the nutrients are transported away from the digestive tract by the circulatory system.)

9.17 The term 'maintenance rations' refers to the ration needed purely to keep a horse healthy. The ration does not allow for extra energy for work.

9.18 A young, growing horse requires high levels of protein in his diet. Vitamin D, calcium and phosphorus are also needed for healthy bone growth.

9.19 Fibre is needed for healthy gut function and to provide a certain amount of energy.

9.20 Carbohydrate provides energy.

9.21 Chaff and sugar beet pulp are bulk feeds.

9.22 Oats are rolled to aid their digestion.

9.23 A sandy-based stream must not be used as a water supply as the ingestion of sand can lead to colic.

9.24 Ponds are unsuitable as a water supply as the water is stagnant.

9.25 a. The horse can become entangled in a haynet, especially if it hangs lower when empty.
b. It is safer to feed hay from the ground.

9.26 In icy weather the ice must be broken and removed from the trough at least twice a day. A ball floating on the water can help to prevent freezing.

9.27 Considerations to bear in mind when feeding the old horse include:
1. The horse may have additional vitamin and mineral requirements which can be met through feeding of a supplement.
2. The aged horse's teeth may be less effective (often with many missing) thus reducing his capacity to chew. In these cases the horse will benefit from being fed sloppier feeds such as a cube mixed with water. Some hay/haylage could be replaced with a shorter forage form such as alfalfa or chaff.
3. Feed companies have a range of products to fulfil the nutritional requirements of the aged/veteran horse. Compare these to each other to find the most suitable for your animal.
4. Check dentition and condition regularly and deal with any problems promptly.

9.28 The horse on box rest should have his diet changed immediately to ensure he is not receiving too much energy for his exercise levels.
Conditions such as equine rhabdomyolysis syndrome (azoturia), lymphangitis, laminitis and weight gain and bad behaviour may occur if too high an energy content is fed.
Reduce the quantity of concentrate fed and ensure plenty of forage (ideally on an ad lib basis).
The type of feed fed is dependent on the horse's condition but any changes to feed type should be introduced gradually.

9.29 When choosing bedding for the horse on box rest it should be as dust-free and free-draining as possible to limit dust spores and ammonia in the stable. In addition it should be non-edible as straw eaten can cause colic as it may impact in the digestive tract. Rubber matting with a topping of paper or cardboard is best. Shavings are an alternative but even 'dust-extracted' versions can be very dusty!
Forage must be of very good quality and dust free. Hay would benefit from soaking or steaming to reduce dust and soften it for ease of chewing and digestion. Ideally it should be fed from the floor. If feeding haylage ensure it is of low

energy value and contains no moulds.

Horses on box rest very much enjoy a nibble of succulent grass so try feeding handfuls of just pulled (not mown) grass or graze in hand if approved by your vet.

Additional forage can be fed via tubs of alfalfa or chaff.

9.30 Trying one or a combination of the following may help to tempt a sick horse to eat:

- Moisten the feed, even making it very sloppy for some horses. Sloppy sugar beet pulp is very useful for this.
- Add molasses to the feed as a temptation (depending on the condition the horse is suffering from, as molasses is very high in sugar).
- Add succulents such as sliced carrots, apples and parsnips.
- Use a horse ball to trickle small quantities of feed and occupy the horse at the same time.
- Feed little and often, removing unwanted feed and discarding quickly.
- Feed from the hand as most horses will take feed this way.

9.31 When watering the sick horse try to use buckets so that you can assess how much he is drinking. Turn off automatic drinkers but make sure that the horse will drink from the buckets, otherwise he will become dehydrated. If he will not drink from buckets, drinkers will have to be used.

Change water regularly to ensure it is fresh; always ensure there is plenty of 'chilled' water available especially overnight where two large tubs are recommended.

Add glucose to water for energy and electrolytes to restore the balance in the horse's body. Always ensure there is one plain bucket when doing this in case the horse dislikes the additives.

10.1 In an ascending order of fitness, i.e. starting with the least demanding discipline:
e. Riding Club Dressage.
b. Working Hunter show classes.
a. Riding Club One-Day Event.
d. BE Novice One-Day Event.
c. Point-to-pointing.

10.2 The following are ways in which exercise alters the horse's body systems:

- Exercise promotes the circulation of body fluids within the circulatory and lymphatic systems, which helps them to function efficiently. It also promotes efficient digestion and removal of waste products through excretions.
- The respiratory system is developed, improving the supply of oxygen to the muscles.
- The muscles become supple and well developed.
- Correctly performed fittening positively alters bone density and thus strength.
- The horse will become mentally relaxed.

10.3 Before starting a fitness programme the following checks should be made:
Feet. The horse must be shod.
Vaccinations must be given as protection against tetanus

and equine influenza.
Worming. All horses should be wormed regularly in accordance with the drug manufacturer's instructions.
Teeth must be rasped annually.

10.4 The early walk work is very important as the horse is normally in 'soft' condition at the start of a fitness programme. Walking gradually tones and conditions the horse's systems in preparation for the fittening programme.

10.5 Begin walking for 20 minutes, increasing to at least 1½ hours by the end of Week 2.

10.6 In Week 3 introduce short spells of steady trotting on good ground.

10.7 Introduce canter work when the horse can trot up a long slope without getting out of breath; this is usually around Week 5.

Introduce canter slowly with short spells (initially 1–2 minutes). Try to begin canter work out hacking in straight lines to avoid injury. Keep to good ground and don't allow the horse to go faster than you wish – a stronger bit may be required temporarily if the horse becomes excitable/strong.

10.8 Excessive trotting, cantering and jumping can lead to concussion and sprain injuries such as splints, sore shins, inflamed joints, tendons and ligaments.

10.9 *In hot weather*: stand horse in the shade and wash off with cold water, sweat-scraping thoroughly immediately afterwards. Make sure you wash off all sweat marks and pay special attention to areas such as the head, in between the legs, the girth and udder/sheath area. Turn the horse out for a roll or stable unrugged. Complete strapping once the horse is dry.

In cold weather: remove sweat marks efficiently with warm water – do not overly soak the horse as he will become cold. Sweat-scrape and rub down with a towel. Apply a cooler or Thermatex rug and put stable bandages on wet legs. If the horse is dry brush him off to ensure no sweat marks remain; don't wet him unnecessarily.

11.1 Minimum stable dimensions:
a. 12.2hh – 3m x 3m (10ft x 10ft)
b. 14.1hh – 3m x 3.65m (10ft x 12ft)
c. 15.3hh – 3.65m x 3.65m (12ft x 12ft)
d. 16.2hh – 3.65m x 4.25m (12ft x 14ft)

11.2 a. The main disadvantage of using breeze blocks to construct stable walls is that they can be pushed over and dislodged if a horse constantly leans or rubs on the wall.
b. To prevent this from happening, metal rods, set in the concrete floor, can be passed through the centre of the breeze blocks for reinforcement.

11.3 The stable doorway should be at least 2.1m (7ft) high and 1.2m (4ft) wide.

11.4   Three qualities of good stable flooring:
1. Non-slippery.
2. Impervious to moisture.
3. Hard-wearing.

11.5   Poor drainage in a stable means that urine will sit on the floor rather than drain away, making the stable smell and the bedding a lot wetter, which can lead to problems with the horse's hooves, e.g. thrush. Poor drainage will lead to additional costs in bedding materials and make mucking out more difficult. Also, when you wash the stable floor, it is difficult to get rid of the water.

11.6   Four disadvantages of using automatic waterers:
1. You cannot monitor how much the horse is drinking.
2. The pipes and bowls freeze in icy weather.
3. The bowls are small and take a while to refill. This may deter a thirsty horse from drinking his fill.
4. If the bowls become unlevel, they overflow, soaking the bedding.

11.7   The quality of air in a stable is affected by the effectiveness of the ventilation. Carbon dioxide is exhaled by the horse and ammonia is released from the urine in the bedding. The air should change frequently to keep it clear. Inadequate ventilation will prevent fresh air replacing the stale air. Dust in the air will also affect its quality.

11.8   Poor ventilation will result in the horse breathing in stale air. Stale air contains ammonia, carbon dioxide and a certain amount of dust. These contaminants will irritate the horse's respiratory tract and cause coughing. In hot weather, a poorly ventilated stable can cause the horse to overheat.

11.9   Ways in which boredom can be reduced:
1. Turn the horse out daily with others for long periods. If this is not possible, lead out and graze in hand.
2. Divide the exercise into two lots. This is only possible if the yard has a large number of staff, or you are only dealing with one horse.
3 Keep the work varied – a variety of hacking, schooling and competing will all make life interesting for the horse.
4. In a large yard a horse-walker can provide a means of exercising horses and getting them out of their stables. Whilst this cannot be a substitute for proper work and turning out, it is better than nothing.
5. Divide up the feeds to adhere to the 'little and often' rule of feeding. Eating helps alleviate boredom.
6. Ensure a constant supply of good quality hay. Use a haynet with small holes so it takes longer for the horse to eat his ration.

11.10   Two reasons why horses may develop stereotypical behaviour:
1. Boredom.
2. Social frustration.

11.11   To control crib-biting:
1. Alleviate boredom and reduce confinement stress.
2. Paint exposed woodwork with creosote, or an anti-chew paste such as Cribox.
3. Fit a muzzle which is designed to allow the horse to eat and drink, but stops him from catching hold of anything with his teeth.
4. A metal grille on the top half of the door will allow the horse to see out but not bite the top of the door.

11.12   Two negative effects on the horse of weaving:
1. The constant swaying places extra, uneven stress on the horse's joints.
2. The horse may lose condition owing to the energy used when weaving.

11.13a. Rough handling or grooming of a sensitive horse, girthing up and feeding titbits can cause a horse to bite. Some horses are naturally more prone to biting than others.
b. To prevent biting, the horse should be tied up when being groomed, rugged or tacked-up. He should be handled firmly yet sympathetically. Serious biters should be muzzled and a grille used on the stable door.

11.14a. The safest way to reprimand a horse is to slap his shoulder and verbally reprimand him.
b. Horses should not be slapped on the face as it can make them head-shy and cause them to pull back, which can lead to an accident.

11.15   The minimum land requirement is 1 acre (0.405ha) per horse.

11.16   The three main soil types are:
Medium loam.
Sand.
Clay.

11.17   Horses grazing on sandy soils can suffer from sand colic as they ingest sand whilst grazing. This can lead to a blockage in the intestine.

11.18   The four main nutrients needed in the soil are:
1. Nitrogen – needed for healthy plant growth.
2. Phosphorus – needed for good root development.
3. Potassium – helps promote good root development and grass growth.
4. Calcium – reduces acidity, which enables the other nutrients to work effectively.

11.19   Two reasons why paddock drainage is important:
1. Poaching is reduced.
2. Well-drained soil allows oxygen to mix within the soil particles. This helps root growth and the breakdown of organic matter. Nutrients are then released into the soil.

11.20 Barbed wire is not suitable for fencing for horses as it causes serious injuries.

11.21 Fence posts should be sunk at least 46cm (18in) deep.
1. Fence posts at a change of direction should be 75cm (30in) deep.
2. Gateposts should be 90cm (3ft) deep.

11.22 Shelter is needed as protection against wind, heat, flies and driving rain.

11.23 Hedges provide good shelter as they are permeable wind-breaks that prevent circular draughts (eddies) from forming.

11.24 Three factors to take into account when siting a field shelter:
1. The shelter should face away from prevailing weather conditions.
2. It should be sited on free-draining land.
3. It should be close to the gate for ease of checking horses, but be far enough away to prevent poaching.

11.25 Three considerations to take into account before using a river or stream as a water supply:
1. There should be safe and easy access to the water.
2. The riverbed should have a stony base, not sandy or muddy.
3. The water should be free-flowing and unpolluted.

11.26 If the land is not free-draining around the water trough, hardcore should be put down, compacted and then have sand laid on top of it.

11.27 Water pipes should be laid 60cm (2ft) underground to prevent them being fractured by heavy machinery, broken during soil cultivations and from freezing.

11.28 Ragwort causes the most cases of poisoning in horses in the British Isles.

11.29 Seneciosis is the term describing the state of permanent liver damage caused by ragwort poisoning.

11.30a. Ragwort should never be cut as this encourages more vigorous growth. It also increases the risk of horses picking up any remnants of the dead plant if all is not removed after cutting.
b. Ragwort can be controlled by pulling up the whole plant, including roots, or by spraying.
c. If ragwort is sprayed the dead plants must be completely removed from the field. This must be done with the utmost vigilance as small amounts of ragwort cause poisoning.

11.31 Buttercups lose their toxicity when dried in hay.

12.1 Two points to consider regarding the fit of the lungeing cavesson:
1. The noseband must be fitted two fingers' width from the projecting cheekbone. If any higher it will rub on the cheekbone; any lower and it will interfere with horse's nasal passages.
2. The noseband and middle strap should be fitted quite securely to prevent the cavesson from pulling around on the horse's face.

12.2 Three reasons for using side-reins:
1. To teach the horse to accept a contact.
2. To encourage the horse to work in a rounded outline.
3. To give extra control over a lively horse.

12.3 To adjust the side-reins:
1. Make sure they are fitted the same height on either side.
2. They should be the same length.
3. With the horse standing with his neck straight and his head in a normal position, the side-reins should just touch the bit rings. As the horse is worked-in the side-reins should be tightened up evenly.

12.4 If the side-reins are fitted too tightly the horse may become upset and run backwards. If very upset he may rear. When working with over-tight side-reins the horse may not go forwards properly and he may overbend.

12.5 If the side-reins are too loose there will be insufficient contact with the horse's mouth so he will be unlikely to work in the correct outline. As he lowers his head there is a danger that, if very loose, the horse may get a foot over the side-rein.
Very loose side-reins will not help control an excitable horse.

12.6 When leading the lunge horse the whip and thong should be under your left arm, pointing back and downward.

12.7 When lungeing you should be positioned in such a way that your body is level with the horse's girth area, slightly inclined towards his shoulder. The whip is held so it points behind the horse's hocks.

12.8 Four points to note regarding the contact on the lunge line:
1. The line should be taut.
2. There should be no twists.
3. The line must never touch the ground.
4. The line must not 'swing' loose and low.

12.9 If you move in front of the horse's shoulder whilst lungeing it would have the effect of stopping the horse from moving forwards. It may also encourage the horse to turn in and face you.

12.10 a To make an upward transition (e.g. from halt to walk or walk to trot) ensure that the tone of voice moves from a low to a higher pitch and speak in an animated and energetic fashion: 'And – walk on'.

b. To make a downward transition (e.g. from trot to walk or walk to halt) use a slow, calm voice moving from the higher to a lower pitch: 'And – woah'.

12.11 a. If the horse falls in on the circle you must correct this by ensuring that the horse is moving with impulsion and is bending in the correct direction as this will mean he is less likely to fall in. Point the whip to the horse's girth area and use the command 'Out' to encourage him to stay out.

b. For the horse who pulls out, repetitive squeezes (of similar strength to the rein aid in a half-halt) on the lunge line can help to keep the horse's head facing the desired way and focus his attention. The use of transitions can also help to focus his mind on the job in hand! You need to maintain a firm contact and try to keep the horse on the circle.

12.12 To warm up the horse before attaching the side reins, walk one circuit, trot two then walk, halt and change the rein. If, at this point, the horse has been very lively, it would be sensible to attach the side-reins to increase your control. If the horse has been quiet, walk half a circuit, trot for one, then walk and halt. Then attach the side-reins.

13.1 It is necessary to adopt the correct riding position:
To balance the rider over the horse's centre of balance, so there is no feeling of a need to grip in order to remain in the saddle at walk, trot and canter.
To harmonise the rider with the movement of the horse to avoid unintentional interference with the horse's action, i.e. the rider should 'go with' the horse.
To establish a light contact acceptable to the horse, through the seat, legs and reins, enabling the rider to apply the aids correctly.

13.2 A straight line from the ear through the shoulder, hip and down to the heel can be 'drawn', as can a line from the elbow, down the forearm to the hand and down the rein to the horse's mouth if the rider is sitting correctly.

13.3 Two main functions of the hands:
1. Passive resistance – when slowing or stopping, the hands cease to allow and reflect the blocking of further forward movement employed by the seat and back.
2. Allowing – the seat, legs and back ask the horse to move forward, and the hands permit the horse to obey by allowing – opening the fist slightly.

13.4 The aids can be divided into natural and artificial:

The natural aids	The artificial aids
Seat	Whip
Legs	Spurs
Back	Martingale
Hands	Various gadgets
Voice	

13.5 The horse's head should not be restricted by the rider's hands as it will impede the horse's forward motion.

13.6 The horse is said to be 'on the bit' when:
- He moves freely forward with controlled impulsion.
- He is straight, accepting and taking the same contact on each rein.
- He accepts the bit without resistance.
- He is submissive to the rider's aids.
- His neck is slightly raised and arched, with the poll being the highest point of the neck. His whole outline gives the appearance of being generally convex (rounded upwards) rather than 'hollow'. The degree of 'roundness' will be dependent on his level of training and the movement being performed.
- His head remains steady, with the front line of the face slightly in front of the vertical.
- He is free from stiffness, in particular through the neck and back.

13.7 A half-halt should be ridden by the rider sitting tall in the saddle, gently closing the legs and deepening the seat followed by a brief closing of the hands on the reins; this whole process lasts around a second. The half-halt is used to prepare the horse for a change in gait or direction and to generally ensure that he is listening and will respond to the forthcoming aids.

13.8 To make an upward transition from halt to walk, keep a light and even contact on the reins, maintain an upright position and squeeze with both legs simultaneously. The rein contact must allow the horse to move forwards. As he moves forwards the leg aids can cease unless he is reluctant to move forwards actively, in which case the leg aid can be repeated.
To move from walk to trot, make sure you have a good quality, i.e. calmly active, walk and apply a preparatory aid. Most horses naturally hold their heads a little higher in trot than walk so shorten the reins slightly in preparation.

13.9 To make a downward transition apply a preparatory aid, then, keeping your legs close to the horse's sides to maintain impulsion, sit tall yet deeply into the saddle and brace your back slightly while applying light resistance with the reins. As the horse obeys your instructions release (but do not lose) the rein contact.

13.10 The functions of the following on a turn or circle:
a. Inside leg – stimulates impulsion and prevents the horse falling in.
b. Outside leg slightly behind the girth – helps to maintain bend and prevent the quarters from swinging outwards.
c. Inside rein – maintains inside flexion

d. Outside rein – prevents excessive inside bend, limits the bend and speed, and controls the horse's outside shoulder.

13.11 'Working on two tracks' means that the horse's right hooves are on one track, his left hooves on another.

13.12 The reasons for selecting the outside diagonal is to ensure that the rider's seat is in the saddle when the inside hind leg is on the ground, prior to propelling the horse forward. The rider can then use back, seat and legs more efficiently to promote balance and impulsion.

13.13 When riding on the left rein you should be rising when the right foreleg and left hind leg are moving forward. Check to see if you are rising as the outside (right) shoulder moves forward and sitting as it comes back towards you. On this rein the right foreleg and left hind leg are known as the outside diagonal and the left foreleg and right hind leg known as the inside diagonal.

13.14 The aids to canter:
For the novice rider this is most easily achieved if the canter strike-off is asked for in a corner of the school when the horse should be naturally bent to the inside. The horse should be established in an active working trot. The rider ceases rising to the trot and gives a preparatory half-halt before asking for the actual transition. Pressure is applied with the inside leg which remains at the girth, and the outside leg which is drawn back slightly, behind the girth.

13.15 If the horse strikes off on the incorrect lead you must make a transition back to trot immediately (this proves to the examiners you knew you were on the incorrect leg), and prepare and ask again on the next corner. If the horse strikes off on the incorrect lead yet again, trot and bring him on to a 20m circle to ask again. Take your time and ensure that the horse is balanced and has a good rhythm before asking again for the canter.

13.16 In a disunited canter the horse moves incorrectly – although he is correct in front, the diagonal is split and the inside hind does not move with the outside fore. It appears that the inside foreleg and inside hind are moving away from each other – the hind leg moves backwards as the foreleg moves forward. This is sometimes termed as 'incorrect' or 'wrong behind'.
The corrections for a disunited canter are the same as for an incorrect lead.

13.17 When holding the reins in one hand, bridge them together and hold both reins in the outside hand. Allow the inside arm to hang down by your side. The whip should be held in the outside hand but positioned so it rests down the horse's inside shoulder.

13.18 a. The preliminary command gives you early warning of what

will be required within the next few strides. It gives you the opportunity to prepare the movement.
b. The executive command is the command which results in the execution of the movement or exercise. It is the culmination of the preparation that preceded it.

13.19 The normal safety distance is a minimum of at least half a horse's length, and a maximum of a horse's length – approximately 2m (6ft 6in). You should be able to see at least half of the tail of the horse in front when you look between your horse's ears.

13.20 Working as a ride means that the other riders in the group lesson follow in single file behind the leading file rider at the front. Working in 'open order' is where the riders in the group do not follow each other, but ride independently. They can pass each other, work at different gaits and different exercises as determined by the instructor.

13.21 Five ways of changing the rein in the arena include:
- F X H or K X M across the long diagonal.
- C X A or A X C down the centre line.
- B X E or E X B across the centre.
- H B, K B, M E or F E across the short diagonal.
- B 10m half-circle right to X; X 10m half-circle left to E (or vice versa).
- Four-loop serpentine from A or C.
- 20m half-circle A to X; 20m half-circle X to C.
- 10m half-circle from F for example, inclining diagonally back to the track at M This can also be reversed – ride a diagonal line off the track to the centre line and 10m half-circle back to the track.

13.22 School protocol includes the following:
- Permission should be gained before entering the arena to ensure the entrance is clear.
- The gate/door to the arena should be closed before ridden work commences.
- Riders altering stirrups and tightening girths at the halt should come in off the track so as not to interfere with those already working.
- The session should commence and finish with the ride lined up off the track.
- Leave plenty of room when passing the ride; do not box other horses in.
- Maintain correct safety distances at all times – minimum of half a horse's length, maximum of one length.
- Having completed an exercise in succession, i.e. one at a time, riders should ensure that they ride their downward transition in plenty of time to avoid running into the back of the rear file.
- When carrying out an exercise in succession – for example, cantering to the rear of the ride – the new leading file should wait to be told to go by the commander to ensure that the previous rider has

completed the exercise safely.

- No rider may dismount or leave the arena without permission from the instructor.

Additional rules when working in 'open order':

- Always pass left to left. This means the rider on the left rein will take the outside track and the rider on the right rein will take the inside track.
- Riders working in walk will take the inside track.
- A rider who wishes to canter whilst other riders are trotting on the outside track, should request 'Track please' so that the track can be cleared.
- Be aware of all other horses to avoid collisions.
- Be careful around young/nervous horses working in open order.
- Only use your whip if you have plenty of space around you.
- It is the rider's job to avoid the instructor, not vice versa.
- Riders performing more advanced movements are given priority in their use of the arena.
- Downward transitions and halt transitions are ridden down the long centre line A to C as much as possible to leave the track free.

14.1 a. A horse should approach a fence actively and straight.
   b. As an approximate guide, the horse should take off between 1 and 1½ times the height of the fence from the ground line (e.g. if a fence is 1.2m (4ft) high, the take-off point should be 1.2–1.8m (4–6ft) from the ground line.
   c. During this phase the horse is airborne with no feet on the ground. He will stretch his head and neck down, rounding his back underneath the rider. This rounding is termed the bascule.

14.2 a. Stirrup leathers need to be shortened when jumping to help maintain balance over a fence.
   b. Stirrup leathers should be shortened 2–3 holes. Ensure you feel balanced and that your legs are not tiring too quickly.

14.3 The five phases of a jump:
   The approach: The horse should be forward, balanced and rhythmical with the rider looking up and ahead, in a slightly forward seat with a secure leg and hand position.
   The take off: The horse will lower his head and stretch his neck before taking off. His neck will shorten as he raises his forehand off the ground, folding his forelegs up. With his hocks underneath him, his quarters bunch as the power of the hind legs sends him up and over the fence.
   The rider will continue to look up and ahead and will fold forward a little more to maintain harmony with the horse. The hands will allow the horse to lift his forehand.
   The suspended bascule: The horse is airborne with no feet on the ground. He will stretch his head and neck down, rounding his back underneath the rider. This rounding is

termed the bascule. The rider should continue to look forward, maintain the body fold with the back straight, the leg position secure and hands allowing the horse to stretch.
The landing: The horse raises his head to balance himself during the descent as he straightens his forelegs in readiness to meet the ground. The horse should round his back to draw his hind legs underneath his body to facilitate the first stride away from the fence. The rider must continue to look forward and up. The upper body should be straightened as the rider starts to sit up again.
The departure: If the landing has been balanced, with the hind legs being drawn underneath the body, the departure from the fence should be balanced, calm and rhythmical, with no loss of impulsion. The rider should sit up properly back into the flatwork position and ride the horse positively and straight away from the fence.

14.4 To influence which leg the horse lands on when landing after a jump – if the next fence is to the right you can indicate the change of leading leg in mid-air by looking to the right, feeling the right rein, very slightly weighting the right stirrup and drawing the left leg back. Do not exaggerate the weighting of the stirrup or you risk unbalancing the horse and ruining the jump.

14.5 If, upon landing, he is incorrect, go forwards to trot before asking for the desired canter lead. Corrections should be made early – preferably before the corner prior to the next fence.

14.6 A horse may refuse to jump for the following reasons:
   1. Lack of impulsion. The horse needs to be ridden actively forwards from the leg.
   2. Loss of rhythm and impulsion owing to the rider being a passenger. You must actively help the horse by keeping him forward, straight and into a contact.
   3. The horse may be genuinely lazy – be ready to give a tap with the whip behind the leg on the approach.
   4. Confusion between speed and impulsion. You must not 'chase' the horse into the fence – you will have less control if the horse is rushing into the fence at speed and when it goes wrong it tends to be more dramatic and more difficult to stay on board.
   5. Dropping the contact a few strides from the fence. This can make the horse feel disconcerted and unsure whether you still want to jump. Your legs must maintain the forward momentum whilst the hands channel it. If these influences are abandoned in the last few strides, the horse is effectively left to make his own decision as to whether to jump or not.
   6. Ungenuine or 'cheeky' horse. The horse may have become disobedient having learned that some riders are weak and ineffective. Ride this sort of horse very positively so he knows you mean business.